International Finance

for non-financial managers

Dora Hancock

KoganPage

First published in Great Britain and the United States in 2018 by Kogan Page Limited

2nd Floor, 45 Gee Street	c/o Martin P Hill Consulting	4737/23 Ansari Road
London	122 W 27th Street	Daryaganj
EC1V 3RS	New York, NY 10001	New Delhi 110002
United Kingdom	USA	India

© Dora Hancocky 2018

The right of Dora Hancock to be identified as the author of this work has been asserted by her in accordance with the Copyright, Designs and Patents Act 1988.

ISBN   978 0 7494 8001 1
E-ISBN   978 0 7494 8002 8

British Library Cataloguing-in-Publication Data

A CIP record for this book is available from the British Library.

Typeset by Integra Software Services, Pondicherry
Print production managed by Jellyfish
Printed and bound in Great Britain by Ashford Colour Press Ltd

For all the strong women in my life

CONTENTS

PREFACE

Over the last 25 years of my working life I taught modules on International Finance at two universities to undergraduates and postgraduates, many of them international students, and indeed sometimes still teach those modules now that I am retired. In common with other teachers, I have learned as much from my students as I have taught them. I have also been very lucky to have worked with some wonderful colleagues who have been generous in sharing their thoughts, ideas and material with me.

International finance and multinational companies have always been fascinating areas of study and have changed almost beyond recognition during my working life. As a student in London I remember the delight of the arrival of McDonald's in the UK and their delicious milkshakes. Changes followed that I could never have imagined. The most dramatic change was the creation of the Internet and the explosion of multinational companies such as Amazon, Starbucks, Google and Facebook that seem to be essential elements of my life today. Other major changes include international travel and the movement of people around the world and, of course, the creation of the euro.

In 2008/09 we experienced the global financial crisis and one way or another the effects of that continue to affect most of us today; its consequences will continue to impact on individuals, companies and countries into the future. My last book was about tax and I never got a really positive reaction to that information. Today when I tell people about this book they are often really interested and many are happy to engage in conversation about it. Over the last 10 years, we have all been exposed to a very large amount of information about international finance and the financial environment. People talk about jobs being moved to low-cost countries and multinational companies avoiding paying tax but they have also come to enjoy world-class goods and services.

We will continue to see change in both the financial environment and the multinational companies we have come to depend on in our daily lives. The UK will leave the EU, artificial intelligence will take many more of our jobs, and climate change will bite ever deeper into our lives.

I hope that you enjoy reading this book as much as I have enjoyed writing it, and that it helps your understanding of international finance and multinational companies, enabling you to better understand the changes to come.

A word about Chapter 1

The first chapter covers the fundamental concepts of finance, risk and return and the maximization of shareholder wealth, moving on to the key ideas of the capital asset pricing model. We finish this first part of the chapter with the ideas of arbitrage and market efficiency. All of these ideas are covered with a brief introduction only. You may already be familiar with these ideas, in which case it is fine to skip to the second half of the chapter when we begin to discuss the ideas of international finance and the theories of foreign direct investment.

ACKNOWLEDGEMENTS

Firstly, I want to thank my editor Catherine Yates, who has been very supportive and encouraging throughout the writing of this book. I'm not sure I could have done it without her help.

I also want to thank MacroTrends, who freely gave me permission to use their charts.

I also want to thank my students and colleagues from whom I have learned so much.

My thanks also go to my husband, David, who is both a great cook and very long-suffering.

Finally, I want to thank all the bankers, governments and managers of multinational companies who never stop providing me with fascinating events to reflect on and discuss with my students.

01
The rise of the multinational and the international monetary system

At the end of this chapter you will be able to:

- state and briefly discuss the fundamental concepts of corporate finance;
- state and briefly discuss the reasons for the rise of multinational companies;
- state and briefly discuss the methods of undertaking expansion into a new country;
- explain how changes in exchange rates affect a company's competitiveness in their domestic market and internationally.

Introduction

This book is mostly about multinational companies, that is companies with a number of foreign subsidiaries which often interact strategically with each other. We will consider how they came to be multinationals, what the benefits and difficulties are for multinationals, and the environment within which they operate. We will also discuss 'local' or domestic firms: firms which largely operate solely in the country in which they are situated. You might work for a multinational or a domestic business but either way you will find useful information in this book. Even purely domestic companies can be affected by the global economy and by international issues, and most will have an international competitor, customer or supplier.

In this chapter, we will explore how multinationals came to exist, take a brief look at the world in which they operate, and then consider how multinationals differ from other businesses. Many of the ideas in this chapter will be revisited in later sections of the book.

The first multinationals appeared in the days of the British Empire in the 1800s and were companies seeking raw materials across the world. As the world has changed since those early days, the multinationals and their reasons for a global presence have also changed.

The political changes in the 1980s, particularly deregulation, the removal of trade barriers and the embracement of free markets, have all reduced costs and increased the opportunities for companies seeking to break out of their domestic borders and become multinationals in their turn.

The Internet and easy transportation have helped to integrate markets and create a global market in which buyers seek high-quality standardized products and the lowest prices possible. Consider that in the UK in 2016, Tata, an Indian company, proposed to merge with its German rival ThyssenKrupp in response to difficult trading conditions partially caused by a fall in growth in China. At the time of writing the future of the Tata-owned steel works in Port Talbot, Wales is uncertain.

In addition to people, goods and services, capital is also highly mobile in this integrated market. The Bank for International Settlements reported that over US $5 trillion a day was traded on global foreign exchange markets in 2016.

Introduction to the world of corporate finance

If you have studied corporate finance before, you might like to read this section to refresh your memory and check your corporate finance vocabulary. If you are new to the subject of corporate finance, this section is designed to equip you with the fundamental ideas from finance which will enable you to understand the world of international finance.

Key concept

The main objective of all companies is to maximize shareholder wealth.

Shareholder wealth

The first assumption of corporate finance is that all companies' main objective is to maximize shareholder wealth. We usually take that to mean that they aim to maximize their value, or market capitalization. This is a better aim than trying to maximize profits because directors might make bad decisions in order to increase profits, such as reducing spending on research and development. This might increase profits in the short term but not in the longer term.

Activity

Find and read your own company's mission statement and find the mission statements for a few other quoted companies. If you are a student and not currently employed, choose several companies that you know of or that interest you.

Here are two multinational companies to start you off:

Vodafone says: *'Our vision sets out our ambition to deliver connectivity and innovative services to improve people's livelihoods and quality of life. Central to achieving this vision is our longstanding commitment to manage our operations responsibly and ethically.'*

Tesco's mission statement is: *'Creating value for customers, to earn their lifetime loyalty.'*

Neither of these refers to their shareholders. Can you find any that do?

In practice, if companies like Vodafone and Tesco didn't focus on their customers they would soon lose business and market value, so these two mission statements are probably consistent with maximizing shareholder wealth.

Risk and return

The relationship between risk and return lies at the heart of finance and yet it is a simple relationship we can all agree on.

When we use the word **return**, we really mean expected, or future, return and we will refer to it in this way from now on. The return may be the profits on a business investment or the dividends and capital growth of a share.

When we use the word **risk**, we are referring to the volatility (how much it might fluctuate by) of the expected return. The higher the volatility, the higher the risk. For example, if there are two shares currently trading at £1.50 each and the first, Share A, had traded at a high of £1.80 and a low of £1 in the last year while the second, Share B, had traded at a high of £1.60 and a low of £1.30 over the last year, we would say that Share A is more volatile, that is, more risky, than Share B. We actually measure risk using standard deviation rather than the range.

Activity

In the graph below, expected return is plotted on the vertical axis and the level of risk is along the horizontal axis.

Figure 1.1   Risk/return trade-off 1

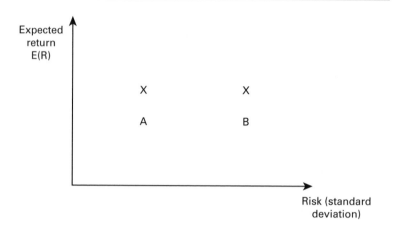

Would you prefer to hold investment A or investment B?

Now in the next graph, decide if you would prefer to hold investment A or investment B.

Figure 1.2   Risk/return trade-off 2

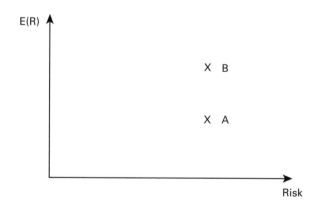

Finally decide if you would rather hold investment A or investment B in the last graph.

Figure 1.3   Risk/return trade-off 3

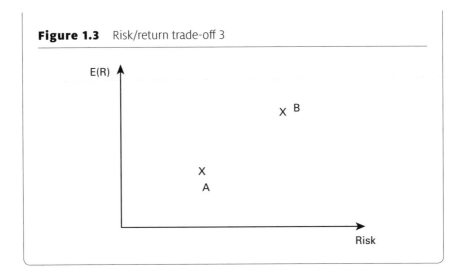

Feedback

We assume that people would prefer less risk than more risk at the same level of expected return, so investment A is more attractive to investors than investment B in the first graph.

We also assume that people would prefer to have more expected return than less expected return at the same level of risk. In the second graph, we would also prefer to hold investment A than investment B.

In the last graph, there is no right answer. Each person will have to make their own decision about which investment they prefer. A offers a higher expected return but also has higher risk than B. Each investor must ask themselves if the additional expected return is sufficient to compensate them for the additional risk taken.

Figure 1.4   Risk/return trade-off 4

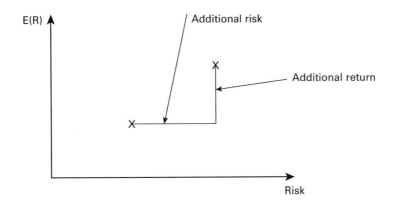

Capital asset pricing model

In this section we have been talking about total risk. But we have a way of analysing risks into two types: **systematic risk** and **specific risk**.

The **capital asset pricing model,** or **CAPM,** defines systematic risks as risks that affect all businesses to a greater or lesser extent, while specific risks affect a specific company. An example of a specific risk is the oil spill where BP was responsible for an environmental disaster in the Gulf of Mexico in 2010.

Figure 1.5   Impact of Gulf Oil Crisis on BP's share price

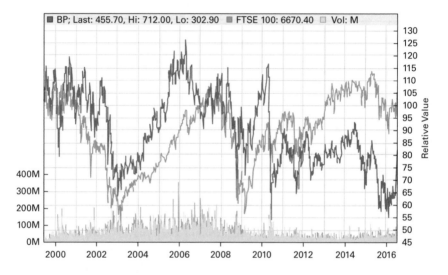

SOURCE   Digital Look

Figure 1.5 shows the share price of BP and the FTSE 100 index. Notice how the share price of BP fell sharply as a result of the disaster while the FTSE 100 index was largely stable.

Systematic risks include interest rate changes, changes in oil prices and events such as the UK referendum on its membership of the EU in 2016. Companies will not be equally affected by systematic risks. Generally, banks and housebuilders are more sensitive to systematic risks than tobacco companies and supermarkets, for example.

The capital asset pricing model argues that investors can diversify away specific risk by holding a number, around 20 or 30, of carefully chosen securities. While their BP holding might have suffered losses, other securities in their portfolio will not have been affected and may even have gone up due to some specific event of their own. Since specific risk can be avoided by diversification, investors need only concern themselves with the systematic risk rather than the total risk, which is made up of both the systematic risk and the specific risk.

So should a multinational company be more interested in its total risk or its systematic risk?

The CAPM suggests it should only be concerned with the systematic risk because the specific risk can be diversified away. But a firm's total risk is likely to have a direct impact on its sales and costs due to third parties' unwillingness to enter into business arrangements with high-risk businesses. We will review this argument again in Chapter 8, when we consider the benefits of hedging to a multinational company.

Arbitrage

Arbitrage occurs when a risk-free profit is made by simultaneously buying and selling an asset in two different markets.

Example

Suppose the exchange rate in London is £1:$1.50 and in New York the exchange rate is £1:$1.45.

The pound is stronger in London than in New York because it will buy more dollars in London than it will in New York.

If you had £100 what would you do?

New York	London
£1:$1.45	£1:$1.50
Sell $145 for £100	Sell £100 for $150

You could exchange your £100 for $150 in London and at the same time you could agree to change $145 for £100 in New York. This is great because you still have your £100 and you have made an arbitrage profit of $5. Without any market correction, you could do this over and over again, assuming there are no transaction costs.

But foreign exchange markets are an example of a **zero-sum game**. That is, the total amount gained by participants exactly equals the total amount lost by other participants. So if you have made $5, it means that others have lost $5.

What do you think would happen to the exchange rates in these two markets?

In London, people would be selling pounds in order to buy dollars, which would increase the supply of pounds and increase demand for dollars.

That would make the pound become weaker and the dollar stronger. Don't worry if this isn't entirely clear. We will revisit this idea in Chapter 6. At the same time in New York, people would be selling dollars in order to buy pounds, and using the same argument, the pound in New York would strengthen and the dollar would weaken.

So the exchange rate in London might move from £1:$1.50 to £1:$1.475 and in New York in might shift from £1:$1.45 to £1:$1.475. Now the exchange rates are the same in both countries and this means that there are no further arbitrage opportunities.

In summary, if there are arbitrage opportunities, we can assume that the markets will react and they will be eliminated.

Market efficiency

We assume in finance that markets are efficient. That is, that prices in capital markets instantaneously react to new information and that prices fully reflect all available information about securities.

When Kraft first announced that it was going to attempt to take over Cadbury, there was an almost instantaneous leap in the Cadbury share price (see Figure 1.6).

Figure 1.6 Cadbury's share price during Kraft's takeover bid

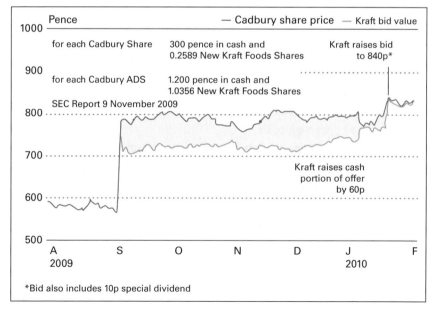

*Bid also includes 10p special dividend

SOURCE Thomson Reuters

The increase in the share price was due to the announcement and is a clear example of market efficiency. Unfortunately, there are plenty of examples of changes in share prices and exchange rates which are not explainable in the same way, so the reliability of market efficiency is questionable. We will assume that it holds in this book but bear in mind some of the difficulties it has faced in recent years.

There are other important ideas in finance that you need to be familiar with but we will talk about them when we need to.

Foreign direct investment (FDI)

When companies invest in physical assets in other countries we call it **foreign direct investment** or **FDI**. There are other ways for a company to trade in a foreign market, for example exporting goods and services or granting a licence to allow their products to be manufactured abroad. Yet FDI is still a popular strategy used by businesses. We will start by considering the theoretical models that attempt to explain why companies undertake FDI and how they are able to compete successfully with the local firms. Then we will compare the theory to what has happened in practice.

Activity

Suppose your company was planning to set up a subsidiary to undertake a new but complementary activity. Your company has two possible sites: the first one is based within 20 miles of its current operations and the second is based in a foreign country 3,000 miles away.

Quickly note down the additional difficulties your company would face if it opted for the foreign country. Consider both internal and external difficulties.

Feedback

Internal difficulties:

- *Additional costs of communication, administration and transportation.*
- *It is likely that everything will take longer to do, which will require increased financing to cover the increased time it takes to receive money from sales.*
- *Controlling the overseas subsidiary will require more time and will cost more. It will also be more difficult to achieve.*

External difficulties:

- *Local firms will be able to compete effectively with you because they will be well known locally and will be held in higher regard than a foreign firm.*
- *Your company is likely to lack local knowledge and reputation.*

The additional difficulties are not trivial and yet companies continue to expand internationally.

Theories of foreign direct investment

Theories of FDI are intended to answer the following two questions:

1 Why do firms go abroad as direct investors?
2 How can overseas firms compete successfully with local firms (where local competitors exist) in host countries, given the disadvantages and problems of operating in a foreign territory?

As we discuss each of these theories, ask yourself if they help you answer the two questions above.

Comparative advantage

Adam Smith was the first to consider the theory of international trade. He argued that each nation would have a comparative advantage over other nations, for example agriculture or mining, and that each country should specialize in producing and exporting the goods for which they have an advantage. Other goods, which can be produced more efficiently by other countries, should be imported.

This model assumes the free movement of goods, largely commodities, but that the factors of production such as capital, labour and raw materials are not mobile. The model is a static rather than a dynamic model. It suggests that the country differences are more significant than the company when assessing competitiveness.

In the 21st century, these arguments are not as compelling as when they were first posited in the 17th century.

Deregulation, begun in the 1980s, the global move towards free-market policies and the removal of trade barriers around the world, together with the Internet, have all contributed to change the business world.

Many countries are becoming more and more homogeneous with similar lifestyles, a highly skilled workforce and economic structure all contributing to the erosion of comparative advantage. Combine this with the ease with which production and capital can be shifted from one country to another, and the shift towards a knowledge-based society rather than one dependent on raw materials, and it is apparent that the differences between companies are more important than the differences between countries.

Market imperfections theory

Capitalist economies such as the UK, the United States and the EU rely on free markets, as far as possible, to allow the economy to run efficiently. In a perfect market, buyers and sellers have access to full information, and products or services are easy to compare because they are the same as each other. In practice, it is hard to find a truly perfect market. Stock markets like the London Stock Exchange are probably as close as we get to a perfect market.

Market imperfections allow businesses to charge more for their products or services than they otherwise could, which means that businesses try to create or exploit market imperfections. For example, some companies invest a great deal of time and money in persuading people or other businesses to buy their products and services by effective use of marketing. Some of the companies running the most successful marketing campaigns are also some of the biggest multinational companies in the world, for example Coca-Cola and McDonald's.

There are other ways of creating market imperfections, for example product differentiation, where companies make relatively small changes to their product to differentiate it from other very similar products in an attempt to make it more attractive to buyers. Companies also use proprietary technology, trademarks and patents to create a competitive edge over other similar products.

Multinational companies may be able to exploit other differences such as managerial and organizational skills and economies of scale to create market imperfections. Tesco used the introduction of the Clubcard to manage their inventory, giving them the competitive edge that enabled them to become the largest UK supermarket chain.

Finally, multinational companies are uniquely placed to benefit from different legislation and economic conditions in different countries. The ability of multinationals to legally pay very little tax has come to the public's attention in recent years and they are also able to raise new funds at very advantageous rates compared to local companies.

Many countries also attempt to protect their own companies and markets by introducing caps or tariffs on imports.

Now we can see that although the local firms have many advantages, local knowledge and reputation for example, multinational companies also have a competitive edge due to the market imperfections created by marketing, as well as different tax laws and other factors.

Product life cycle theory

Broadly there are four stages in a product's life cycle:

- introduction;
- growth;
- maturity;
- decline.

Figure 1.7   Four stages of a product's life cycle

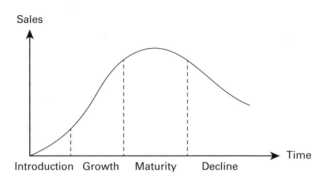

The life cycle can be repeated around the world, so for example, as tobacco sales fell in countries like the United States and the UK, the tobacco companies expanded into new markets such as India and China to find new customers and began the cycle all over again.

Proponents of the product life cycle theory argue that the location of production is dependent on the stage of the life cycle.

When a product is first introduced, it is produced locally. Production is likely to be on a fairly small scale, which means the benefits of manufacturing abroad are not so great, and enables the additional costs of manufacturing abroad to be avoided. The product is likely to be highly tailored to the domestic market, with some exports to similar countries also taking place.

In the next stage, growth, production is much higher, there is interest in the product from abroad, and the benefits of the economies of scale make moving manufacturing to a lower-cost country to reduce costs desirable. Manufacturing abroad is also likely to help to penetrate new markets, increasing growth further. This is likely to increase interest in the product from potential competitors who will introduce similar products. The company is likely to respond by finding ways to differentiate its product to retain its market share. The growth stage moves into maturity and then saturation when the market is no longer growing and sales are reduced by substitutes. Throughout this time, the pressure is on to further reduce costs to maximize profits.

Finally, the product moves into decline and poorer countries are its only remaining markets, leading to production in developing countries.

The maturity phase makes it essential that the lowest-cost producer is used for manufacture to maximize profits in a contracting industry.

International portfolio diversification theory

Diversification is one of the most important ideas in finance, and multinational companies are ideally placed to take advantage of it.

For more information on the benefits of diversification, find out more about portfolio theory. We won't spend much time discussing portfolio theory in the book but will focus on its application to multinational companies here.

Before you work through the next example, we need to introduce some ideas about **exchange rates.**

Currencies are stated at their rate of exchange with each other. Today the exchange rate between the pound and the dollar is quoted as £1:$1.46. That is, if you exchange £1 for dollars you will receive $1.46 and if you have $10 you will be able to get £6.85 ($10/1.46).

If the exchange rate changes to, say, £1:$1.40 then we say that the pound has weakened against the dollar; that is that the pound is worth fewer dollars than it used to be. Equally the dollar has strengthened against the pound; that is that our 10 dollars can buy more pounds than formerly.

Don't worry if you are not entirely sure about these ideas. We will return to them again in detail in Chapters 3 and 6.

Example

Suppose you are working for a purely domestic company manufacturing, say, tableware. Suppose the country in which you operate experiences a rise in the value of its currency, perhaps due to a rise in economic activity generally. Demand for dinner services might go up as people have more money to spend but how do potential overseas companies view your market now?

It is sometimes easier to understand a situation if we put some numbers in.

Suppose our company is selling a dinner service for £200 and the exchange rate with another country was £1:€1.10 but has now moved to £1:€1.30.

A competitor in the eurozone might be able to export and sell a dinner service for €240. How much would they have to sell a dinner service for if they needed to receive €240 at each of the two exchange rates?

At an exchange rate of £1:€1.30 they would have to sell their dinner service for £184.62 (€240/1.30), whereas when the exchange rate was £1:€1.10 they would need to sell their dinner service for £218.18.

The stronger currency makes it easier for the overseas company to enter the market and to price their product to make it very competitive with the domestic company's product.

When the domestic company's currency appreciates, they find that their market becomes more attractive to companies in other countries.

> What could our domestic company do to protect itself against the risks
> caused by the domestic currency becoming stronger or appreciating?

One effective step the company could take is to seek other markets for its products in other countries. While the pound might have strengthened against the euro, it might have fallen against a different currency. In that case, our company might find that it is more competitive in this new market given that it is now in the position of being able to sell goods more cheaply in the new market than it could have before.

We are suggesting that by becoming a multinational company we can begin to reduce some of the risks that we are faced with. Other risks will increase but as we will see in later chapters the benefits of diversification generally outweigh the increase in other risks.

The eclectic theory

The **eclectic theory** (Dunning, 1980) is also called the **OLI Model** or the **OLI Framework,** where OLI stand for Ownership advantages, Location advantages and Internalization advantages.

Ownership advantages cover everything from patents and trademarks owned by the company to good entrepreneurial skills. Disney is an example of a company with trademarks that are very valuable.

Location advantages might be due to the physical location such as the availability of raw materials, local economic conditions such as a low-wage economy, or local legislation such as low rates of tax or limited regulations.

Internalization advantages refer to the ability of a company to produce its goods and services more effectively than others could.

The eclectic theory argues that FDI will only occur when the incoming firm has a unique competitive advantage which more than compensates for the disadvantages of competing with domestic firms:

- it is more profitable to produce in the local location than the home location;
- the firm benefits more from controlling the foreign business activity than it would from using an independent local company to provide the service.

Now we have established why companies become multinationals, let's consider the criteria that a multinational might use to decide where to extend their activities in terms of both market seeking and production.

While the decision to manufacture may appear to be different to the decision on which markets to target, in practice, markets tend to be created and grow when manufacturing is undertaken locally. Multinationals understand this and will look to locate in countries where the differences between costs of production and benefits from accessing the market are at their highest.

It is necessary not to just consider labour costs but to consider the labour cost element per unit of production. In other words, productivity is a crucial factor to consider and in practice there is often a significant difference in real wages even between countries at a similar level of economic development. In addition, the local availability of essential raw materials is a factor.

The current size of the potential market is only one factor to consider; the potential for growth, the stage of economic development in the country, and the presence or absence of local competition are also considerations.

The political and legislative environment also needs to be considered. Does the country have trade barriers which limit the potential to export to the country, thus increasing the attraction of inward investment? Companies like Toyota and Nissan chose to build plants in the UK in response to restrictions on the import of foreign cars into the UK. Government policy will affect the investment decision in other ways. Is the economic policy one which offers a stable environment for future growth; are there fiscal incentives to encourage inward investment? Does the regulatory regime provide safeguards to protect assets? Is the social environment likely to encourage inward investment?

How should companies behave in the global economy they find themselves in? When considering where to locate production, where to seek new markets and where to raise capital, managers must consider the global economy rather than just the domestic one.

A brief history of multinationals

We have already suggested that the first multinationals arose in colonial times and that they were raw material seekers; companies like Shell and BP are still raw material seekers today.

The next multinationals were those seeking new markets in which to sell their goods and services. Companies like Coca-Cola, McDonald's, Microsoft and Apple are truly global companies selling their goods around the world. These companies found that by operating internationally they were able to take advantage of economies of scale, especially in research and development and marketing.

More recently we have seen multinationals who have sought to reduce their costs by manufacturing in economies with lower costs, often because they pay lower wages. Companies such as Dyson, which began as a UK domestic firm, expanded into international markets firstly by selling into them and then moving production from the UK to Malaysia. James Dyson moved production to reduce costs, to be close to similar producers and to be closer to the important markets of Australia and New Zealand.

Some companies enter new markets as knowledge seekers, looking to learn more about how their competitors operate by entering their domestic markets. That knowledge can then be used in their own domestic markets against those competitors.

There are other reasons to become a multinational. Many service companies, or suppliers of components, followed their customers in order to ensure they didn't lose their own domestic business. Firms of accountants, for example, followed their clients into new countries and bought up local accountancy practices to ensure they could continue to provide a full service to their clients.

Finally, companies may become multinationals in order to exploit financial market imperfections; for example they may be able to reduce taxes, thus lowering their costs, and are likely to be able to reduce their cost of capital.

Most importantly of all, the benefits of diversifying away risk make internationalization very attractive.

The process of expanding internationally

Companies usually follow a series of steps on the road to becoming a multinational. They begin with strategies which don't require much investment, such as exporting, and then progress through working with local firms on joint ventures, licensing or franchising until they are ready to undertake FDI by setting up their own operation and moving from distribution to production and after-sales services.

Exporting

Exporting doesn't require much investment and the profits are immediate. As a result it is a low-risk way of enabling a company to learn about the market, especially customer demand and trading conventions. If they are successful they are likely to switch to using a local agent and ultimately to setting up a sales subsidiary and distribution facility. But it is unlikely that a company can maximize profits from a market by exporting alone.

Licensing and franchising

Some companies elect to license or franchise their product in another market rather than produce and sell it themselves. The main advantage of this approach is that it doesn't require high levels of investment and is relatively low risk, but as with exporting it also generates relatively low returns.

There may be other issues too. The company may encounter problems with maintaining quality and may also find that the licensee exports some of its product, turning it into a competitor in other markets. The licensee is also gaining experience and reputation, and at the end of the licence period may launch its own product and become a formidable competitor.

Overseas production

Once production is also in the local country it will be easier to satisfy local demand, particularly satisfying local tastes, reducing lead times and providing an after-sales service. Demand for products is likely to be increased when buyers can see that local jobs have been created and that the company is committed to the market. At the same time, the company is gaining additional knowledge about the market and its competitors, and will often have gained access to local experts to work on research and development.

Competitive advantage and the route to international growth

In order to be successful, a multinational company must have an advantage over its competitors. That advantage may take a number of forms. In order to choose the most successful route to becoming a multinational, a company must identify its competitive advantage and play to its strengths.

An advantage generated by assets like trademarks makes licensing an attractive route, while if the company has particular marketing or organizational skills which would be difficult to convey to another business, it might be better to begin with exports and move directly to setting up a subsidiary when exports are no longer appropriate.

Summary

In this first chapter we have set out some of the fundamental ideas of finance. The relationship between risk and return is easy to understand and appears also easy to forget, as we will see in the next chapter. The benefits of diversification are very significant and are key drivers to becoming a multinational. A multinational faces several risks that don't trouble a purely domestic company but the benefits of diversification, such as reducing exposure to political uncertainty in one country, far outweigh the additional risk.

We also began to introduce some of the ideas about exchange rates such as a currency strengthening, also called appreciating, or weakening/ depreciating.

We then moved on to a review of the theories on foreign direct investment. The theory of comparative advantage did not anticipate that countries would become more homogeneous over time. Clearly the market imperfections theory explained the behaviour of multinationals who arrange their affairs to reduce their tax liabilities. The product life cycle theory described the behaviour of a number of well-known companies such as Dyson and Apple.

While considering the international portfolio diversification theory, we began to appreciate how significant exchange rates are for the competitiveness and profitability of businesses. We were also able to understand the benefits to a company of moving into new, international markets.

In the next section, we further explored reasons for companies becoming multinationals, despite the difficulties, by looking at their history. Throughout history, companies have spread in waves around the globe.

The raw material seekers were followed by those seeking new markets and then the mature businesses seeking to reduce their costs. Few expansions are planned in advance; most are in response to opportunities or threats facing the company.

Finally, we briefly discussed the forms international expansion can take. Some businesses move through the forms as they evolve into multinationals; others identify a strategy that suits them and repeat it over and over again in each new country or region of the world.

Questions

Question 1

If you are a retired UK resident and you invested your life savings of £500,000 in long-dated UK government bonds to provide an income for yourself, what risks, if any, would you be taking with this investment? Long-dated bonds will not mature, or be repaid for many years.

Hint: think about what your return would be in different economic scenarios and for each one consider whether you would have more or less spending power in real terms.

Question 2

The efficient market hypothesis claims that securities are priced to reflect all available information about the security. In recent years, new ideas such as behavioural finance have begun to question the extent to which the efficient market hypothesis can be applied to stock markets and other financial markets. By reading Malkiel (2003) or other articles, consider how useful you think the efficient market hypothesis is in explaining the behaviour of markets today.

Question 3

By undertaking some research about Dyson, the company founded in 1987 by James Dyson, assess the theories of foreign direct investment.

Question 4

Compare and contrast the behaviour of Apple and Google to their business models and their treatment of business partners to assess methods used by those two companies to expand their businesses internationally.

02
The institutions and participants that make up the global financial system

At the end of this chapter you will be able to:

- identify and discuss the participants in the global financial system, particularly the role of central banks;
- discuss the need for banking regulation and supervision and the difficulties faced by legislators;
- briefly describe what happened in the global financial crisis.

Introduction

The *Financial Times* defines the global financial system as:

> This is the interplay of financial companies, regulators and institutions operating on a supranational level. The global financial system can be divided into regulated entities (international banks and insurance companies), regulators, supervisors and institutions like the European Central Bank or the International Monetary Fund. The system also includes the lightly regulated or non-regulated bodies – this is known as the 'shadow banking' system. Mainly, this covers hedge funds, private equity and bank-sponsored entities such as off-balance-sheet vehicles that banks use to invest in the financial markets.

The global financial system has grown over recent decades to meet the needs initially of international trade, and today to meet the complex needs of companies, investors, governments, banks and everyone seeking to borrow or invest money or to use a currency other than their domestic currency.

One way or another almost all of us have some contact with the global financial system. Holidaymakers will be affected by changes in exchange rates, finding their holiday more or less expensive than in previous years. Oil and fuel are priced in dollars so the fall in the value of sterling following the Brexit vote led to an increase in fuel prices across the UK. In practice, there are also links between the interest rates that different countries charge and this impacts on the cost of borrowing for most of us.

In this chapter we will focus on the participants in the global financial system, especially the banks and the regulators. In later chapters we will study the markets that are part of the global financial system.

A brief background to the UK banking system

The first bank was set up in Amsterdam in the 16th century and by the 17th century had spread to the UK. Banks quickly put in place a range of services they could charge customers for, including **bills of exchange**, where the bank paid out cash to anyone holding a document signed by the customer instructing the bank to make such a payment on or after a specific date.

By responding to the increasingly complex needs of their customers, the UK banks became world leaders in banking innovation, creating the financial instruments that their customers needed to conduct their international trade. Exporters often faced problems financing their business. Their customers would pay them with a bill of exchange but the exporters would need the money earlier than the specified date. The banks offered a discounting service where they would pay out a smaller amount of cash on the bill of exchange earlier than the specified date. Some banks became discount houses because of their willingness to do this.

Cheques and overdrafts were created in the 18th century and banks settled their accounts with each other by meeting in a physical location at the end of each working day.

Through the 18th and 19th centuries, banks became more important, offering more services and spreading geographically to meet the needs of businesses and individuals. Some of the names we are so familiar with today, such as Barclays, were founded at this time.

At the end of the 18th century, the first merchant banks were set up to provide the services needed by the new exporting companies who were benefiting from the Industrial Revolution. By 1826, a national network of 20 banks was established.

The Bank of England was created in 1694 to enable the government to raise money to finance the war with France. Subscribers were enthusiastic about the project and the bank raised £1.2 million in a few weeks. Subscribers became the owners of the bank. In addition, to continue to meet the government's demands for new finance and the issuance of new coins, the bank offered banking services to the public, accepting deposits and discounting bills. The bank began to issue bank notes, which were widely accepted as currency.

Government debt increased and by the end of the 18th century the bank was no longer exchanging bank notes for gold. During this time, other banks were also issuing bank notes, which were also vulnerable to counterfeiting.

In the middle of the 19th century the Bank of England was given a monopoly on issuing bank notes, Scottish banks were still able to issue bank notes but they had to be backed by holdings of Bank of England bank notes. To reduce the risk of inflation, the bank was only allowed to issue new notes if matched by an increase in its holding of gold. After this it decided to stop offering commercial banking facilities and instead to focus on being banker to the government, developing the concept of lender of last resort.

Central banks

Most countries have a central bank. In the UK it is the Bank of England, in the United States it is the Federal Reserve, and the eurozone has the European Central Bank (ECB) which, together with the central banks in each member state, makes up what is called the eurosystem. The exact status and role of each bank vary, though many were originally based on the Bank of England model, but there are some activities that are undertaken by almost all central banks.

Generally, central banks act as banker to the government. That is, they accept receipts paid to the government such as tax payments and make payments for the government's expenses such as paying civil servants. This is achieved by the government having a bank account with the central bank which then operates in the same way as any other current account. There are other flows of cash through the government's bank account with the central bank. The central bank doesn't generally lend money to the government but it will often play a role in raising money for the government by issuing and redeeming financial instruments such as bills and bonds. Government bonds are held for investment purposes by financial institutions and individuals in the domestic market. In the UK about a third of government bonds, also called gilts, are held overseas. But the full scope of the role of central banks generally far exceeds acting as banker to the government.

Central banks usually play a role in monetary policy. Some central banks, such as the European Central Bank, have full independence. That means that they are free to set monetary policy, interest rates and money supply, and take the necessary actions to achieve the targets set.

In contrast, the Bank of England has instrument independence where the government sets the policy but the bank is free to take any necessary action to achieve the targets. Prior to 1997, the Bank of England was not independent; the government set the targets and determined the action to be taken to achieve them. The Bank of England was simply the agent of the government. But the evidence is that in countries where the central bank is independent, inflation levels are lower. This might be partly because governments can be tempted to manufacture a boost to the economy prior to elections, leading to inflation rising after the election as more money chases the same amount of goods.

In 1997, the Bank of England was granted instrument independence by the new Labour government. The Treasury remained responsible for setting the inflation target and the Bank of England is charged with achieving the inflation rate set. In addition, the Bank of England is charged with maintaining a safe and stable financial system. This is termed instrument independence. That is, the Bank of England is given its targets but is free to achieve them as it sees fit. In contrast, the European Central Bank (ECB) has full independence and sets its own targets in addition to being free to determine how to achieve them.

In the UK, the Bank of England is responsible for printing bank notes and the Royal Mint is responsible for minting coins of the realm. While many transactions today are electronic, via card payments or bank transfers, the amount of cash in circulation is significant for the amount of credit available in the economy. One might expect a central bank to print sufficient additional cash to cover any growth in the economy as well as replace old or damaged notes. In practice, they sometimes print more cash in order to provide a boost to the economy.

Since the global financial crisis, the UK central bank, in common with some other central banks, has been practising '**quantitative easing**'. Quantitative easing describes the action of the central bank entering the market and buying back government and sometimes corporate bonds, thus electronically 'printing' money. This is intended to increase private spending in order to increase demand in the economy which should help to create growth and increase inflation, which at the time of writing is below the government's target of 2%. Clearly this is a delicate operation, as too much quantitative easing could lead to inflation significantly exceeding the government's target.

Central banks are often responsible for issuing government bonds, though in the UK it is the responsibility of the UK Debt Management Office. Government bonds, called **gilts** or **treasury bills**, in the UK have the same risk and return relationship as almost every other investment. Thus, if investors begin to question the ability of the government to pay the interest due or repay the capital, the cost of issuing new debt will rise, perhaps substantially increasing the cost of borrowing.

Governments understand that if they printed as much money as they might like to it would lead to higher levels of inflation and in extremis to hyperinflation and the currency becoming virtually worthless.

UK gilts can be issued in currencies other than the pound sterling. In the past, they have even issued shares in the currency of China, called renminbi bonds.

Activity

Why would the Bank of England wish to issue bonds denominated in a currency other than sterling? Who bears the risk if bonds are issued in sterling? How does that change if the bonds are issued in renminbi?

Feedback

This is a very interesting question which goes to the heart of the global financial system. We need to start by identifying the risks.

If the Bank of England issues bonds in sterling there is effectively no credit risk. The bank will always be able to pay capital and repay the bond when it is due to be redeemed. It might do this by issuing more bonds. If it was unable to issue more bonds then it could print money. If the bonds are held by a UK citizen, either a company or an individual, then there is no exchange rate risk in that the proceeds will not be converted to another currency. As we will see, exchange risk isn't just about converting currency but for the moment we will ignore this. The only risk then is that the individual's purchasing power could be eroded by the effect of inflation. The value of their investment might fall in real terms if inflation is high. Part of the interest payment is compensation for inflation as we will see in Chapter 6.

What about international holders who will want to convert the pounds they receive into their own currency?

This group is exposed to exchange risk. If the pound depreciates between the date of the purchase of the bond and the date the bond is redeemed, or sold if earlier, the amount of foreign currency received at the end of the period will be less than the amount of foreign currency spent on the bonds in the first place.

Now let's consider what happens if the Bank of England issues renminbi bonds.

Since the Bank of England cannot print yuan, presumably there is some default or credit risk. But in practice, the Bank of England can always sell sterling bonds or print sterling to use to buy yuan, which means that there is effectively no credit risk.

What about the exchange risk?

Now the Bank of England will have to buy yuan in the open market in order to repay the debt, unless they issue new renminbi bonds when they effectively defer the risk. So the Bank of England takes all the exchange risk on these bonds. Of course, the holder of the bond may want to convert the yuan into another currency but that is beyond our considerations now.

There are other reasons for issuing a renminbi bond, the most important one being to enable investors to diversify into different currencies. But from the above we can see that holding bonds issued by the Bank of England will be less risky to Chinese investors if they are denominated in yuan.

As a result, governments generally prefer their independent central banks to make these decisions to ensure that printing money is an economic rather than a political decision.

Central banks generally also act as banker to the commercial banks. Commercial banks are required to maintain an account with the central bank which does not pay interest but must have sufficient funds in it for day-to-day transactions. At the end of each day, the central bank will aggregate the daily transactions between the commercial banks and net the balances off.

In addition, the Central Bank usually acts as 'lender of last resort' to the commercial banks. This means that the central bank will lend money to any bank which finds that it is running out of cash. One of the early signs of the scale of the problem of the global financial crisis in the UK was that Northern Rock couldn't raise sufficient money in the money markets to meet its debt obligations as they fell due and it was obliged to borrow from the Bank of England. The service is very important because it enables banks' customers to have confidence in the bank because they are assured the Bank of England will always save the banks from collapse. In Chapter 5 we will consider the Scottish Referendum and the plan to use the pound as the Scottish currency. Had that happened, the Scottish Banks would not have been able to rely on the Bank of England as the lender of last resort and that might have led to a loss of confidence in the Scottish banks.

In response to the global financial crisis, the Bank of England reduced its base rate from 5% to a historic low of 0.5% by January 2009, where it remained until the summer of 2016, when rates were reduced even further to 0.25% in response to the vote to leave the EU. This move was possible because of the very low inflation and was necessary to support the economy and encourage investment.

Activity

So how low can base rates go? See if you can find out if there are countries with lower interest rates than that of the UK.

Feedback

Well, in practice, several central banks have used negative interest rates, that is, they charge depositors a fee for the money they deposit with them, over the last few years. The ECB has had a negative marginal deposit facility rate for the last two years and the Bank of Japan moved into negative interest rates in January 2016.

Most governments have a target for inflation of around 2% but at the time of writing many countries, including the UK, have inflation below that target. By lowering interest rates, banks hope to encourage spending over saving to stimulate their economies and raise inflation towards the target rate.

A further role of most central banks is the management of the country's foreign reserves. **Foreign reserves** are made up of gold, foreign currencies (mostly the US dollar but also the euro, the pound sterling or the Japanese yen) and the IMF **Special Drawing Rights** (**SDRs**). We will discuss SDRs in Chapter 3. The foreign reserves are used to reduce the volatility of the exchange rate by enabling the central bank to step in and buy or sell their own currency to change the equilibrium of supply and demand.

Banking supervision and regulation

The world has suffered banking crises for almost as long as we have had banks. The first major crisis was in 1763 when a Dutch bank collapsed and the crisis spread to Germany and Scandinavia. Banking crises have remained a feature of the banking system since then. The global financial crisis of 2008 was probably the biggest one so far but it almost certainly won't be the last.

The problem with banking crises is that they often have a substantial adverse impact on businesses and the economy because organizations and individuals can't borrow the money they need to invest. The crises also carry the risk of contagion where the failure of one bank leads to the failure of otherwise successful businesses and other banks and can spread between countries.

Other businesses do not generally have such a substantial impact on the economy as a whole if they fail, so governments generally attempt to supervise and regulate banks in a way that they don't with most other businesses.

Before we move on to consider supervision and regulation in detail we will assess the fundamental issues that led to the global financial crisis. We can then consider supervision and regulation in the context of the crisis.

The global financial crisis

We are going to set out a brief overview of the causes of the global financial crisis, how the crisis unfolded, and how the regulators responded.

The origins of the crisis date back to 2000, when central banks reduced interest rates in response to low levels of inflation and over the following years maintained that low level partly because of a desire to mitigate the uncertainty caused by terrorist attacks and wars. At the same time, the citizens of the emerging markets in Asia were saving money, providing a ready supply of cash to the West and contributing to the continuing low interest rates, the euro was launched, allowing some countries in Europe to borrow at much lower rates than before, and America was borrowing money from the Asian savers to cover their substantial current account deficit.

While the low interest rates encouraged borrowers to take on debt, they dismayed savers who wanted higher returns than their traditional low-risk investments, such as government bonds, were providing.

The bankers, along with most other people, had forgotten the relationship between risk and return in the stable economic environment they found themselves in. In order to increase returns, they took on additional risks such as borrowing money to invest, lending to riskier individuals and businesses, and investing in new securities such as credit default swaps, whose risk characteristics were not well understood.

Some European banks were borrowing at very low rates in the United States and using the money to buy securities offering high returns with unclear levels of risk.

Not everyone was convinced by these complex financial instruments. In 2002, Warren Buffett, the CEO of Berkshire Hathaway, famously described derivatives, one type of complex financial instrument, as 'weapons of mass destruction', citing the range of variables that affected value, the dependence on the creditworthiness of the other party to the transaction, the ease with which risk could be shifted from one party to a contract to another, and the long duration of some of the resulting financial positions as reasons to be concerned about the financial system at that time.

In the United States, bankers were using the cheap money to provide mortgages to people who were not as creditworthy as previous borrowers had been. These were called **sub-prime mortgages**. Mortgages appeared to be very low risk because if the borrower defaulted the bank could repossess the house. Given this apparent low risk, the bankers lent money to people who were increasingly unlikely to be able to pay their mortgage. But borrowing short term in money markets and using the money to lend to people for 25 years or even longer is in itself a risky activity. If the supply of cheap money fell, banks would soon be in difficulties as they would be unable to raise the money they needed to maintain their position. Many people were offered low introductory rates and had little chance of paying their mortgage once the rates rose after a couple of years. House prices responded to this increased funding by more than doubling in value between 2000 and 2006, further fuelling a belief that houses were a safe investment which provided high returns.

Collateralized debt obligations (CDOs)

A CDO is a tradeable derivative. That means that it can be bought and sold on a suitable stock exchange where its current value is found by the law of supply and demand and that its value is based on the value of some underlying security.

In the case of a CDO, the underlying security is a pool of debt or loans made to individuals who are committed to making interest payments and to repaying the capital in line with a formal agreement.

So, when you buy a CDO you are buying an income stream received from the original borrowers. These promised payments are the collateral that makes the CDO valuable. This process of pooling mortgages and using them to create CDOs is called securitization.

The pool of debt on which a CDO is created is potentially made up of loans made for a variety of reasons: mortgages, car loans, bonds and so on. The financial intermediaries, primarily in Wall Street, took a pool of debt and then divided it into tranches, that is slices or parts, in such a way that the senior tranches received the income first and more junior tranches only received income once the amount due to the more senior tranches had been paid.

That makes the senior tranches less risky and the junior tranches more risky. As a result, the senior tranches receive a lower return than the junior tranches, as you would expect.

The financial intermediaries then called upon the credit rating agencies, Standard & Poor's, Moody's and Fitch, to rate the CDOs they had created.

It is clear in hindsight that the credit rating agencies did not understand the CDOs well enough to accurately rate their creditworthiness. They appear to have given all the senior tranches a triple-A rating because they were backed by mortgages and were protected from some default by the junior tranches who had to bear the loss of default first. The junior tranches generally gained a BBB rating which was still an investment-grade rating. The confidence shown by the credit rating agencies in CDOs was probably due to the fact that if borrowers defaulted on their loans the lender would be able to repossess the property the mortgage was secured on and sell that. A widely held belief that house prices would only go up then made the CDOs look very attractive.

The financial intermediaries responded to this strategy by taking some of the junior tranches and combining them into a new CDO which led to some now appearing to be low-risk senior tranches. The credit rating agencies were now willing to give these new senior tranches a triple-A rating even though they had previously given exactly the same security a BBB rating.

Another derivative, **credit default swaps (CDSs)**, were also being used on Wall Street at this time. The buyer, or holder, of the CDS paid an amount, called a premium, to insure against the default of a debt instrument. If the instrument defaults, the seller of the CDS has to pay the agreed amount to the holder of the swap.

Credit default swaps enabled investors to bet against the CDOs and some made a great deal of money when mortgage holders were unable to make the due payments.

The availability of CDSs and the reduction in the number of mortgages made led to the development of **synthetic CDOs** towards the end of the boom period which led to the global financial crisis. A synthetic CDO was made up of CDSs and other derivatives rather than a pool of debts and was cheaper and easier to create. The synthetic CDO was effectively a bet on the default of some underlying tranche of mortgages and other debt. By

2006, synthetic CDOs were worth as much as US $5 trillion, more than any other CDOs.

European banks were also attracted to borrow by the very low interest rates in the United States and were also experiencing an expansion in the financial sector caused by the introduction of the euro. Like other investors, they used the money they borrowed to buy CDOs in order to obtain a satisfactory return.

But as homeowners found paying their mortgages impossible and houses were repossessed, house prices began to fall and the risky nature of the sub-prime mortgages and thus CDOs became apparent. In the United States, house prices fell by a third between the middle of 2006 and the start of 2009. Securities which had been thought to be safe were suddenly worthless. The money markets stopped working and the supply of cheap credit dried up, leading to banking failures such as Lehman Brothers in the United States and Northern Rock in the UK.

Throughout the build-up to the crisis, regulators around the world failed to take action to stop the banks' risky behaviour. Once the crisis took hold, the regulators were inconsistent in their response and allowed Lehman Brothers to collapse, increasing the risk of other banks failing.

Businesses in other sectors which had had no involvement in the activities of the bankers suddenly found that they couldn't access credit and some failed as a result. Many had to defer planned investment and the global economy contracted.

In many ways, the global financial crisis was typical of banking crises, which tend to occur when economies are booming and new opportunities for investment present themselves. People become overconfident of the new assets available to them, be they railways or complex financial instruments, and an asset bubble ensues where prices rise quickly and without any fundamental reason for their increase. Eventually, people question the value of the assets and the bubble bursts, as house prices, followed by CDOs, did this time.

The global financial crisis is widely accepted as a consequence of the failure of banking regulation. This failure is perhaps best illustrated by Alan Greenspan, Chairman of the Federal Reserve from 1987 until 2006, who wrote in 2007: '*Why do we need to inhibit the pollinating bees of Wall Street?*'

Greenspan was implementing the 1980s philosophies of Thatcher in the UK and Reagan in the United States, who favoured deregulation and liberalization, preferring to rely on market forces than regulation.

Supervisory authority

When we look at the supervision and regulation of the banking sector there are a number of elements we need to consider. The first is the structure of the supervisory authority: is it a single organization or is the role split between more than one organization? Prior to the global financial crisis, regulation in the UK was split between three organizations: the Financial Services Authority (FSA), the Bank of England and the Treasury.

In a survey of 180 countries on banking regulation covering 1999 to 2011 by Barth, Caprio Jr. and Levine (2013) it was found that only 10 out of 136 countries used multiple agency regulators, with the rest relying on a single regulator. Interestingly, those 10 using multiple agency regulators included many of the countries that were hit hardest by the global financial crisis, for example the United States, the UK, Denmark, Germany and Iceland.

Eighty-nine of the countries used their central bank as the single regulator and nine of the 10 using multiple-agency regulation used the central bank as one of their regulators, meaning that 38 countries did not give a regulatory role to their central bank.

Countries adopt a variety of organizational structures to regulate their banks. The World Bank undertakes regular surveys of countries to assess their regulation of the banks. The most recent was in 2011/12 and was particularly focused on the global financial crisis and its aftermath (World Bank, 2013). They tried to identify differences in supervision and regulation between countries that were seriously affected by the global financial crisis, such as the United States and the UK, and countries that were not, such as Australia and Canada. The researchers were also interested in how supervision and regulation had changed as a result of the global financial crisis.

The researchers found that there were significant differences between the two groups:

> First, crisis countries had less stringent definitions of capital and lower actual capital ratios. Second, banks in crisis countries faced fewer restrictions on non-bank activities such as insurance, investment banking, and real estate. Third, regulations concerning the treatment of bad loans and loan losses were less strict in crisis countries. Finally, in crisis countries, there were weaker incentives for the private sector to monitor banks' risks.

The Bank for International Settlements

The Bank for International Settlements was set up in Basel, Switzerland after the end of the First World War, to facilitate German war reparations. Its role quickly shifted to focus on encouraging international cooperation between central banks, who effectively run it, as only central banks own shares in it. Around 60 central banks are members of the BIS. The 1944 Bretton Woods Conference (discussed in detail in Chapter 3) agreed to close down the BIS despite the British delegation arguing for its survival, but after the conference the decision was reversed. In the 1990s, the BIS became an increasingly global institution.

In some ways, the Bank for International Settlements, which is owned by the central banks, can be considered to be the banker to the central banks, offering daily settlement between the banks and taking on the role of lender of last resort.

The BIS has the following aim:

Promoting global monetary and financial stability through international cooperation.

Today it seeks to make monetary policy in its member countries more predictable and transparent.

The BIS also takes an active role in banking supervision, which we will talk about in the next section. For now it is enough to say that it aims to regulate capital adequacy and encourage reserve transparency.

The need for banking regulation

We have already seen that the failure of a bank may lead to contagion and be a serious risk to the banking sector and the entire economy. There are also other reasons for banking regulation.

The first is termed **information asymmetry**. This means that when a business or individual approaches a bank to, for example, buy a service, the bank knows much more about its products than their client and regulation is necessary to protect the client from bad practice on the part of the bank.

Given all the scandals in the banking sector in the last few years, you might be surprised to find that this problem is well understood and attempts have been made to regulate for it.

Example

Perhaps the biggest scandal so far has been the misselling of PPI (payment protection insurance) which is estimated to be going to cost the British banks a total of £45 billion. To put that in context, the NHS is planned to cost about £117 billion pounds in 2016/17. This is a major reason for the desire to improve banking regulation.

The second reason for needing banking regulation is the fear that people will lose the money they have deposited in the bank. We are not talking about the shareholders, who accept that the value of their investments may go up or down, but depositors who are seeking a safe place for their wealth. In the UK, the government guarantees the deposits of investors up to the value of £75,000 in any one group of banks.

If a bank failed, its depositors would find that they were unable to access their normal banking facilities, which today could quickly mean that they couldn't buy food or pay for transport. It is important that people have confidence in the banking sector.

Banks, in practice, are very closely linked together and routinely borrow and lend to each other. They also hold each other's securities as part of their day-to-day investment business. The failure of one bank will put pressure on other banks because assets would suddenly become worthless. And this is likely to be happening at a time when the banking system as a whole is under the same kind of external stress which led to the failure of the first bank. This domino effect is termed contagion and is a major concern of regulators, who are concerned not only with the survival of individual banks but also with the safety of the banking system as a whole.

Finally, banks in distress are likely to sell some of their paper assets to provide a much-needed cash injection to their operations. But selling assets increases the supply of assets at a time when demand is unlikely to be increasing, thus leading to a fall in value of other assets.

Given all of this it is easy to see why governments are eager to regulate their banks.

Regulation

Bank regulation usually takes a number of forms. The regulator is likely to limit the individuals and organizations undertaking banking operations by licensing banks and requiring individuals to be approved. The regulator is likely to set out requirements for the amount of capital that the bank has in reserve.

These regulations are likely to cost banks money in terms of compliance and having to hold more cash than they otherwise might have chosen to. In addition, the regulation is likely to restrict new entrants into the market, thus reducing competition. These costs are not insignificant.

There are additional problems with banking regulation, the first being the problem of **moral hazard**. Moral hazard can occur when the natural relationship between risk and return is disrupted by regulation and so individuals do something that they would not otherwise have done. In the case of banking regulation, individuals know that their deposits are protected up to £75,000, and so it doesn't matter how risky the bank is in which they put their money: it is safe anyway. In which case a depositor need only concern themselves with the return offered by the bank.

This means that banks are competing with each other in terms of the return they can offer alone. Risk is no longer a factor.

So a bank might choose to lend to risky organizations and individuals in order to generate the highest possible return, since in terms of lending the normal risk and return relationship we discussed in Chapter 1 still holds. The bank which takes the greatest risk is able to generate the highest return and so can offer the best rates to savers. The regulation protecting savers is actually encouraging banks to behave in a risky fashion.

A second problem with banking regulation is that it is increasingly a global issue and effective regulation is difficult without international cooperation.

Banking regulation in the UK

After the global financial crisis and change of government in 2010, the system of regulation of banks in the UK was changed.

Under the current system of regulation, the Bank of England took on responsibility for the financial markets' infrastructure. The Financial Conduct Authority took on responsibility for ensuring that financial markets operated effectively and the Prudential Regulatory Authority (PRA) has responsibility for the regulation and supervision of around 1,700 banks and other financial firms.

One of the biggest differences from the previous system is that the PRA is forward looking, assessing the level of risk in organizations and the potential impact on the stability of the financial system.

Summary

In this chapter we have discussed the global financial system, the organizations that underpin it and the participants who operate within it. We have focused on the role of central banks and regulation, including the difficulties of regulating the global banking system. Here we have focused on the Bank of England and the regulation of banks used in the UK, partly because it has changed in recent years. Most countries face similar dilemmas and adopt similar solutions as the UK has done. In subsequent chapters we will further consider the role of the central bank and what happens if a country joins a currency union, such as the eurozone, rather than maintaining an independent central bank. Finally, in this chapter we began our discussion of the global financial crisis and the role that regulation took in countries' ability to deal with the crisis. Again, in subsequent chapters we will return to this to consider the impact of the global financial crisis on the global financial environment today.

Questions

Question 1

As part of banking regulation, the Bank of England undertook a stress test of the UK banks in 2017, as they do every year. In July 2016, *Forbes* published an article claiming that the stress tests were irrelevant because banks which failed were not penalized for their failure (Worstall, 2016). By reading the financial press, assess the benefit of the Bank of England's stress test in the light of the *Forbes* article.

Question 2

In this chapter we focused on the role of the Bank of England. By visiting the websites of the Bank of England and the European Central Bank, compare and contrast their roles in the countries which they serve and the global financial system.

Question 3

In January 2017, the Bank of England reported that household debt, excluding mortgages, had risen by 10% over the previous year and now stands at the highest level since 2008 at the start of the global financial crisis. At the same time, house prices are at an all-time high and as inflation returns, interest rates will eventually increase. By researching the financial press and credible websites such as the IMF and the Bank of England, consider the extent to which the UK is at risk of a financial collapse.

03
The history of exchange rates, the IMF and the World Bank

At the end of this chapter you will be able to:

- discuss the historic arrangements for calculating exchange rates;
- critically evaluate the changing role of the IMF and the World Bank.

Introduction

In this chapter we will study briefly the history of exchange rates. While this history is very interesting, our real reason for this is that there is much to learn from the past about today's exchange rate regimes. We will also discuss the setting up of the IMF and the World Bank and assess their roles over their first 50 years. In Chapter 4 we will assess their actions during the global financial crisis and the subsequent euro crisis over the last few years.

Gold – the gold standard, 1876–1913

International trade probably initially relied on bartering goods but as it increased, better ways of paying for goods were needed. This was initially through the use of gold coins but there proved to be some difficulties in both the actual weight of the coins, older coins tending to be worn away, and the metallic composition of the coins, with some countries putting more gold in than others.

In the 18th century, bank notes were introduced which were convertible into a set amount of a metal; silver and gold were popular and sometimes both were referenced in what was known as a bimetallism. This led to the introduction of the gold standard in 1876, which stated exactly how much currency could be exchanged for a fixed amount of gold. Under the gold standard, governments committed to buying or selling gold at that exchange rate. This worked well because, due to its nature, the value of gold relative to goods and services has historically proved stable over time. This brings stability to the currencies pegged against it, giving low levels of inflation.

However, there are some difficulties with using a gold standard. Under a gold standard, the level of inflation is dictated by the rate at which gold is mined. Most gold is mined in Russia and South Africa. Large gold reserves found in South Africa at the end of the 19th century led directly to a 4% increase in worldwide inflation in a single year. Any disruption to the mining of gold risks global deflation. Equally, increases in global production in excess of mining always risk deflation.

Most countries were members of the gold standard until the start of the First World War, when it was abandoned; it was not reintroduced at the end of the war because of the poor liquidity of the Bank of England.

There are some difficulties with using a gold standard, though. One significant one is that a government needs to have sufficient gold to underpin its currency in issue. Holding gold has costs attached to it. First, it has to be mined, processed, transported and protected from theft. In addition, the money invested in gold can't be invested in assets which provide a return that might be interest or profits so there is an opportunity cost associated with holding gold. Over time there was a shift away from holding gold reserves to holding foreign currency, which could be used to settle transactions with other countries without using gold and which provided a return in the form of interest.

Gold Exchange Standard and beyond, 1925–44

In 1925, the Gold Exchange Standard was adopted by the major trading nations. A gold exchange standard doesn't require a government to agree to exchange currency for a fixed quantity of gold. Economists came to realize that gold was effectively an international currency but was not necessary for a national currency. All that was needed was to hold sufficient gold to pay international debts at a fixed rate for the other currency. This works provided the other country is also part of the gold standard.

As you might have expected, the Gold Exchange Standard, applied to weakened economies, created deflation and contributed to turning the recession of 1929–31 into the Great Depression of 1931–41. Those countries which were not part of the Gold Exchange Standard, or left in 1929, such as Argentina and Brazil, largely avoiding the Great Depression, and countries which left the Gold Exchange Standard in 1931, such as the UK, Germany and Austria, were able to recover more quickly than countries like the United States and France, who remained members until 1933 and 1936 respectively. In the case of the UK, it was forced to abandon the Gold Exchange Standard in 1931 after speculative attacks on the pound sterling. The British government was then able to use monetary policy to stimulate the economy.

After the end of the Gold Exchange Standard, currencies effectively floated freely, which meant that the law of supply and demand led to considerable volatility of the exchange rates. The situation was made worse by speculators holding currencies they considered strong and selling short currencies they thought would fall in value, leading to even more volatility. This volatility had been thought to limit the free flow of trade internationally. In addition, governments tried to restrict imports in order to protect their own economies and even sought to devalue their own currencies in order to make themselves more competitive internationally. These activities led to the Great Depression.

In 1934, the United States moved to a modified gold standard by devaluing the dollar and only trading gold with foreign central banks rather than private citizens. From 1934 to the end of the Second World War, once again exchange rates were theoretically determined by the currency's value in terms of gold but by the end of the Second World War, only the dollar remained as trading currency that was convertible.

Key concept

Selling short means selling something you don't actually have or entering into a contract to supply something you don't currently have. Probably the simplest example of this with currencies is to borrow money in a foreign currency.

Activity

Suppose you are based in the United States and you believe that the pound sterling is going to fall. How could you use a bank loan and foreign exchange to make a potential profit?

Feedback

Let's put some numbers to this problem. Suppose the current exchange rate between the pound and the dollar is £1:$1.30 and that you can borrow and lend at 0%, which isn't far from the truth at the time of writing.

We could borrow £1,000 in London and convert it into $1,300 to put on deposit in New York. At the end of a year, the exchange rate might have moved to £1:$1.20, and we could convert our dollars back into pounds: $1,300 can be converted in £1,083 ($1,300/1.2). We can use these pounds to repay our loan of £1,000, giving us a profit of £83 (£1,083 - £1,000).

However, this is not an arbitrage opportunity and were the exchange rate in a year's time to be £1:$1.50 we would only be able to buy £866.67 ($1,300/1.5) leaving a loss of £133.33 (£1,000 - £866.67).

This is a very simple example of selling short and the profits are unlikely to be really high. But by using derivatives such as options and futures contracts, you can sell short on a spectacular scale and potentially make handsome profits, at the risk of course of losing a fortune.

Key concept

We talk about currencies in a fixed exchange rate regime like the gold standard devaluing (revaluing) if their value falls (rises) against other currencies in the fixed rate system, that is the currency can buy less (more) of the foreign currency than it used to. In a floating rate system we talk about currencies depreciating (appreciating) rather than devaluing (revaluing).

If a currency changes its value – suppose it devalues against the currencies of its trading partners – there can be a significant impact on the economies of the countries involved.

At the time of writing, the pound sterling has depreciated against the dollar as a result of the vote to leave the EU in June 2016. Prior to the vote, the pound was trading at around £1:$1.46 but it quickly fell to around £1:$1.30. The pound also fell against the euro and other currencies.

Activity

State the impact on the following groups of people when the pound fell against the dollar as it did in 2016:

1 British people planning a holiday considering going abroad or holidaying in the UK.

2 Americans planning a European holiday and considering Britain along with other EU countries as their destination.

3 British exporters.

4 British importers.

Feedback

The weakening pound made holidays abroad more expensive for Britons, many of whom responded by taking holidays in the UK.

For Americans it meant that their dollars bought more pounds than in the past, making the UK an attractive destination.

British exporters were able to sell goods for fewer dollars than previously, as it takes fewer dollars to buy the same number of pounds, thus increasing demand for UK exports.

Imports would become more expensive as it takes more pounds to buy the dollars needed for the goods or services imported.

Activity

Given the impacts identified in the previous activity, what is the likely short-term impact on the UK economy?

Feedback

The depreciation gives a big boost to the UK economy, with Britons buying more domestic goods and services such as holidays because they are cheaper than the goods and services of other countries. Equally, British goods and services are now cheaper across much of the world than formerly and so international demand for those British goods and services increases.

This effect was seen in 1992 when the UK withdrew from the European Exchange Rate Mechanism (ERM) and the pound depreciated by around 15%.

A currency is said to devalue if its value against another currency is fixed, that is there is a fixed exchange rate and it becomes necessary to change the fixed exchange rate to reflect the lower value of the currency.

Bretton Woods 1944

Towards the end of the Second World War, the 44 Allied nations sent delegates to Bretton Woods, New Hampshire to what became known as the Bretton Woods Conference. At the end of the conference they signed the Bretton Woods Agreement, which set out a system of rules, institutions and procedures to regulate the international monetary system. The aim of the agreement was to prevent a recurrence of the Great Depression and the risk of another war.

The agreement set up the International Monetary Fund (IMF) and the International Bank for Reconstruction and Development (IBRD), now part of the World Bank. The IMF and the World Bank are part of the United Nations (UN).

The Bretton Woods Agreement didn't believe the gold standard could operate successfully or that the weakened pound could act as a reserve currency, so instead introduced a fixed exchange rate with the US dollar as a reserve currency. It also didn't believe that the gold standard, with its fixed exchange rates, would succeed when economic policy was focused on reconstruction rather than exchange rate stability. It also seemed unlikely that the production of gold would be sufficient to cope with the growth in international trade and investment.

The agreement established a fixed price of $35 an ounce of gold and the US government committed to converting dollars into gold at that price, making the dollar a very attractive security to hold because it offered the low risk of gold along with paid interest. There was then a system of fixed exchange rates between member states and members were asked to commit to the convertibility of their own currency into other currencies and to free trade. This is called a **pegged rate currency system**, which we will discuss in more detail in Chapter 5.

Members were required to determine the peg by reference to the reserve currency, the US dollar, and then to maintain the exchange rates within a 1% band around the exchange rate with the dollar, called the peg. Later on, the band was increased to 2.25%. In order to maintain the exchange rate, governments would have to buy and sell foreign currency or gold in order to use the mechanism of supply and demand to achieve their target exchange rate. The US government then pledged to maintain the value of the dollar at $35 to an ounce of gold. The dollar was then the only convertible currency (convertible into gold) and all other currencies were pegs against it, making it effectively the world currency. In practice, most international transactions were priced in dollars.

Governments could seek a realignment against the dollar if they were unable to maintain the peg. If they wanted to adjust the peg by more than 10%, they had to seek IMF approval, which would only be granted if there was a 'fundamental disequilibrium'. Countries were specifically forbidden to devalue in order to increase their own competitiveness. Unfortunately, the IMF didn't specify what a fundamental disequilibrium was, which created uncertainty.

The original aims of the IMF and World Bank

The initial aims of the IMF can be found on the IMF website, **imf.org**:

The purposes of the International Monetary Fund are:

(i)   To promote international monetary cooperation through a permanent institution which provides the machinery for consultation and collaboration on international monetary problems.

(ii)   To facilitate the expansion and balanced growth of international trade, and to contribute thereby to the promotion and maintenance of high levels of employment and real income and to the development of the productive resources of all members as primary objectives of economic policy.

(iii) To promote exchange stability, to maintain orderly exchange arrangements among members, and to avoid competitive exchange depreciation.

(iv) To assist in the establishment of a multilateral system of payments in respect of current transactions between members and in the elimination of foreign exchange restrictions which hamper the growth of world trade.

(v) To give confidence to members by making the general resources of the Fund temporarily available to them under adequate safeguards, thus providing them with opportunity to correct maladjustments in their balance of payments without resorting to measures destructive of national or international prosperity.

(vi) In accordance with the above, to shorten the duration and lessen the degree of disequilibrium in the international balances of payments of members.

The World Bank had the objective of 'reducing poverty'. This was to be achieved by providing loans to developing countries in order to:

- encourage foreign investment;
- promote international trade; or
- facilitate capital investment.

The World Bank is now made up of five different organizations:

- International Bank for Reconstruction and Development (IBRD);
- International Development Association (IDA);
- International Finance Corporation (IFC);
- Multilateral Investment Guarantee Agency (MIGA);
- International Centre for the Settlement of Investment Disputes (ICSID).

The World Bank provides loans to developing countries. Its actions must generally meet a tripartite goal of encouraging foreign investment, promoting international trade or facilitating capital investment. The first recipient of World Bank aid was France, which received US $250 million in loans, with strict conditions. As many Europeans looked to the Marshall Plan, rather than the World Bank, for post-war aid, the bank gradually shifted to serve mostly non-European, developing countries.

Special Drawing Rights

In 1969 the IMF created a unit of account called the Special Drawing Right (SDR) which has a currency code XDR and is defined and maintained by the IMF. The value of the XDR is a weighted average of key international currencies and is reviewed by the IMF every five years. The weightings are based on each currency's current level of use in international trade and national foreign exchange reserves.

The most recent review was in November 2015 and it was implemented in October 2016. For the first time, the renminbi or Chinese yuan was included in the basket. There are now five currencies in the basket:

Table 3.1 Special Drawing Right currencies

Currency	Weighting
US dollar	41.73%
Euro	30.93%
Chinese yuan	10.92%
Japanese yen	8.33%
British pound	8.09%
Total	100%

It is an international reserve asset which supplements the existing foreign exchange reserves. It acts as a unit of account for the IMF and also for other organizations. Some countries use the SDR as a base against which to peg their currency. Individual countries hold SDRs in the form of deposits with the IMF. They form part of the country's international monetary reserves along with official holdings of gold, foreign exchange and its reserve position with the IMF. Members can also settle transactions among themselves by transferring SDRs.

IMF: up until the end of the 1990s

The IMF uses what it calls a quota system to determine a member's position within it. The quota is currently a weighted average of a country's gross domestic product (GDP), its openness, that is its openness to trade, or lack of trade protectionist policies, economic variability and amount of international reserves. Each country's quota is denominated in Special Drawing Rights (SDRs), the IMF's unit of account. The IMF uses a quota formula to help assess a member's relative position.

A country's quota has a number of implications. The first is that the quota is the amount that a country is required to contribute to the IMF funds: a quarter has to be in the reserve currencies (dollar, euro, yen or UK pound) while the rest can be in the country's own currency. These funds are then available for the IMF to lend to member countries in need of financial support. The second is that the quota is closely linked to the percentage of votes that a country has; the higher the quota, the higher the proportion of votes. However, since the global financial crisis there has been some revision of votes, with up to 6% of the votes moving away from over-represented countries to countries which are highly dynamic or have very low incomes. Finally, the quota establishes the maximum amount a country may borrow from the IMF. A country can borrow up to 200% of its quota a year and up to 600% of its quota in total, although this upper limit can be increased in exceptional circumstances.

The quotas are reviewed every five years but a country's quota can't be increased without its consent.

Structural adjustment programmes (SAPs)

When the IMF or the World Bank lend money to a member country it is accompanied by an SAP, which sets up conditions which must be complied with in order to qualify for the loan. The SAPs have attracted considerable criticism for the impact they can have on the people of a country.

The aim of the SAPs was to address the course of the crisis, which might have been budget deficits, high levels of inflation or price controls, often on staple items such as rent, fuel and basic foodstuffs. This was achieved by compelling a country to reduce its fiscal deficits, often by cutting government spending programmes and thus reducing government borrowing and by encouraging a country to adopt more market-based policies including privatization, deregulation and reducing trade barriers. This general approach was often referred to as the Washington Consensus, and was a generally accepted strategy for creating economic growth by encouraging productivity.

The Washington Consensus or neoliberalism

The Washington Consensus was an agreement among the international financial institutions (IFIs) about the approach needed to create reform in countries seeking help from the IMF and the World Bank. It evolved as a response to the crises in Latin America in the 1980s.

The term was coined by the economist John Williamson, who produced a 10-point list of policies which together made up the Washington Consensus. These were:

1   There should be fiscal policy discipline. Governments should avoid large fiscal deficits relative to their GDP.

2   Public spending priorities should shift away from subsidies towards investment in areas likely to result in high returns.

3   There should be tax reform to broaden the tax base and lower marginal rates of tax.

4   Interest rates should be determined by the market and should be positive and moderate in real terms.

5   Exchange rates should be competitive and designed to create rapid growth in non-traditional exports.

6   There should be trade liberalization to reduce restrictions on imports. Any trade protection should be via low and relatively uniform tariffs.

7 Barriers to foreign direct investment (FDI) should be lowered to encourage increased FDI into the country.

8 State enterprises should be privatized.

9 There should be deregulation, that is of regulations to restrict the entry of new firms or competition except on the grounds of safety, environmental and consumer protection and the overseeing of financial institutions.

10 Secure intellectual property rights (IPR) without excessive costs.

Overall there should be a reduced role for the state, which should allow market forces to prevail.

The Washington Consensus was widely criticized for increasing poverty and creating social instability, and there have been a number of criticisms of the work of the IMF, the World Bank and the SAPs during this time.

They have been accused of threatening countries' national sovereignty by imposing policies on countries who have no choice but to comply. The privatization of state-owned industries means that the now foreign-owned industries now focus on profitability rather than the public prosperity. Finally, the insistence on cutting budget deficits leads to cuts in key social spending such as education and health, both of which are likely to already be underfunded, leading to social unrest and ultimately damage to economic growth.

There were some specific criticisms of the IMF during this time. For example, Joseph Stiglitz, the Nobel Prize-winning economist and former chief economist of the World Bank, highlighted that the IMF required the Korean Central Bank to focus on reducing inflation during the 1997 Asian Financial Crisis because the IMF believed that lowering inflation should be the primary objective of all central banks even though monetary policy did not play a part in the currency crisis and Western banks do not have a primary objective of fighting inflation. Stiglitz went on to claim that the IMF's economists did not have adequate knowledge of the countries they were advising and without a good understanding of the government they used a 'one size fits all' Western economic policy and focused on economic models without considering how economies work in practice. The IMF was criticized for the speed with which they insisted that reform policies were introduced. In practice, privatization often leads to job losses. If governments are forced to privatize state-owned enterprises without a welfare system to support the people who lose their jobs, the policies may fail. Ideally a government should create an environment in which jobs are being created, for example by having low interest rates in order to compensate for the job destruction that privatization often brings. Stiglitz also claimed that there was a lack of transparency in the deals between a government and the IMF, with deals kept secret even from the World Bank, even if the World Bank was also working in the country. That prevented opposition politicians and other pressure groups from criticizing the IMF's policies in their country.

Government ministers felt powerless to criticize the IMF in case they jeopardized the funding that their countries needed and so the IMF was free to push for change with limited opposition to their proposals.

IMF: the current role

The IMF was required to play a key role in the aftermath of the global financial crisis of 2008. It revisited its core purposes and in 2010 adopted the following goal:

> Working to foster global monetary cooperation, secure financial stability, facilitate international trade, promote high employment and sustainable economic growth, and reduce poverty.

Today the IMF has 189 members, the most recent being South Sudan which joined in 2012.

The head of the IMF is Christine Lagarde, a French national. Traditionally the head of the IMF is a European and the head of the World Bank is a North American.

The United States has a current quota of SDR 83 billion; the UK's current quota is SDR 20 million. You can find a full list of member states and their quotas on the IMF website: **https://www.imf.org/external/np/sec/memdir/ members.aspx**.

The quota was roughly doubled in January 2016 to increase the IMF's resources which can be used to lend to member countries in need of support.

In his book *The Euro*, published in mid-2016, Joseph Stiglitz, talking about neoliberalism, also referred to as market fundamentalism and enacted in the Washington Consensus set out above, wrote:

> Market fundamentalists believed, for instance, that if only the government would ensure that inflation was low and stable, markets would ensure growth and prosperity for all... They are held with such conviction and certainty, immune to new contrary evidence, that these beliefs are rightly described as an ideology.

He went on to say:

> Similar ideas pushed by the IMF and the World Bank around the world led to a lost quarter-century in Africa, a lost decade in Latin America, and a transition from communism to the market economy in the former Soviet Union and Eastern Europe that was, to say the least, a disappointment.

After neoliberalism

At the time of writing there seems to be a growing backlash against neoliberalism. We will see what the IMF had to say about it in Chapter 4. Economists Joseph Stiglitz and Thomas Piketty, to name but two, argue that change is inevitable. We have seen the UK vote to leave the EU, something unthinkable only a short time ago, and the election of Donald Trump for president in the United States and Jeremy Corbyn leading the Labour Party in the UK.

This is partly a response to the global financial crisis and its consequences and a reaction to poor or no growth and growing inequality in many Western countries. There has been almost no growth in the eurozone since 2009.

I won't speculate about what is to come. My point is that the era of neoliberalism may be drawing to a close.

Summary

We began this chapter by studying the organization of exchange rates over the last 150 years. This was partly to create a context for our study of the current environment, particularly the supranational organizations like the IMF and the World Bank, but also because there was much to learn about the difficulties of basing a currency on gold or using fixed exchange rates.

We began to consider the consequences of changing exchange rates on the economic decisions and activities of residents and businesses in different countries.

We moved on to discussion of the changing role of the IMF and the World Bank and made some attempt to assess both. We finally defined neoliberalism and by considering some recent events in politics noted that neoliberalism's domination of global economics since the 1980s might be on the wane. In Chapter 4 we will return to the current role of the IMF when we discuss the euro crisis and particularly the Greek crisis.

Questions

Question 1

Visit the IMF and World Bank websites and investigate the range of activities they each undertake.

Question 2

Suppose that you are a UK citizen and you believe that the pound is going to fall to $1.15:£1 by the end of 2019. You have savings of £20,000 which you do not expect to need to access in the next three years.

How could you act on your belief to take advantage of the exchange rate movement?

What risks, if any, does your plan expose you to?

Question 3

As the UK prepares for Brexit, do you consider that they are following a neoliberal agenda?

04

The euro and the global financial environment post the global financial crisis

At the end of this chapter you will be able to:

- discuss the euro, its history, benefits and disadvantages;
- discuss the cause of the euro crisis and its consequences;
- critically evaluate the role of the IMF in the bailout of Greece;
- explain the impact of the euro on the cost of government debt.

Introduction

In 2002 the euro was adopted by 12 of the European Union (EU) countries and today is the legal currency of 19 of the 28 EU countries, together with four more countries from outside the EU who have also adopted it. In this chapter we will evaluate the success of the euro and its problems. The EU countries using the euro make up the eurozone. In some ways, the euro has been a resounding success; it is now the second most used reserve currency in the world, second only to the US dollar and accounting for a little less than a quarter of global reserves, but it has not emerged unscathed from the global financial crisis. Some countries adopting the euro found that they could borrow at much lower interest rates than before and, in the case of Greece, were able to borrow money that the country could never repay.

When the governments were under pressure to bail out the banks after the global financial crisis, the euro crisis hit them and Greece defaulted on much of its debt.

A very brief history of the euro

The desire to introduce a single currency in the EU has been a long-held vision in Europe and the path to its creation dates back to the 1960s. Once the Bretton Woods currency agreement failed and currencies floated freely, the introduction of a single currency was seen as a way to eliminate exchange rate volatility. In March 1979, the European Monetary System (EMS), which used the **European Currency Unit (ECU)** was launched. The ECU was a basket of a fixed amount of EU currencies. The aim of the EMS was to establish a zone of exchange rate stability which would encourage trade and growth. The EMS was also intended to accelerate the convergence and integration of economic policies within the EU which would pave the way for a single currency. The ECU was used as a virtual currency to settle accounts between the EU central banks and was used in official EU business. ECUs were also often used in international credit and bond markets.

Countries were required to maintain their currency within a specified margin, originally 2.25% either side of a central rate against the other currencies. If a currency was at risk of moving outside the specified range, the government would be required to intervene by adjusting their official interest rates or by buying and selling currencies. In the long term, the only successful strategy is to adopt converging monetary policies.

The Maastricht Treaty of 1993 laid the foundations for an economic and monetary union, part of which was the introduction of a single currency, the euro.

The European System of Central Banks was set up in 1998 and the euro was launched in 1999 as a virtual currency; it became the legal currency in issue in all the eurozone countries in January 2002.

The euro and the global financial crisis

Only a few years after its adoption, the euro faced a test on a scale few had anticipated. The global financial crisis revealed weaknesses in the financial and economic position of some members of the eurozone and the system was tested almost to breaking point.

Some of the euro crisis in 2009 had its roots in the period leading up to the creation of the euro. At the end of the 1990s, stringent criteria were set for membership of the eurozone including low inflation, low currency volatility, and caps on budget deficits and government debt. But some governments, Greece in particular, undertook some creative accounting, including off-balance-sheet activities and the use of complex financial instruments to conceal their true debt. Greece was spending much more than it was collecting in tax and thus was running up more and more debt.

Greece's main industries are tourism and shipping and both are very sensitive to economic downturns, which meant the global financial crisis had a significant effect on the Greek economy.

In 2009, the new Greek government became more transparent in its financial dealings and creditors began to worry about their ability to service their existing and future debts, as it eventually became apparent that the Greek budget deficit was much higher than the 3% maximum allowed under the Maastricht Treaty. Such a situation is referred to as a structural deficit and can be very difficult to reduce or eliminate. While Greece was clearly in the most difficulty, other countries also breached the Maastricht Treaty rules and were causing concern. These included Portugal, Italy, Spain and Ireland – together with Greece, the so-called PIGS countries.

At the same time as these countries joined the eurozone they were forced to deal with the deregulation and financial liberalization that were part of the growth of the single market, and globalization increasing the pressure on their economies to modernize. During the early years of the euro there was also a growing trade gap between the northern eurozone countries like Germany and their poorer southern neighbours. Finally, these countries faced the difficulty of bailing out banks who had run into serious difficulties as a result of the global financial crisis. The result of the bailouts was to convert banking debt into sovereign debt, thus adding more debt to already overstretched governments. The countries were forced to seek help from other member states, the European Central Bank and the IMF.

Until the autumn of 2009, eurozone governments had been able to borrow at around the same rate as each other. Creditors believed that a euro was a euro and it didn't matter which government issued government bonds denominated in euros. But they soon realized that some countries did suffer from credit risk and their interest rates, including long-term rates, quickly rose, In the case of Greece, within two years they had risen to nearly 30%.

The ECB undertook a number of initiatives to support countries in difficulties, including the European Financial Stability Facility (EFSF) and European Stability Mechanism (ESM). In addition, interest rates were lowered and the ECB lent over a trillion euros at very low rates to support members in financial difficulties.

In practice, the countries most affected, Greece, Portugal and Ireland, together only accounted for around 6% of the eurozone's GDP and so economically the impact on the area was not great. However, the political concerns about the euro and the eurozone were considerable. Greece received financial support in 2010 and again in 2011.

By 2014 the financial position had significantly improved for most of the PIGS countries.

The euro since the global financial crisis

While the global financial crisis began as a banking crisis, it soon became apparent that some governments were also in financial distress. The flip side of the low returns to investors since 2000 was the availability of large amounts of borrowings at very low cost. This was even more true for some of the eurozone countries like Greece, Spain, Ireland and Portugal whose governments found that their credit rating was far better in euros than in their original currency and who used the opportunity to borrow heavily.

In the wake of the global financial crisis and the subsequent recession, these countries found that they couldn't borrow more money to refinance their debt or to bail out their own banks. Their costs of borrowing soared, to as high as 60% annual interest in the case of Greece. Many countries held bonds in other countries in the eurozone, leading to a fear of contagion, that is that the crisis would engulf much of the eurozone and might threaten the euro itself. Greece was hardest hit by this new crisis, partly because previous governments had concealed the size of its budget deficit in earlier years. Greece was forced to seek help from supranational organizations such as the European Central Bank, the International Monetary Fund and the European Financial Stability Facility (EFSF) which was created in 2010 to deal with the now-sovereign debt crisis gripping the Southern European eurozone members. Greece's lenders were forced to accept a debt restructuring, which means that some of the debt was cancelled in 2012. Ireland, Portugal and Spain also needed to ask for financial assistance, but let's continue our focus on Greece in the case study below.

CASE STUDY   Greece and the financial crisis

In the summer of 2016 the Greek debt crisis continued, with further assistance of over €10 billion needed to allow Greece to pay its debts as they fell due and to pay arrears on domestic debt. To access this funding the Greek government had to undertake fiscal reform. This brings the total cost of the bailout to Greece so far to €170 billion, which is only a little less than the annual gross domestic product (GDP) of Greece. The EFSF expected Greece to need additional assistance in the months and years to come.

In January 2017, the IMF produced its annual report on Greece. In the report, the IMF questioned whether it would participate in lending more money to Greece because they argued that 'Greece cannot grow out of its debt problems'. The IMF forecast that Greece's debt-to-GDP ratio would rise from 180% to nearly 300% by 2060 if debt restructuring wasn't provided to the country. To put that in perspective, at the time only Japan and Zimbabwe exceeded this ratio, Italy and

Portugal owed around 130% of their GDP, Ireland around 120%, the United States, Italy and France around 100%, the UK around 90% and Germany around 70%.

Fears that there wouldn't be another bailout forced up Greece's bond yields to as much as 9% by reducing the value of the bonds. The Greek government also resisted a debt restructuring after better than forecast economic performance. Some of the northern eurozone countries, Germany, Finland and the Netherlands, had lost confidence in the ability of the European Commission and other EU organizations to manage the Greek bailout and were insistent that a deal would require the participation of the IMF, risking another Greek debt crisis.

By April 2017, all the parties, including the IMF, were able to agree a reform package for Greece that enabled it to repay debts that were due to be repaid in the summer of 2017. The Greek authorities have agreed to tax and pension reforms to increase its before-interest budget surplus by 2% and the deal was likely to include some debt relief which was unclear at the time of writing. It is evident that Greece will continue to need financial support for some years to come.

Activity

Now that we have reviewed the Greek debt crisis, pick one or two of the other PIGS countries, Portugal, Ireland, or Spain or you might pick Italy, and research the extent to which they have recovered from the global financial crisis and the euro crisis. You will want to consider sovereign and consumer debt, the stability of the banking system and the growth of GDP to answer this question. If you pick Italy you might want to start by looking at the stability of the banks.

The IMF's role in the euro crisis

In Chapter 2 we evaluated the performance of the IMF and the World Bank in the 21st century. In this chapter we will look at the IMF's role in the euro crisis in more detail.

In July 2016, the IMF's Independent Evaluation Office (IEO) undertook an in-house review of its work bailing out Greece, Ireland and Portugal. During the euro crisis, the IMF worked with the European Commission (EC) and the European Central Bank (ECB); together these three were termed the Troika. The EC represented the eurozone member states in the partnership. This mix of political and financial organizations ran the risk of political influence affecting technical judgements of the IMF staff.

The internal report was very critical of the role of the IMF in the euro crisis. The chairman of the IEO argued that the IMF had never expected to have to 'bail out' an EU member state and had no strategy for dealing with such a situation. The IEO found that the IMF was too enthusiastic about the euro and that while it had correctly identified the key issues surrounding the euro crisis it had seriously underestimated the magnitude of the risks or their consequences.

The IMF was also found to have significantly overestimated expected economic growth, especially in Greece. The IEO went on to claim that the IMF had repeatedly given way to political pressure from various European governments and that the executive board of the IMF, responsible for the day-to-day lending decisions, were sometimes inadequately briefed in meetings. Some claimed they learned more from newspapers than from their briefings. It argued that the IMF's response was unclear and uneven, and found that key decisions had already been made in Europe prior to the IMF becoming involved in the Greek rescue which led to a failure to restructure Greek debt during the first bailout of the country in 2010. The IEO found that the IMF disregarded its own protocols by giving Greece financial assistance when it couldn't guarantee that the financial aid would be enough to bring the country's debt under control or help the country's economy recover. Such support had not been given to other IMF member states, particularly developing and emerging market economies. Eswar Prasad, a former IMF official, claimed that 'Political factors seemed to play a bigger role than pure technical considerations in matters involving advanced economies'. It appeared that the political considerations of creditor countries were given sufficient weight by the EC that sometimes IMF staff felt pressured into a suboptimal outcome.

The head of the IMF, Christine Lagarde, accepted that some of the criticism was justified and that internal procedures should be improved but refused to take action against political interference. She argued that the IMF actions in the eurozone had been a 'qualified success'. On the Greek bailout she said:

> While initial economic targets proved overly ambitious, the programme was beset by recurrent political crises, pushback from vested interests, and severe implementation problems that led to a much deeper than expected output contraction.

She went on to say that:

> Greece undertook enormous adjustment with unprecedented assistance from its international partners. This enabled Greece to remain a member of the euro area – a key goal for Greece and the euro area members.

The report confirms that there was tension between Germany and the IMF, with Germany seeking continued assistance to Greece and the IMF undecided on further funding but declaring that any future bailout would have to be linked with a clear, detailed Greek debt restructuring plan before it could be approved.

In February 2017 it was unclear whether the IMF would participate in a third rescue programme for the country. Germany threatened to stop lending if the IMF pulled out but the IMF stated that it would only continue in return for meaningful debt relief, which Germany resisted. The IMF's reluctance is perhaps understandable given that inspectors from the IEO concluded that the decision to participate in the first, 2010, bailout without debt restructuring undermined the project from the beginning.

The IEO concluded that:

The IMF Executive Board approved a decision to provide exceptional access financing to Greece without seeking pre-emptive debt restructuring, even though its sovereign debt was not deemed sustainable with a high probability.

It went on to say:

The risk of contagion was an important consideration in coming to this decision. The IMF's policy on exceptional access to fund resources, which mandates early board involvement, was followed only in a perfunctory manner.

Although the report makes it clear that Greece itself made little progress with politically difficult measures to overhaul its public finances; the country remains mired in crisis and in debt. At the heart of it all, from the IMF's perspective, are concerns that the fund yielded to political pressure from European governments and some member states believe that the IMF 'bent the rules' in its work in Greece and treated a developed economy in a more favourable way that its treatment of less-developed economies.

This prompted the inspectors to demand sharper protections against political interference in technical analysis by the fund. IMF chief Christine Lagarde says no, but critics see plenty to bolster their conviction that the fund's strategy in Europe was different to its engagements in emerging markets. At the very least, this will increase the stakes when the ever-divided creditors of Greece return to the negotiation chamber in the autumn.

The director of the Hellenic Observatory at the London School of Economics, Kevin Featherstone, argued, in an echo from the past, that the principal beneficiaries of the Greek bailouts were the financial institutions rather than the Greek people, with over 80% of the rescue package used to refinance old government debt which was largely held by financial institutions outside Greece. This effectively shifted debt from private financial institutions to European taxpayers on a massive scale.

While there has been agreement on a further rescue package for Greece in spring 2017, we are living in politically interesting times and with elections in France, Germany and Italy in 2017 after the UK Brexit vote in 2016, the euro is going to continue to face a somewhat uncertain future.

Adopting a single currency

The benefits of adopting the euro have been widely promoted by its advocates. When countries use a single currency, they are effectively adopting an extreme version of a fixed exchange rate. This brings the benefits of a fixed currency as well as its limitations. The specific arguments used to introduce the euro were:

- Elimination of currency risk so that companies don't have to concern themselves with the difficulties of exchange rate movements. When trade is undertaken with businesses located outside the eurozone all companies based in the eurozone will face the same levels of exchange risk, which will promote competitiveness. We will discuss this in detail in Chapter 5.

- Cheaper transaction costs because there is no need to exchange currency.

- Transparent price differences between firms making or selling similar products in different countries. This should increase competitiveness, which is good for consumers and will force companies to achieve performance targets, making them more efficient.

- Encouragement of long-term business arrangements between firms in different countries.

- Increasing inter-country business, leading to increasing trade flows. The evidence is that increasing trade flows increases the wealth of a country.

- Increasing merger and takeover activity in the eurozone, creating larger companies able to operate internationally because the price to pay for a target company should be easier to determine.

- All this should lead to economies becoming more integrated, even countries not in the euro such as the UK, because of the economic weight of the countries in it.

It was also argued that the euro would have a positive impact on financial markets:

- Share prices would be more comparable, increasing competition. Of course, as the economies become more highly correlated, share prices should also become more highly correlated. While this does increase transparency, it does also reduce the benefits of diversification we considered in Chapter 1.

- Investors would be free to invest in other countries without exchange risk. It is this that we will consider in more detail in the next section of this chapter.

- More cross-border investment in real assets than in the past. In addition to creating larger companies capable of competing globally, this will bring real benefits to the poorer countries in the eurozone by bringing into the country the management, marketing and technical skills that they need.

- All of this will help to create deeper capital markets, making it easier for companies to raise large amounts of capital and enabling more large deals to be made.
- A large, highly integrated block of countries should be better able to absorb global shocks.

It was even argued that the governments of some countries would be able to borrow more cheaply once in the eurozone. While this was true, we will see in the next section that it wasn't always a good thing.

Of course, it was widely accepted that there were some disadvantages of the euro, particularly:

- A strong euro would make it difficult for exporters who face competition from China. In practice, the euro is not as strong as the German mark it replaced, so Germany in particular actually benefited from a somewhat weaker currency.
- It was seen that there was a risk that a financial crisis in one nation would infect the whole zone. Within 10 years that risk did materialize but to date the crisis has been contained.
- The unified monetary policy limits action that can be taken to support slow-growth countries by, for example, reducing interest rates, and may spur inflation in high-growth countries.
- It was thought that by using a single currency, businesses would set up all over the eurozone, thus benefiting those countries that did not have a well-developed economy. However, in practice, companies tended to set up in the same areas as other similar companies, rather like computer companies are drawn to Silicon Valley and defence companies are drawn to the M4 corridor in the UK. There are some good reasons for this, such as access to highly skilled staff, and so the use of a single currency was not enough on its own to persuade companies to move to new areas.

The euro and government debt

In this final section we are going to discuss what it means for a country's national debt to adopt the currency of another country or group of countries as their currency. We will use the eurozone countries to provide examples for our points but this section applies to any group of countries using a single currency.

We will begin by considering the nature and especially the risks of government debt. We tend to consider government debt as being free of default or credit risk; that is that there is no possibility of a government failing to make interest payments or of repaying the debt on the due dates. In the case of most countries, if they are facing difficulties making payments they can simply issue new debt to raise the cash they need to service the debt already in issue. Of course, in practice it is more complicated than this but essentially this is true.

Activity

Suppose you bought a 10-year government bond that didn't pay interest but repaid your capital and an amount in lieu of interest in 10 years' time: we would call such a bond a zero-coupon bond. If the government has no default risk then does this mean that the bond is risk free?

Feedback

Well, no, it doesn't. Your real return on the bond will be affected by the rate of inflation over the period in which you held the bond. The higher the rate of inflation, the lower your return.

Now we can consider the relative positions of a UK investor and an investor in a eurozone country, Spain or France for example. Suppose our investors wish to invest in government bonds. Our UK investor can choose to invest in UK government bonds or the bonds of another country. In practice, most investors invest their money in their own country's bonds because:

- It is easier and cheaper to invest in the government bonds of the investor's country. Information is more freely available for domestic bonds than international bonds and agents will charge less for their services.

- Investors receive their income – salaries, trading profits and investment income – predominately in their domestic currency and incur taxes and most expenses in their domestic currency. If you invest in the bonds of another government you have to accept that if the exchange rate changes your investment might be at risk. For example, if our UK investor buys US government bonds and then the dollar loses value against the pound then the UK investor will receive lower returns from the investment than they expected and the pound value of the investment will also fall.

In contrast, our eurozone investors can choose to hold government bonds in any of the eurozone countries without any exchange risk. The information they need is easily available since all money is denominated in euros. Generally, people hold government bonds to earn a return while avoiding taking risk and so our investor would consider the risk and return characteristics of bonds in a number of countries and then buy bonds in the one that best matches their requirements.

After a crisis like the global financial crisis, consumers and companies often lose confidence and reduce spending, repay debt and increase savings. This leads to the private sector being investors and our UK investor has two investment choices for their money:

- Buy government bonds, effectively lending money to the government, which tends to be a net borrower after such a crisis and in need of borrowing money to repay its liabilities. Companies themselves are generally not seeking to raise funds.

- Invest in foreign securities such as foreign government bonds or shares in foreign companies. These investments tend to lead to a fall in value of the domestic currency as supply of the domestic currency increases and demand for foreign currency also increases.

A French or Spanish investor immediately after the global financial crisis has more choices than the UK investor:

- They can still buy government bonds but can choose between any government in the eurozone without taking on exchange rate risk.
- They can also invest in foreign securities, and provided they invest in another eurozone country, they are not facing the exchange risk faced by the UK investors. A Spanish investor could buy German bonds without having to be concerned about any exchange risk since both countries use the euro.

Our Spanish or French investor then is free to select the government bonds that provide the lowest level of risk. Since Germany is the largest country in the eurozone and is seen as the strongest economy, many investors choose to hold German government bonds rather than their domestic currency. This has pushed the price of German bonds up and thus the yields down. At the time of writing, the yield on 10-year German government bonds is only 0.2%, while French government bonds are returning 0.93% and Spanish government bonds a massive 1.67%. In contrast, UK government bonds are returning only 1.05% despite the Brexit vote and the uncertainty about the future value of the pound and the prospects for the UK economy. These results are perhaps even more surprising when we also consider the government debt-to-GDP ratios for these countries. We generally take for granted that the more an entity owes, in this case a government but it could be an individual or a company, the higher the required return on their debt to compensate for the risk of a government default.

Table 4.1 The cost of government debt of EU countries in 2017

	Yield on 10-year government bonds	Government debt as percentage of GDP in 2016/2017
UK	1.05%	89.2%
Germany	02%	71.2%
France	093%	96%
Italy	2.3%	132.7%
Greece	6.66%	176.9%

(continued)

Table 4.1   *(Continued)*

	Yield on 10-year government bonds	Government debt as percentage of GDP in 2016/2017
Portugal	3.86%	130.4%
Spain	1.67%	99.2%
Netherlands	0.45%	65.1%

From the above table, there does appear to be some correlation between the yield and the amount of government debt but France, Spain and the UK have similar levels of government debt and yet Spain's yield is significantly higher than the UK or France. It is easy, given Brexit, to see why the UK's rate should be higher than France but we need to consider why Spanish rates are so much higher than the UK rate. These are two countries of similar size and debt obligations.

A significant difference between government debt in the UK and in a eurozone country like Spain is that the UK is always able to raise additional money if needed and so investors can be sure that the bonds are indeed free of default risk. In contrast, Spain does not have its own central bank and cannot freely print euros. If investors generally begin to lose confidence in the ability of the government to raise new funds in capital markets they may begin to demand some return for the perceived additional risk. While a country like Germany has the confidence of the market and so can borrow at 0.2%, another country like Greece cannot be so sure of market confidence and so has a risk premium on its debt, taking its bond yield to over 6% at the time of writing. But the loss of value caused by inflation we discussed above is also a kind of default risk. The difference between the loss caused by inflation and the loss caused by default is that bond holders have some warning of increasing inflation and so can take action to protect their investment, while default is often unpredicted, giving investors no opportunity to protect their investment.

We might have been too quick to consider the erosion in value of a bond to be akin to default risk. Take our UK investor and suppose he has a mortgage and some investments in government bonds. Then while inflation might reduce the value of his bonds it will equally reduce the real value of the mortgage. If we consider a similar investor in Spain, if the government were to default on the debt the investor would suffer a loss on their investments which would not be matched by a similar loss on their liabilities.

Summary

The euro, its creation, objectives, the euro crisis and its current situation formed the first part of this chapter. We found that the driver to creating the euro was more political than financial and that while strict financial and economic entry criteria were set, the politicians sometimes allowed their vision to overrule those criteria when determining whether a country should be admitted to the eurozone or not.

In the second part of the chapter we assessed the impact that the global financial crisis had on countries in the eurozone and the subsequent Greek crisis. The role of the IMF was scrutinized.

In the final part of the chapter we reflected on the consequences for government default risk of using a single currency with other countries. It became apparent that the euro introduced default risk into government debt and this increased the cost of borrowing.

Questions

Question 1

The Ditchley Report, which was published by the Centre for European Reform (CER) at the beginning of 2016, reports on the conference held by the CER in Oxfordshire in November 2015 with the title 'Has the Euro been a Failure?' and can be found here: **https://www.cer.org.uk/sites/default/files/Ditchleyreport_11Jan16.pdf**.

There are other discussions on whether the euro has failed, particularly in Joseph Stiglitz's book *The Euro: And its threat to the future of Europe*. However, there has been change since the Ditchley Report, most notably Brexit and the election of President Trump, and Stiglitz has his critics.

By reviewing the serious press, revisit the arguments put forward by the panellists at Ditchley and consider the extent to which their concerns remain significant today in a post-Brexit European Union.

Question 2

Returning to the impossible trinity, given the eurozone countries have a single central bank, the ECB and free flow of capital across the countries in the eurozone, do you think it is a problem that each country has its own fiscal policy?

Question 3

Plot the exchange rate between the euro, the US dollar and the pound since the euro was created. Can you see a long-term trend? Is the euro strengthening or weakening against other reserve currencies?

05
Exchange rate regimes

At the end of this chapter you will be able to:

- critically evaluate fixed and floating exchange rates;
- discuss the criteria used by countries to determine their optimal exchange rate regime;
- explain the concept of the impossible trinity.

Introduction

One of the tasks of almost all governments is to decide on their exchange rate policy and then to arrange for its implementation.

This is an important and complex decision. As we saw in Chapter 3, historically there was an emphasis on stable exchange rates because it was thought that stable exchange rates helped to create a stable economy and increase international trade.

While stable exchange rates are still seen as being desirable it has become apparent that there are other desirable features of exchange rate systems; unfortunately it is not possible to have them all at the same time.

In this chapter we will discuss the range of exchange rate regimes used around the world today. We will evaluate the benefits and disadvantages of many of them and try to understand why different countries use different exchange rate systems.

At one extreme are fixed exchange rates where governments fix the amount of currency of one or more other countries that can be exchanged for their currency. Sometimes the fixed rate is legally binding on a government; at other times the government retains the freedom to change the fixed rate.

At the other extreme is a pure floating rate system where governments adopt a laissez-faire approach to exchange rates.

As we will see, in practice countries often choose a policy which is not at one of these two extremes.

How do exchange rates work?

The UK uses indirect quotes for exchange rates. Today's exchange rate with the dollar is £1:$1.4619. Indirect quotes tell us how much foreign currency is needed to buy one unit, in this case £1, of the domestic currency.

In contrast, direct quotes tell us how much domestic currency one unit of foreign currency will buy. For example, in the United States the exchange rate with the euro today is $1.11107:€1.

The exchange rate between the pound and the dollar is £1:$1.4619. A month ago the exchange rate was £1:$1.45664. We say that one of these currencies is getting stronger, or strengthening, and the other is getting weaker.

A currency gets stronger if it can buy more of the foreign currency than it could before. In this case, £1 used to buy $1.43664 but now it can buy $1.4619, which is more than before. Hence over the last month the pound has strengthened and equally the dollar has weakened because it doesn't buy as many pounds as it did a month ago.

A currency that gets stronger is said to be appreciating in a floating rate system. If it is getting weaker we say that it is depreciating.

In a fixed rate system we use the terms revaluing or devaluing to mean the same as appreciating and depreciating. In practice, the terms appreciating and revaluing are used interchangeably just as depreciating and devaluing are.

Why does the exchange rate matter to businesses and their managers?

It is easy to see how companies which rely on imports or exports are affected by exchange rates.

Example

Columbo, a UK domiciled company, has a turnover of around £10m a year. Half its sales are to the eurozone and all of those sales are invoiced in euros. Columbo has a net profit margin of 8%.

Find the highest and lowest exchange rates between the pound and the euro in the last 12 months.

On the day I looked this up, the exchange rate was £1:€1.31. The highest exchange rate in the last year was £1:€1.44 and the lowest was £1:€1.24.

Because Columbo invoices its exports in euros, the amount of sterling it gets for the euros varies depending on the exchange rate.

With an exchange rate of £1:€1.41, if Columbo sells €100 of goods it gets £70.92 (€100/1.41).

But when the exchange rate is £1:€1.24, the €100 of sales will give £80.62 (€100/1.24), nearly £10 additional revenue and additional profit.

Using today's exchange rate, Columbo has £5m or €6.55m of sales into the eurozone, giving an 8% net profit of €0.524m or £400,000.

But when the exchange rate was £1:€1.44, the profit would have been only £364,000 and when it was £1:€1.24 it would have been £423,000. That is a range of profits of nearly £60,000 (£423,000–£364,000). Such volatility makes it difficult for exporters to price their goods or services so that they are both competitive and profitable.

Work out the range for the dates that you have used.

Importers have similar difficulties when dealing with floating exchange rates. They will have to pay for the goods or services they are importing in a foreign currency and make their sales in pounds. If the pound is high, or strong, they do well but with a weak pound their profit is often eroded unless they can increase their prices in the UK.

So exporters and importers find life difficult if exchange rates are volatile but what about domestic companies who don't have imports or exports?

While some domestic companies are protected from exchange rate changes others are not.

Activity

Consider a company providing UK-only holidays, perhaps a company offering cottages to rent or a boat hire company. Since all of its expenses and all of its income are in pounds sterling, it doesn't suffer from the same kind of fluctuation as Columbo does.

But it does suffer from exchange risk. What happens to a UK holiday company when the pound is strong?

Feedback

If the pound is strong, UK holidays become more expensive and foreign holidays cheaper. Not only are UK holidaymakers more likely to go abroad but foreign tourists may also decide that the UK is too expensive and take their business to another country.

This is an example of exchange risk, but we call it economic risk. We will look at this in more detail in Chapter 8.

IMF AREAER 2014

Each year the IMF publishes its Annual Report on Exchange Arrangements and Exchange Restrictions. While the most recent couple of editions are expensive, early ones are freely available on the IMF website and make very interesting reading.

In the report from 2014, the IMF identifies the following exchange rate systems.

Pegs

A pegged exchange rate system may be a hard peg or a soft peg system.

A hard peg system involves either using the currency of another country or a currency board arrangement.

A soft peg system which may be a conventional peg, have horizontal bands, have a stabilizing arrangement or have a crawling peg system. In practice, very few countries use horizontal bands or crawling pegs, while conventional pegs and stabilizing arrangements are widely used.

Floating

Floating systems may be managed, with governments interfering in markets, usually in an attempt to stabilize the exchange rate rather than achieving a target rate. Or they may be independent, called freely floating, where markets are left to determine the exchange rate. This is achieved by the law of supply and demand. That is, if people want to buy a currency, the demand for it goes up and the currency appreciates in value, while if they want to sell it, supply goes up and the currency depreciates in value.

Managed system

There are a number of other systems which are designed to manage the exchange rate system. The IMF report found that there was a move towards more stable exchange rate systems, particularly the use of soft pegs.

More countries are considering other factors as well as exchange rates when determining their monetary policy, whereas in the past the focus was more on exchange rates.

Generally, there was a move towards greater transparency and increased financial liberalization, particularly of capital flows.

We will look very briefly at each of these systems but our focus will be on the broader fixed and floating systems.

Fixed rate exchange rate systems

These are also called pegged rate systems. They may take the form of a hard peg, where the government cannot change the exchange rate policy, or a soft peg, which is under the direct control of a government or its agents.

In a fixed rate exchange rate or conventional peg system the government of a country pegs or fixes its currency against the currency of another country, often a major currency, particularly the US dollar, which is the world's major reserve currency. Alternatively, the peg may be against a basket of currencies.

Once the exchange rate has been fixed, it will be announced and the government is committed to exchanging currency at the published rate. The government will need to take any necessary action to maintain the exchange rate. For example, if the currency is under pressure to devalue against the pegged currency, a government might buy its own currency in foreign markets to increase demand for its own currency. If this is done, the government will need to use its foreign currency reserves to buy its own currency. Equally, if the currency is at risk of appreciating, the government might wish to sell its own currency in foreign exchange markets in order to increase the supply of its own currency. In practice, this is unlikely to be a successful strategy so the government will have to resort to increasing or reducing the demand to hold its own currency by increasing or decreasing interest rates.

Hard peg

A hard peg gives a government no opportunity to interfere with the exchange rate policy. The country either uses the currency of another country – for example Zimbabwe uses a number of different currencies, though may return to the Zimbabwe dollar in the future – or a currency board, which is independent of the government and whose role is to buy or sell currency at the fixed rate in order to maintain the fixed rate. A country with a currency board in place will need very high foreign reserves in order to achieve their aim.

Soft peg

Under a soft peg system it is unlikely that a government will be able to maintain an exchange rate indefinitely and at some point a realignment will be necessary. This is often delayed by politicians so that when the realignment finally comes it is relatively large and causes a shock to the country's economic system.

A stabilizing arrangement is an informal policy to maintain the current exchange rate within a narrow band for a period of time, often a number of months.

Soft peg systems are the most popular choice for countries today, accounting for 43% of all countries in 2014.

If a government elects to fix their currency, all their monetary policy decisions will have to be primarily focused on supporting the exchange rate rather than addressing any of the country's other needs. A government might have an overheating housing market and to address that it might wish to increase interest rates, or it might wish to reduce unemployment by reducing interest rates to boost investment by businesses. But if it has a pegged exchange rate system it must first consider the impact of a change in interest rates on its exchange rate.

Ultimately a pegged rate system is only going to be successful if the two countries involved have similar levels of inflation. We will discuss this in Chapter 6. Empirical evidence suggests that the use of a pegged exchange rate has the effect of reducing the inflation rate. This is probably mostly because of the economic and monetary discipline that is needed to maintain the pegged rate.

A pegged exchange rate requires a government to maintain foreign currency reserves to support the currency when necessary. This can be expensive.

Advantages and disadvantages of fixed rate exchange rate systems

The obvious reason for using a fixed rate system is that the exchange rate will be stable against the currency you are fixed against. If exchange rates are stable it should be easier for companies to export their goods and services to businesses or individuals in other countries because they can remain competitive. Equally, stable exchange rates reduce risk and that makes foreign direct investment into a country more attractive. Most countries welcome inward investment as a boost to the economy in supporting jobs and job creation. Finally, the economic discipline required to sustain a fixed exchange rate also tends to lead to lower inflation, which encourages investment. Lower inflation also leads to lower expected inflation, which in turn leads to lower wage increases.

However, there are some significant disadvantages to using a fixed exchange rate policy. A country with a fixed exchange rate policy must generally prioritize that over all other economic objectives such as reducing unemployment. A fixed exchange rate policy also makes it impossible for a currency to react to short-term shocks so it lacks flexibility. It can be very difficult to set the fixed rate appropriately and if it is set too high, for example, it can reduce the competitiveness of exporters. Finally, a country in a fixed rate exchange system won't be able to benefit from the automatic realignment of a floating rate system to help to address a current account imbalance.

CASE STUDY Switzerland

In 2011, at a time when many major currencies were experiencing high levels of volatility, the Swiss decided to impose a cap on the franc against the euro. The franc was not allowed to be worth more than 1.2 francs to 1 euro. Remember that if the franc appreciates it will take fewer francs to buy a euro.

Activity

Given the global economic situation in 2011, only a couple of years after the global financial crisis and with the euro crisis creating great uncertainty, why did the Swiss choose to cap the franc against the euro?

Feedback

The Swiss economy is generally thought to be well run by the government and the central bank. The country is not running a budget deficit and given the uncertainty surrounding the reserve currencies, the dollar, the pound and the euro, investors sought a safe haven in Switzerland. But as other countries have found in the past, the pound in 1992 for example, the Swiss became concerned that with a very high-valued currency they would become uncompetitive. This was important because 70% of Switzerland's GDP comes from the exports of goods and services. Capping the franc was a way of protecting the economy.

The Swiss supported the cap by increasing the supply of Swiss francs and buying euros, and the franc appreciated by more than the cap. By 2015 this activity has led to the Swiss government accumulating very substantial foreign reserves, about $480 billion worth of foreign currency. If the European Central Bank continued with a policy of quantitative easing, that is printing euros, it would require the Swiss to print even more francs in order to maintain the cap. This caused the government difficulties with its voters, many of whom worried that printing francs on that scale would lead to high levels of inflation. In fact, high inflation probably wasn't a risk for the Swiss but people did worry about it. In addition, by capping the franc to the value of the euro, as the euro depreciated during the euro crisis so did the franc, which led to the Swiss National Bank suggesting that capping a depreciating currency was not sensible.

At the beginning of 2015, the Swiss National Bank announced that with immediate effect it would no longer cap its exchange rate with the euro but would allow it to float. The market quickly responded and the Swiss franc appreciated in value, rising from 1 euro:1.20 francs to a high of 1 euro:0.85 francs at one point on the following day, an appreciation of nearly 30%, which is a very large increase. The Swiss stock market collapsed because the appreciating currency made Swiss companies less competitive globally and some hedge funds reported large losses as a result of the change in exchange rate policy.

Figure 5.1   Euro: CHF 2010 –2017

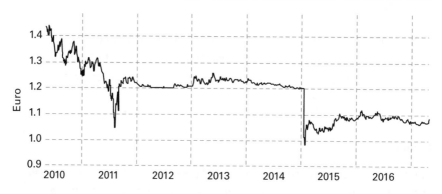

SOURCE EC

The graph clearly shows the cap being introduced in 2011 and the consequent fall in the value of the Swiss franc (CHF), which was fully reversed at the beginning of 2015 when the value of the Swiss franc rose to around 1.1 francs to 1 euro.

Floating and freely floating exchange rate systems

Like fixed rate systems, floating exchange rate systems come in a variety of forms. Broadly, a floating rate system depends on the market forces of supply and demand to determine the exchange rate. As economic conditions change, market participants will revise their current and expected future needs for currency and the exchange rate will change as a result. It will not generally be possible to predict these changes and so the exchange rate will fluctuate randomly.

Clean float

A clean floating rate system depends entirely on market forces to determine the exchange rate or value of the currency. Governments do not have a target exchange rate and do not interfere in the markets to attempt to affect the exchange rates. Under a clean float system, rates may fluctuate significantly. The UK government operates a clean float and has done since 1992 when it left the Exchange Rate Mechanism.

Dirty float or managed float

Under a managed floating system governments, via their central banks, intervene directly in the foreign exchange markets in order to influence the exchange rate. The evidence is that such activities are widespread. There are a number of reasons for government intervention in foreign exchange markets.

Governments may simply wish to reduce the high levels of volatility often seen in a pure floating rate system. These high levels of volatility create uncertainty and can have an adverse impact on the economy and on international trade. A sudden appreciation might disrupt the export market and a sudden depreciation might increase the rate of inflation. A second reason is to address irrational or short-term fluctuations in exchange rates which might be difficult for those trading internationally and which will not have a long-term effect. In practice, it isn't easy to distinguish between irrational fluctuations and a fundamental adjustment.

Sometimes governments operate a floating rate system publicly but privately are committed to fixed value against another currency or basket of currencies. From 1987 until the UK joined the Exchange Rate Mechanism, the Chancellor of the Exchequer, Nigel Lawson, unofficially pegged the value of the pound against the German mark. This tended to lead to the pound being overvalued compared to the mark and also led to the pound entering the ERM at an unrealistically high rate. Exporting nations tend to be very wary of seeing their currency appreciate against their trading partners because of the impact on the competitiveness of their industries.

At its simplest, a floating exchange rate is set by economic principles of supply and demand in the foreign exchange market. If demand for a currency goes up then other things being equal we would expect to see the currency appreciate in value. Equally, if the supply of a currency goes up, through a government printing money for example, then we would expect to see the currency fall in value or depreciate.

Now we've considered the characteristics of the major exchange rate systems we can turn our attention to their relative merits and investigate the reasons for some countries choosing fixed rate arrangements while others opt for floating rate systems.

Advantages and disadvantages of floating rate exchange rate systems

In a floating rate system the government, or its agents, do not have to decide what the exchange rate should be.

In theory, floating rate systems have a very effective self-correcting system.

Example

Suppose there are only two countries in the world, North and South, who trade with each other. Suppose North wants to buy wheat from South at a cost of $1,000 Southern dollars and South wants to buy oats from North at a cost of £1,000 Northern pounds. If the current exchange rate is $1:£1 then each country will have the foreign currency they need to buy the goods they want from the other country.

Suppose now that North wants to buy wheat from South but South does not want to buy goods from North. The importers in North will have to buy Southern dollars in order to pay for the wheat they want to buy. This will increase the demand for Southern dollars and the supply of Northern pounds. We would say that South has a positive Balance of Payments with North and North has a negative Balance of Payments with South. As demand for Southern dollars increases, the value of Southern dollars will increase, just as we see house prices increase when demand for housing increases. That means that it will cost more Northern dollars to buy Southern dollars than in the past. Equally, the supply of Northern dollars will lead to a fall in the value of the Northern dollar. The exchange rate might move to $1:£0.9. The effect of this change is that wheat will become more expensive in North, which presumably will reduce demand for wheat, and oats will become cheaper in South, which, providing oats are price elastic, will increase demand for oats in South.

The more successful country will have a positive balance of payments with the less successful country. But the exchange rate movement will reduce demand internationally for the goods from the more successful country and increase demand for goods from the less successful country until the trade between the two countries is once again equalized.

In practice, while this self-correcting facility does appear to take place to some extent, some countries have had a long-term positive or negative

Figure 5.2   The pound-dollar exchange rate showing the impact of Brexit

SOURCE Macro Trends

Figure 5.3   The impact of the Brexit vote on the FTSE 100

SOURCE Macro Trends

balance of trade with the rest of the world which has not been eliminated by floating exchange rates.

Countries with floating rate systems should, according to the parity laws we will look at in the next chapter, adjust for different levels of inflation in different countries, allowing them to maintain their competitiveness.

There are some disadvantages to floating rate policies. There is evidence that exchange rate volatility is higher than would have been predicted by the exchange rate models because market participants react, and often over-react, not only to changes in economic activity, inflation and so on but to expectations about future economic conditions.

The pound fell sharply against the dollar as a result of the Brexit vote despite the long time period between the vote and Britain actually leaving the EU. At the same time as the pound fell, the stock market soared, suggesting that investors in shares believed that for the time being at least, the future looked promising.

Why do countries have different exchange rate policies?

You can already make an attempt to answer this question but it is worth spending some time considering it in detail.

Activity

Spend a few minutes considering what a country's policies, particularly economic policies, might be. You could start by thinking about what the British government policies were regarding the vote to leave the EU.

Feedback

These are some of the economic policies that a government might have:

- *to reduce unemployment;*
- *to reduce inflation;*
- *to reduce interest rates;*
- *to affect trade balances, for example to increase exports;*
- *to increase economic growth.*

Activity

Now consider carefully which exchange rate policy might help a government achieve each of the economic policies we just identified. Let's do the first one together to start you off.

To reduce unemployment a government needs to see jobs created. That would happen if imports were reduced, exports increased and/or interest rates were reduced. If a fixed rate policy were adopted, a country would have to focus on maintaining the exchange rate and might have to keep interest rates higher in order to support it. With a freely floating policy, the government would be free to reduce interest rates to provide a boost to economic activity. Reducing interest rates should reduce demand for the currency too, leading to a reduction in demand for imports, which will now be more expensive, and an increase in demand for the country's exports. So a country whose main policy is to reduce unemployment will find a floating exchange rate will suit their needs better than a fixed rate, all other things being equal.

Feedback

Don't worry if you didn't get all of these right; it is complex and simply thinking about how to achieve a policy will help you even if you didn't come to the right conclusion. A 2003 IMF working paper, 'Evolution and Performance of Exchange Rate Regimes' addressed exactly these issues (Rogoff et al, 2003).

Reducing inflation. If a fixed rate policy is used it requires fiscal and monetary discipline to maintain the fixed exchange rate. The first priority of the government has to be focused on the exchange rate. This tends to lead to a lack of fiscal or monetary stimulus to the economy to boost growth and that leads to lower inflation rates. Floating rate policies do not require this discipline and so are less likely to lead to lower inflation. However, to operate a fixed rate policy it is necessary to hold substantial foreign reserves. In order to generate a return on those reserves the central bank often lends the reserves to other banks, which enables them to lend more; thus holding high levels of reserves has an inflationary effect. The empirical evidence is that despite this it has been found that a fixed rate exchange rate system tends to lead to lower inflation. However, the main beneficiaries of this feature of fixed exchange rate policies are found in developing countries and emerging markets. Mature economies do not appear to benefit to the same extent, if at all.

Reducing interest rates. As we will see in the next chapter there is a relationship between inflation and interest rates and generally countries with high inflation will also have high interest rates. For this reason, the arguments for achieving lower interest rates are the same as those for lower inflation.

Increasing economic growth. Applying the above arguments, particularly on reducing unemployment, would suggest that a floating rate policy might enable governments to adopt the policies which would create economic growth. The empirical evidence is that countries in the developed world who use floating rates do enjoy higher growth in GDP per head but the same benefit is not apparent in developing countries and emerging markets. This difference is perhaps due to a lack of credibility of developing countries with floating exchange rates. That is, there is a lack of confidence that they will be able to control inflation without the discipline of a fixed exchange rate policy.

The IMF paper also analysed the impact of the exchange rate policy on the volatility of economic growth and found that all countries enjoyed lower volatility of economic growth if they adopted a fixed rate exchange rate policy.

Improving trade balances is also complicated. We have seen that floating rates are self-correcting and so should prevent a trade imbalance becoming structural, but several countries with floating rates, for example the United States and the UK, are running large trade deficits. Emerging markets tend to believe that using fixed rates to remain competitive with their customers helps to protect their exports.

Evidence

The above-mentioned 2003 IMF working paper considered the exchange rate policies of many countries. The results revealed that the exchange rate policies the countries stated they used were often not the same as the policies actually used. We considered one example of this earlier in this chapter when we saw that from 1987 to 1991 the UK claimed to have a freely floating policy while the Chancellor of the Exchequer Nigel Lawson was actually using a soft peg with the German mark.

The findings contradicted the idea that countries would take a polarized stance on exchange rate policy, either opting for a freely floating exchange rate policy or a hard peg policy; many countries used an intermediate regime such as a managed float or a soft peg.

They found that emerging markets, which are fast-growing, transitional economies lacking integration with other economies, preferred fixed or semi-fixed exchange rate regimes because they can offer some support for efforts to reduce inflation without compromising economic growth. However, as they grow and develop more open capital markets and the mature financial infrastructure they need, they benefit from shifting towards a more market-orientated exchange rate. One reason for this is that fixed rate regimes are vulnerable to speculative attacks on their currencies like the one that forced the pound out of the ERM in 1992.

They also found that developed economies gravitated towards floating exchange rates which provided the best opportunities for growth without risking inflation, provided that they had other strategies for managing inflation such as an independent central bank with an anti-inflationary mandate. In addition, the more developed the economy, the greater the benefit to be gained from adopting a floating exchange rate policy.

Apart from emerging markets, countries tended to remain with their chosen exchange rate policy for many years, with only 7% of countries other than emerging economies changing in any one year between 1940 and 2001.

Finally, the researchers found that for an exchange rate policy to be successful its policy must be consistent with the underlying macroeconomic goals of the country.

CASE STUDY China and China's changing exchange rate policy

China enjoyed unrivalled levels of growth throughout the 1990s and the early years of the 21st century. This growth led to it becoming the second largest economy in the world and put it on track to be the largest economy in the not-too-distant future. Much of this growth came initially from exports, and government policy was for China to continue to grow by exporting.

To maintain the high rate of growth it was essential that China remained competitive in the countries it exported to. By keeping the exchange rate low, China was able to sell goods to its trading partners at competitive prices. So for many years China pegged its exchange rate against the US dollar, the currency of its major customer. The peg was carefully managed by the People's Bank of China to keep the exchange rate between the yuan or renminbi and the dollar low.

But more recently the Chinese government has adopted a broader economic strategy, seeking to encourage domestic consumption, and at the same time the yuan has been seen to strengthen against the dollar.

In the summer of 2015, China changed its exchange rate policy by taking account of the previous day's trading when setting the exchange rate for the day. This means that market activity will be included in the exchange rate set. The news triggered a nearly 2% devaluation of the yuan.

The question is, why did China make this change and why did it lead to a fall in the value of the yuan?

China has a long-term goal of making the yuan a major currency internationally and ultimately for the yuan to be a reserve currency along with the US dollar, the UK pound, the euro and the Japanese yen. It campaigned for the yuan to be one of the currencies to be included in the basket of currencies that makes up the IMF's Special Drawing Rights (SDR) (see Chapter 3 for more details) which was achieved on 1 October 2016. This is significant progress towards becoming a reserve currency. But before that can happen the Chinese government needs to liberalize its Capital Account, develop its financial markets so that they can operate independently of the government, and ensure that the legal system is more robust and credible. The change in determining the value of the yuan is one small step towards liberalizing financial markets.

But an alternative explanation might be the recent serious fall in growth of the Chinese economy with falling exports. The devaluation caused by the change in how the exchange rate is calculated made China's exports more competitive. This devaluation was not popular with the United States because it makes it harder for them to compete with China.

Currency union

Mark Carney, Governor of the Bank of England, suggested that a currency union made business sense when countries enjoyed a significant amount of cross-border trade. But the price to be paid for a currency union is a loss of economic independence.

The lack of a lender of last resort is considered by some to be an advantage by reducing moral hazard and forcing banks and savers to be more cautious once their 'safety net' has been removed.

Scottish referendum on independence in 2014

One of the key issues in the Scottish referendum campaign was the currency that would be used by an independent Scotland. During the campaign, Alex Salmond, who led the campaign for Scottish independence, announced that an independent Scotland would use the pound rather than join the euro or set up their own currency. This is called sterlingization which, while not a currency union, has many of the same features.

UK politicians generally objected to this plan but in practice couldn't have prevented an independent Scotland from using the pound. There are many examples of countries using the currency of another country. Panama has used the US dollar as its currency for over 100 years. Today Kosovo uses the euro while not being a member of the European Union. In 2014, with the eurozone still dealing with the aftermath of the global financial crisis, joining the eurozone and adopting the euro were not seen as an attractive option for Scotland. In addition, Scotland has far more trade with the rest of the UK than with the rest of the eurozone, so retaining the pound had more benefits.

If Scotland had continued to use the pound they would have benefited from the ultimate in exchange rate stability with the rest of the UK by using the same currency. But there were some disadvantages to the plan too. The most obvious is that the Bank of England sets the monetary policy for the UK and after independence it would set monetary policy to suit the remaining part of the UK, meaning that an independent Scotland would have to accept the monetary policy set by the Bank of England without reference to the needs of Scotland. For example, if the Bank of England felt it needed to raise interest rates to deal with an overheating housing market in England, Scotland would also have to deal with higher interest rates even if its economy indicated that rates should not increase. This really brings into question how independent Scotland would be if it used the pound. The Governor of the Bank of England, Mark Carney, said that a currency union with the UK would be incompatible with an independent Scotland.

But there were other problems to an independent Scotland using sterling. Currently the Bank of England acts as lender of last resort to Scottish banks. This means that if any UK bank is unable to raise money to remain in business, the Bank of England will lend them sufficient money to remain trading. This happened to Northern Rock at the start of the global financial crisis. Without a lender of last resort, banks that are in financial difficulties may fail, threatening the stability of the banking system and leading to individuals and businesses losing money. The banking system in Scotland is too big, with assets over 10 times Scottish GDP, for a Scottish government to bail them out. At the time of writing the Scottish banks are not in good financial health, so this was a real risk. Several Scottish banks reacted to the announcement by declaring that if there were an independent Scotland they would relocate to England.

An additional problem would have been the ability of an independent Scotland to raise money if they used the pound sterling. When the British government needs to borrow money it issues government bonds, called gilts. Investors are willing to buy the bonds at an interest rate which doesn't include a risk premium because they are confident that the government will be able to pay the interest and repay the capital. They are confident because the UK government has the ability to print pounds if necessary. In practice, if the government did print money in this way they would increase the supply of pounds which would probably lead to inflation and the erosion of the value of the pound but such consequences take time and lenders feel that they could sell their bonds before such actions significantly eroded the value of their sterling.

But an independent Scotland using the pound wouldn't be able to print money to repay their debt and thus Scottish bonds would not be risk free and would attract a higher interest rate. So it would cost an independent Scotland more to borrow money.

The impossible trinity

Economists have identified three characteristics of an exchange regime that we generally agree are desirable. You might want to spend a few moments thinking about what they are before you read further.

The three desirable characteristics of an exchange rate system are:

1 **Stability**. This has historically been seen as an essential element of exchange rate policy because it is thought to provide economic stability to a country and to encourage international trade. From the early gold standard arrangements to the Bretton Woods agreement, exchange rate stability has been a key goal. Exchange rate stability was also one of the drivers for the introduction of the euro.

2 **Free flow of capital or a lack of capital controls**. In the 21st century, countries seek to attract investment into their country from outside and also wish to allow their own citizens to be able to transfer money out of the country. In the UK in particular, trillions of dollars flow in and out of the country each day due to the size and success of the banking sector.

3 **Independent monetary policy**. An independent monetary policy allows governments to make decisions about interest rates in particular that are in the interests of the country rather than in response to pressures from the global economy.

Unfortunately it has become apparent, both from theories and from evidence, that it is not possible for a country to enjoy all three of these characteristics at the same time.

Consider a theoretical country which has a stable exchange rate and free flow of currency. Suppose the central bank decided to increase interest rates to try to reduce a rise in house prices.

Such a move will lead to an increase of capital flowing into the country, increasing demand for the currency and increasing the exchange rate.

This country has free flow of capital and an independent monetary policy but the exchange rate is not stable. The UK is an example of such a currency.

Now consider a country in a currency union like the eurozone. The exchange rate with trading partners is fixed by using a single currency and the eurozone enjoys free movement of capital between countries. But individual countries within the eurozone have relatively little freedom to adopt a monetary policy that suits their economy. An example of a country which might have wished to have such freedom would be Greece, a eurozone country.

Finally, consider China, which is currently wrestling with exactly this dilemma, or as it is sometimes called, this trilemma. China appears to believe that while it can't achieve everything it wants it can achieve most of what it wants. In 2016 China appears to seek fairly stable exchange rates, accepting some devaluation of the currency, some free flow of capital, while imposing some restrictions on the movement of capital and an independent monetary policy which is focused on managing the economy rather than supporting the currency. At the time of writing, the currency is falling in value, the flow of capital out of the country is accelerating, and China's foreign reserves are being run down at an alarming rate.

Most larger economies choose to have free flow of capital and an independent monetary policy, and accept more volatile exchange rates.

Summary

In this chapter we learned about the terminology of exchange rates and continued to investigate the impact of exchange rates on the relative competitiveness of two countries. We discussed the different exchange rate systems that are used in the world today which range from fixed at one end to freely floating at the other. We then focused on the priorities of a government and how those impact on the choice of exchange rate policy. We then used a couple of cases, Scotland and China, to consider how the choice of exchange rate policy might impact on those countries.

Finally, we discussed the impossible trinity, so named because there are potentially three things a country might seek when determining the exchange rate policy but in practice only two of the three can be achieved at any one time. This forces governments to make choices.

Questions

Question 1

Pick two or more countries which appear to be economically similar but have adopted different exchange rate regimes. Investigate why each has chosen their exchange rate regime.

Question 2

If you were running a business, which of the three desirable characteristics of an exchange rate would you choose to operate with?

Question 3

For your own company or for a company listed on a stock exchange such as the London Stock Exchange, undertake an analysis of the accounts to assess the risk faced by the company from fluctuating exchange rates.

Hint: use the income statement to find the net profit margin and then identify the country to which the company has the largest proportion of imports or exports. Finally, use information about exchange rates to determine the amount of volatility in the two currencies in the last year or five years. How much do exchange rates have to fluctuate to erode the profit margin? How much have the exchange rates fluctuated by?

Resources From the IMF:
http://www.imf.org/external/pubs/ft/fandd/2008/03/basics.htm

06
Parity conditions and forecasting exchange rates

At the end of this chapter you will be able to:

- use the terminology of exchange rates;
- state and explain the five parity conditions;
- discuss the limitations of currency forecasting.

Introduction

We have spent some time discussing how exchange rates arise. We've considered the impact of market forces on exchange rates and identified some of the factors that influence exchange rates such as recessions and government policies.

But in practice, one of the most important things that companies want to do is to forecast exchange rates. We saw in Chapter 5 the effect that exchange rates can have on business transactions and profitability. In this chapter we are going to discuss the variables such as inflation and interest rates that can be used to help to predict future changes in exchange rates.

We need to start with some terminology and then we'll think about what we might expect to happen to the exchange rate of two currencies given information about the two countries.

Key concept

Spot rate: The spot exchange rate is the exchange rate of two currencies today. The spot rate between two currencies will vary from day to day and the rate you are quoted depends on who you are and which market you go to. The rate you would be offered for your holiday currency will be different to the rate that your company might be quoted if they sought to exchange millions of pounds in a single transaction.

Activity

How many different spot rates can you find for the exchange rate between two major currencies? You could pick reserve currencies like the US dollar, the euro or the pound sterling, and you could look at tourist rates as well as sites like **ft.com**, **bbc.co.uk** or **digitallook.com**. Write down some of the numbers you find because we'll use them in the feedback section.

Feedback

I found a sign in London giving the following information about tourist exchange rates in April 2017:

EXCHANGE RATES

	BUY	SELL
EUR	1.1976	1.17
USA	1. 29	1.24
AUD	1.72	1.65
CZK	33.00	30.00
CAD	1.75	1.68
CHF	1.27	1.21
TRY	4.75	4.55

The first column of numbers is headed 'buy' and tells you how much foreign currency you will have to provide in order to receive £1. This is called the ask or offer price.

The second column of numbers, headed 'sell', tells you how much foreign currency you will receive in exchange for £1. This is called the bid price.

Notice that the bid price is always lower than the ask price.

The difference between the ask and bid prices is called the spread and the currency trader makes their money from the spread.

Have another look at the table above and see if you can say anything about the spreads.

The size of the spread of the dollar quotes is 4% ((1.29 − 1.24)/1.29). Compare that to the size of the spread of the Czech Republic Koruna which is 9.1% ((33 − 30)/33). Why is there such a big difference in the size of the spread? The explanation gives us an insight into an important characteristic of financial markets. The dollar is the most traded currency in the world. That leads to fierce competition between traders and it also means that because of the high volume of trade it is easier to establish a price. In contrast, we say that the koruna is thinly traded, which means that not only is there less competition but also that it is more difficult to establish a price and so traders set a wider spread to be sure of not making a loss. Perform the same calculation on some of the other currencies given above, and when you come across exchange rates in your daily life. It is likely that you will find the spread is smaller when you are considering reserve currencies and other widely traded currencies.

At the same time as the above table was seen, the published exchange rate for the dollar was around $1.2848:£1. This rate is roughly the midpoint of the ask and bid wholesale prices rather than the tourist rates we have above.

I'm sure it is no surprise to you to realize that tourists get a much worse deal than large MNCs and other major currency participants.

Key concepts

Ask or offer price: the price you will have to pay to receive £1.

Bid price: the amount of foreign currency you will receive in exchange for £1.

Spread: the spread is the difference between the bid price and the ask price.

Forward rate: the forward rate is the exchange rate of two currencies at a future date.

The forward rate is very useful to companies because there is often a time lag between the date of making a decision, such as quoting for an order denominated in a foreign currency, and receiving payment. A company can use the forward rate to help them give a quotation which is both profitable and competitive. Too high a quote will be uncompetitive and the company might not win the business; too low a bid might win the business but mean that the company can't make a profit.

In addition, a company can choose to buy a forward rate contract now. If they do that they will be certain about how much of their home currency they will receive for a given amount of a foreign currency by locking into an exchange rate for the contracted amount of currency on a particular date in the future.

> ## Example
>
> Suppose the spot rate between the euro and the pound was £1:€1.20 and the 12-month forward rate was £1:€1.30. A company could arrange with their bank to buy euros today at €1.20 to the pound or to buy the euros in 12 months' time at €1.30 to the pound. It wouldn't matter what the spot rate was in 12 months' time. Our company is contracted to buy them at €1.30. We will discuss this in more detail in Chapter 8.

Forward rates are only quoted for a few months, up to around 12 months into the future. That might be good enough for many purposes but when a company is planning for the longer term, perhaps considering investing for the long term in another country, being able to forecast exchange rates can play a key role in the decision-making process.

Forward premiums and forward discounts

A foreign currency is at a forward discount if it is expected to fall in value over the period of time, that is, it is expected to buy less of the domestic currency than it is able to buy today.

A foreign currency is at a forward premium if it is expected to appreciate over the period of time, that is, it is expected to buy more of the domestic currency than it is able to buy today.

$$\text{Forward premium or discount} = \frac{\text{Forward rate} - \text{Spot rate}}{\text{Spot rate}} \times \frac{360}{\text{Forward contract number of days}}$$

Parity conditions

Economists have identified a number of factors which might be expected to have a direct impact on future exchange rates between currencies. These are called the five parity conditions and they are:

- purchasing power parity;
- the Fisher Effect;
- the International Fisher Effect;

- interest rate parity; and
- forward rates as unbiased predictors of future spot rates.

These parity conditions don't compete with each other; they are linked together.

We'll discuss each one in turn, starting with an example to begin to understand the arguments for each of the conditions before considering how they all fit together.

Purchasing power parity

Suppose that two countries have a long shared border with a large proportion of residents able to travel to the other country to buy goods if they want to; online purchases can also be freely made in either country by the residents of both.

Suppose that both countries sell identical smart phones. Residents of the first country, Uno, can buy the phones from a domestic supplier for Uno $1,000. Residents of the second country, Duo, can also buy phones from their own domestic supplier for Duo 2,000fr.

Activity

What do you think the exchange rate might be between Uno dollars and Duo francs? How many francs do you think one Uno dollar might buy?

Feedback

If $1,000 will buy the same phone as 2,000fr then you would expect the exchange rate to be $1,000:2,000fr if $1 could be exchanged for 2fr.

Activity

What would happen to phone sales if the exchange rate wasn't $1:2fr? Suppose it is $1:2.2fr? How much would an Uno resident have to pay for a phone bought in Duo?

Feedback

Suppose you are a resident of Uno. You have a choice of buying a phone from the local company for $1,000 or buying it from the Duo company at a cost of 2,000fr, which at an exchange rate of $1:2.2fr is the equivalent of $909.

While some customers might still buy their new phones locally, many will switch to buying their phones from the Duo domestic company at the lower price.

This is the essence of **purchasing power parity**, which argues that prices of similar goods should be the same around the world, an idea called the **law of one price**. If the prices are not the same then consumers will undertake arbitrage activity where they take advantage of price differences in two markets to make a risk-free profit, or reduce their costs.

But unless the only things that all consumers buy in the year are smart phones, the exact exchange rate won't just depend on the different costs of a phone, it will depend on the prices of many goods and services.

Activity

Think about trips abroad you might have taken or online prices that you have seen. Do you believe that the law of one price holds in the world today?

Feedback

One index that compares prices around the world is the Economist's Big Mac *index. You can find it here:* **http://www.economist.com/content/big-mac-index.** *In practice, while the Big Mac index has some advantages, it has some serious limitations. When you buy a Big Mac you are buying a service as well as a good. If you are in Berlin and you want to buy a Big Mac you don't have the opportunity to buy it in Paris instead of Berlin. The location of the Big Mac is an important consideration. You might like to find out if iPhones cost the same amount in every country. If they don't, why doesn't everyone buying an iPhone order it from the cheapest supplier, wherever they are based?*

Purchasing power parity ignores the impact of restrictions on free trade such as tariffs and quotas as well as local taxes. Companies also often create restrictions of their own such as the zone system on DVDs and other methods of product differentiation.

Activity

Returning for the moment to our smart phone customer, suppose the exchange rate is $1:2fr and that the law of one price holds. Now suppose that expected inflation is 2% in Uno and 10% in Duo. How much will the phone cost in each country in one year's time if the actual inflation is as expected?

Feedback

In a year's time the phone will cost $1,020 ($1,000 x 1.02) in Uno and 2,200fr (2,000 x 1.1) in Duo.

What would the exchange rate have to be in a year's time to prevent consumers buying from one company in preference to the other company?

The new exchange rate would have to be $1:2.156fr (2,200/1,020).

According to purchasing power parity, then future spot rates will adjust in line with inflation to maintain the law of one price.

Key concept

The equation for purchasing power parity is:

$$\frac{e_0}{e_t} = \frac{(1+i_h)^t}{(1+i_f)^t}$$

where

e_0 is the current exchange rate;

e_t is the predicted spot rate at time t;

i_h is the annualized domestic inflation rate between time 0 and time t;

i_f is the annualized local, or foreign, inflation rate between time 0 and time t.

There are some significant problems with using purchasing power parity in practice.

The first is that it relies on expected inflation to predict the future spot rate and predicting inflation is not something we are always good at.

The second is that to calculate inflation we depend on a basket of goods and services. The basket is based on what consumers spend their money on and if it isn't properly set up it is going to give inaccurate results. Another complication of this is that the people of Uno and Duo won't have the same basket of goods.

Finally, in practice, prices are often 'sticky'. Providers know that there can be a cap on what they can charge for their goods and services and they can't charge more than that.

Over the very long term, perhaps 30 years, the evidence is that purchasing power parity does indeed hold but in the short term it isn't as useful as our next measure.

Activity

One interesting outcome from this is that it isn't the level of inflation in Uno or Duo that determines the exchange rate: it is the inflation rate differential. In our example, Uno had lower inflation than Duo. Which currency has appreciated?

Feedback

The exchange rate has moved from $1:2fr to $1: 2.156fr. Uno will buy more francs next year than it does this year, so Uno has appreciated and Duo has depreciated. Under purchasing power parity, the country with lower inflation than other countries will see its currency appreciate.

Before we move onto the next parity condition there is one last important lesson we can learn here. We call all the exchange rates we have so far calculated the **nominal exchange rates**, that is, the rates that are actually quoted. The move from $1:2fr to $1:2.156fr is a change in the nominal exchange rates but has it made a difference between the competitiveness of the two countries? The answer is that it hasn't. Neither phone seller has an advantage over the other due to exchange rate changes. We would argue that there hasn't been a change in real exchange rates.

Supposing the exchange rates hadn't changed due to the inflation rate differentials, perhaps because the two countries had a fixed exchange rate policy. Now is there a difference in real exchange rates? Would one company be able to sell phones for less than the other one?

Activity

At the end of a year, how much would a resident of Uno have to pay for a phone from each company if nominal exchange rates didn't change?

Feedback

At the end of the year a phone from the Uno company would cost $1,020 ($1,000 x 1.02). The Duo company will be selling phones for 2,200fr (2,000 x 1.1) and the Uno resident would have to spend $1,100 (2,200/2) on a phone from the company in Duo. Similarly, the Duo resident could buy a phone from the Duo company for 2,200fr or spend 2,040fr (1,020 x 2) buying a phone from the Uno company.

Clearly while there has been no change in nominal rates there has been a change in real rates and the Uno-based company is now more competitive than the Duo-based company as a result.

The Fisher Effect

The **Fisher Effect** gives us a relationship between inflation and interest rates.

Activity

Returning to the example above, we know that expected inflation in Uno is 2%. Suppose the banks in Uno offer to pay interest on deposits at 3%. Roughly how much better off would a saver be if they put $100 in a bank account for a year?

Feedback

At the end of the year our investor will have $103 ($100 x 1.03) in the bank. But goods that would have cost $100 a year ago will now cost $102 ($100 x 1.02). Our investor appears to be $1 better off because they deposited their money in the bank for a year.

So while the bank is offering a nominal interest rate of 3%, after adjusting for inflation of 2%, the real interest rate is closer to 1%.

In reality the equation for the Fisher Effect is a little more complicated than that and the equation we shall use is:

$$(1 + \text{nominal rate}) = (1 + \text{real rate})/(1 + \text{expected inflation rate})$$

Or, rearranging $(1 + \text{real rate}) = (1 + \text{nominal rate})/(1 + \text{expected inflation rate})$

Putting our figures into the equation we get:

$$(1 + \text{real rate}) = 1.03/1.02 = 1.0098$$

which is almost but not exactly 1%.

The empirical evidence is that generally investors are able to make a small positive real return on their savings. However, as can be seen from the graph of UK inflation and base rates between 2003 and 2015 (Figure 6.1), the cuts in interest rates at the end of 2008 led to interest rates being below the rate of inflation for several years. While interest rates were higher than inflation for a short period in 2015, in 2017 interest rates continue to be lower than inflation in the UK. When interest rates are lower than inflation it encourages households to spend money rather than save it, which has the effect of boosting the economy. It is generally agreed though that healthy economies have positive real returns on savings.

Figure 6.1   UK inflation and base rates

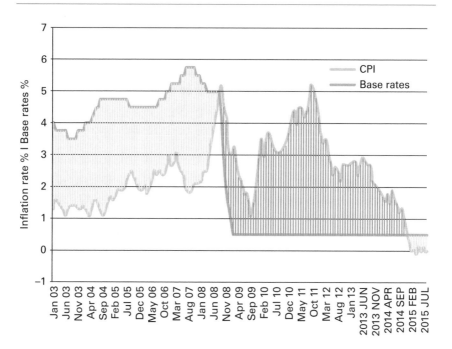

If countries have different real interest rates then arbitrage opportunities would exist. This means that capital would be taken out of countries paying lower real interest rates and flow into countries offering higher real interest rates. Remember that several trillions of US dollars a day flow through foreign exchange markets and we can see that it is likely that enormous sums of money will flow between countries with different real interest rates. As money flows out of the country paying lower rates, interest rates will rise in order to attract more savings. At the same time the country with the higher interest rates will find it has more cash than is needed and interest rates will fall. This process will continue until the rates in the two countries are broadly similar.

If arbitrage leads to differences in real interest rates being eroded and if real interest rates can be defined in terms of nominal interest rates and expected inflation rates then we can conclude that the differences in nominal interest rates in two countries must be approximately equal to the differences in expected inflation in the two countries.

The International Fisher Effect

Interest differentials are unbiased predictors of future changes in the spot rate. In particular, currencies with lower interest rates are expected to appreciate against currencies with higher interest rates.

Example

This is easiest to see with an example before we consider the equations. Returning again to Uno and Duo, suppose that the interest rate in Uno is 5% and in Duo it is 12%. The spot rate is $1:2fr. What is the expected future spot rate?

Solution

If an Uno resident had $1,000 they could invest it for a year and earn $50 ($1,000 x 0.05) interest, giving them a total of $1,050 ($1,000 x 1.05) at the end of the year.

Instead they could convert their dollars into Duo francs, getting 2,000fr ($1,000 x 2). Then the francs could be deposited for a year in Duo at an interest rate of 12%, giving total interest of 240fr (2,000fr x 1.12) and a total in the bank of 2,240fr (2,000fr x 1.12).

Activity

If the exchange rate at the end of the year was expected to be $1:2fr, what would our intrepid investor decide to do?

Feedback

If our investor chose to invest in Duo and end the year with 2,240fr in their account they could exchange them for $1,120 (2,240fr/2) which is more than the $1,050 they would earn if they deposited their money in Uno. So with an exchange rate of $1:2fr, many Uno savers would choose to deposit their money in Duo banks. That would lead to a lack of savers in Uno, forcing banks to offer increased interest to attract savings and a glut of savings in Duo, leading banks to reduce rates paid to depositors to discourage savings.

Activity

Can you work out the expected future spot exchange rate that would prevent savers moving their deposits from one country to the other? You can think about arbitrage activity to answer this. What is the exchange rate that would mean that investors could not make a higher return on their investment by investing in the other country?

Feedback

If the amount you would receive at the end of the year was the same in both countries for a deposit of $1,000, there wouldn't be any incentive to deposit money in the other country. So if the exchange rate meant that $1,050 is exactly equal to 2,240fr or $1:2.133fr (2,240/1,050) then there would be no incentive for our savers to move money from one country to the other. In other words, there would be no arbitrage opportunities if the exchange rate were $1:2.133fr. At any different exchange rate, assuming there were no transaction costs, there would be an arbitrage opportunity.

Put algebraically we can say that the equation for the **International Fisher Effect** is:

$$\frac{(1 + r_h)^t}{(1 + r_f)^t} = \frac{e^0}{e^1}$$

where

r_h is the expected return from investing at home;

R_f is the expected return from investing abroad;

t is the period t which is the end of a year in our case;

e^0 is the spot rate $1:e^0$fr;

e^1 is the expected future spot rate $1:e^1$fr;

Putting our numbers into the equation we have:

$$\frac{1.05}{1.12} = \frac{2}{2.133} = 0.9375$$

In the real world it is usually much more complicated than this example.

There are many different interest rates in each country and exchange currency generally costs money, mostly from the bid–ask spread.

Despite this, the empirical evidence is that the International Fisher Effect holds in the long run and also in the short run for countries experiencing high levels of inflation. It does not appear to hold in the short run for countries with low levels of inflation.

Interest rate parity theory

Interest rate parity is concerned with the relationship between interest rate differentials and the difference between spot and forward rates. Again we will rely on the law of arbitrage to demonstrate this.

Example

We are going to return to the example of Uno and Duo. Remember that the spot rate is $1:2 francs.

Nominal interest rates this time are 3% in Uno and 11% in Duo. We are going to use this information to calculate the forward rate.

Figure 6.2   Solution

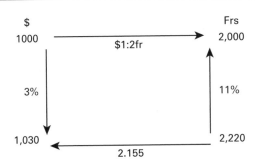

In order for an arbitrage opportunity to exist it must be risk free. Fortunately, an investor can enter into a series of contracts now which remove any uncertainty from the transactions.

Suppose our intrepid investor considers they might be able to obtain a higher return in Duo than they can in Uno.

They could borrow money in Uno at 3%, convert it into Duo francs at $1:2fr and deposit it in Duo at 11% interest. At the end of the year our investor can take his money out of the Duo bank and change the francs back into dollars. Our investor can lock into all three of these contracts today and hence know with certainty exactly how many Uno dollars they will receive in one year's time.

If our investor uses a forward contract they can be sure of exactly how much they will receive in dollars at the end of the investment period. If interest rate parity holds then:

$$\frac{1 + r_h}{1 + r_f} = \frac{e_0}{f_1}$$

where

r_h is the prevailing interest rate in the home country;

r_f is the prevailing interest rate in the local, or foreign, country;

e_0 is the spot rate;

f_1 is the forward rate at the end of the period.

The forward rate as an unbiased predictor of the future spot rate

When a financial institution, such as a bank, quotes a forward rate they use all available information about a currency to make their quote. In addition to interest rates and expected inflation they will factor in other political and economic data. Banks will input all this information into a model to calculate the forward rate. Suppose one bank's model was very cautious compared to other banks? It would generally offer a worse quote than other banks. Investors would soon realize they could have got a better deal from another bank and our cautious bank would soon lose much of its business.

Now suppose one bank believed that one currency was going to appreciate substantially over another currency. Suppose HSBC thought the pound was going to be much stronger than other banks believed. HSBC might offer a 12-month forward exchange rate of £1:€1.25 while other banks were offering the same contract at £1:€1.20. Companies and others wanting to buy euros in 12 months' time would flock to HSBC to buy a forward contract but investors seeking to sell euros in 12 months' time would use other banks offering a better rate. Arbitragers will spot an opportunity to enter into two forward contracts, one to buy euros at £1:€1.25 from HSBC and a second contract to sell euros and buy pounds at £1:€1.20 at another bank, making a risk-free profit in 12 months' time.

Given this, we can see that the forward rate is going to be set by a consensus of those active in foreign exchange markets. This means that the forward rate will fully reflect all available information about the currencies. You might recognize this argument from the efficient market hypothesis, a key idea in finance.

In the next 12 months, it is highly likely that some unexpected things will happen. For example, there was a general belief that the UK would vote to remain in the EU in the 2016 referendum. In the event, the vote was to leave and we saw an immediate reaction in the currency market, with the pound falling by more than 10% against the dollar. In a 12-month period there may be several unexpected events; some will be positive and some will be negative. For this reason it is unlikely that the future spot rate will equal the forward rate for that day but since these unexpected events are as likely to be positive as negative the forward rate is as likely to be an overestimate as an underestimate of the spot rate on that day. We therefore consider the forward rate to be an unbiased estimator of the future spot rate, that is, as likely to be too high as too low.

If this is not entirely clear, consider an example from nature. Pregnant women are given a due date for the birth of their baby: consider this the forward rate. In the event, only about 4% of babies are actually born on their due date but the remaining babies are as likely to be born before their due date as after it, making the due date an unbiased estimator of a baby's actual birth date.

Zero-sum games

Before we go any further there is one last thing we need to say about foreign exchange markets. They are what is called a **zero-sum game**. A simple example of a zero-sum game is a game of poker between a small group of people. If between them a group has £1,000 to play poker with at the beginning of the evening, then by the end of the session they will still, between them, only have £1,000. The only thing that has changed is the people holding the money. So if someone has more money at the end than they did at the beginning that is because other people have less money at the end than they did at the beginning.

That means that if you are able to make money from exchange rate activity, someone else is losing money. It is highly unlikely that other market participants will sit by watching you make money; they will take steps to stop you, which might be that exchange rates or interest rates change by reacting to market conditions.

Currency forecasting

We have now evaluated five different parity conditions which can be used to forecast exchange rates.

One thing that market participants would like to be able to do is to be better at forecasting exchange rates than other market participants. If they could do that, they could take advantage of market imperfections to make more money than other participators can.

If you are going to be better at forecasting exchange rates than the market as a whole, you need to be able to do one or more of the following:

1 Have a better model than anyone else for forecasting. This might work for a while but market forces will soon arrange for others to also have a better model.

2 Have access to better information than other investors, which might be having access to the information more quickly than others. This is relatively unlikely because markets have strict rules about information and it is a breach of those rules for some investors to have information before others. In the UK it is a criminal act to undertake what is known as 'insider dealing', which means acting on information not widely known, and people have gone to prison for it.

3 Take advantage of small short-term deviations from an equilibrium. In practice, foreign exchange markets often overreact to new information. For example, when the UK voted to leave the EU on 23 June 2016, the exchange rate was £1:$1.49 but by the end of the next day the pound had fallen to $1.37:£1. By 7 July the pound had fallen to $1.29 but bounced back to $1.33 by the 14th. In subsequent weeks and months the pound continued to fall and settled at around $1.25:£1. That represented a depreciation of the pound of around 16% ((1.49 − 1.25)/1.49). An investor might have chosen to speculate that the value of the pound on 7 July was an overreaction to the Brexit result and that the pound would recover as the market fully adjusted for the result of the Brexit vote. Such an investor could buy pounds on 7 July and sell them once the pound had recovered.

Traders are well aware of this tendency and it is an important way that they make money. There are other times in which there might be a deviation from an equilibrium.

4 Successfully predict government intervention in the foreign currency markets. This can be a successful strategy in a fixed rate system where it becomes possible to accurately predict the steps taken by the government, or their agent, the central bank, to changes in the exchange rate.

Summary

In this chapter we stated, discussed and tested the five parity conditions of exchange rates. These parity conditions are very important because they are used to forecast exchange rates, something that every MNC needs to do for most of their activities that involve budgeting, including production planning and decision making.

This chapter also provided you with an opportunity to calculate changes in exchange rates given certain conditions.

In practice, forecasting exchange rates is a very difficult thing to do, as changes are not just caused by changes in fundamentals such as interest rates or inflation but also by changes in confidence or market sentiment; we have seen on many occasions that market sentiment leads to very substantial shifts in exchange rates that would be very difficult to forecast using the fundamentals.

Questions

Question 1

Suppose the majority of the countries in the world decided to move towards fixed exchange rates using purchasing power parity to establish the exchange rates. Once set, countries would be required to use monetary policy to maintain the exchange rate.

What are the difficulties with using purchasing power parity to set the exchange rates in the first instance?

Question 2

Suppose Uno and Duo decide to fix their exchange rate at $1:2fr but inflation proves to be at 6% in Uno and 4% in Duo. Is the Uno dollar appreciating or depreciating against the Duo franc?

Question 3

At the time of writing, interest rates are at a historic low with no sign of them rising. At the same time inflation is also very low. To what extent do you agree that it makes sense to borrow money now when it is cheap?

Question 4

Suppose the spot rate is $0.9:€1 and that the annual interest rates are 3% in the United States and 1% in the eurozone. The 12-month forward rate is $0.91:€1. Your foreign exchange model suggests that the euro is going to appreciate to $0.93:€1 over the next year as the economy improves.

How could you use borrowing, lending or forward contracts to make an arbitrage profit in this situation?

07
Foreign exchange markets

At the end of this chapter you will be able to:

- discuss the foreign exchange markets and their participants;
- explain how interest rate swaps, currency swaps and other derivatives work and how they can help reduce costs or uncertainty.

Introduction

The foreign exchange market is a truly global 24-hour-a-day market, starting in Sydney and Tokyo and over the course of the day moving to Hong Kong and Singapore, through Bahrain to Frankfurt, Zurich and London before ending in New York then Chicago and finally San Francisco and Los Angeles.

The foreign exchange market is essential for virtually all international trade. At its simplest, the market allows one currency to be exchanged for another but the market also offers the opportunity to speculate on currencies and to lock into a future exchange rate. In this chapter we will begin by considering the size and scope of the market and the various participants who operate in it. We will then discuss the construction of swaps, both interest rate swaps and currency swaps, and explore the ways in which companies and others can exploit market imperfections by using swaps to reduce their costs of borrowing. We will finish by considering other derivatives offered by the markets that enable companies to fix interest rates in periods of uncertainty.

Size of international currency markets

The currency markets are the largest and most liquid of all markets, with several trillion dollars being traded every day across the world.

The Bank for International Settlements (BIS) undertakes a survey of the size and structure of the international currency markets once every three years. The latest report was published on 1 September 2016 (BIS, 2016). The size of trade is measured in US dollars and since the dollar has appreciated since the last survey it has made the size of trades not involving the dollar appear to be smaller. This is a perennial problem with any study involving foreign exchange.

For the first time since the survey began in 1986 there was a small fall in the daily turnover of currency from $5.4 trillion to $5.1 trillion, largely accounted for by the fall in spot trading. This seems likely to be due to exceptionally high turnover when the last survey was undertaken in April 2013 rather than an indication of a new trend.

Trading in the spot market had declined from $2 trillion a day to $1.7 trillion a day but the turnover of swaps rose by 6% to $2.4 trillion a day, accounting for 47% of the total market. Forward contracts increased their market share by 1% to 14% while options fell by 1% to 5%.

The US dollar remains the dominant traded currency, being on one side of 88% (up from 87%) of all transactions. Emerging markets currencies increased their share of the market: up to 4% for China's renminbi at the expense of the euro, fallen from 33% to 31%; the yen, fallen from 23% to 22%; and the Australian dollar, fallen from 9% to 7%. The UK pound increased its share from 12% to 13%.

Five centres – the UK, the United States, Singapore, Hong Kong SAR and Japan – accounted for 77% of all trade. The UK share of the market fell from 41% to 37%, while markets in the Far East accounted for an increasing share of the market, reaching 21% in 2016. The US share was unchanged at 19%. We can see then that London is the most important foreign exchange trading centre, with almost twice as much trade as the second largest centre, the United States. Most foreign exchange markets do not have a physical trading floor, relying on telecommunications networks.

The foreign exchange market is made up of a retail market and an inter-bank or wholesale market. The main participants in the wholesale foreign exchange or currency markets are financial institutions, multinational companies, governments, speculators and hedge funds.

Speculators and arbitragers, both of whom are often employed by major banks, work for themselves to make a profit. Speculators seek to identify currency, or securities, whose price is likely to change significantly in the short term because the speculator believes they have information that the market has failed to factor into the share price. An example might be a belief that the UK would vote to leave the EU at a time when the widespread belief was that the result would be to remain. A speculator might then buy shares that they thought would increase in value if the vote was to leave, intending to sell them once the result of the vote was announced and reflected in the share price.

Speculators are taking considerable risks in the hope of high returns.

> **Key concept**
>
> **Arbitragers** seek inconsistencies in the two different markets in order to make a risk-free profit. By their actions they help to increase efficiency between markets.

Regulation

Currency markets are unregulated, unlike most other financial markets, meaning that participants self-regulate and have to rely on the creditworthiness of the other participants.

The strict rules on insider dealing that regulate other markets do not apply to foreign exchange markets.

There are no restrictions on the size of any transaction and shorting currency is both allowed and widespread.

In the foreign exchange markets, participants act on their own account. In other markets, participants use brokers to execute trades for them. The brokers are paid a commission for each transaction but there are no commissions in the foreign exchange markets. Dealers make their profits from the bid–ask spread we talked about in Chapter 6.

> **Key concept**
>
> Prices are quoted to four decimal places and 0.0001 is named a pip. So a pip represents 1/100th of 1% of a unit of currency.

The foreign exchange market is essentially there to enable participants to exchange one currency for another but it also offers credit for international trade while goods are in transit and provides opportunities to hedge transaction exposure.

Central banks buy and sell their country's foreign exchange reserves and may choose to intervene in an attempt to change their currency's exchange rate.

Transactions in the foreign exchange market

We have already seen that there are three main types of transaction in the foreign exchange markets: spot, forward and swaps. There are other transactions, such as futures and options, but these three make up the majority of the market and are the ones we will focus on.

Spot transactions

A spot transaction is one in which a buyer and seller, almost always banks, agree to exchange a given amount of currency at a given exchange rate. The currency is exchanged 'immediately', which in practice means within two working days, although the US and Canadian dollars are settled on the following working day. Transactions between a bank and a customer wouldn't necessarily take two days. Most dollar-denominated transactions are settled through the Clearing House Interbank Payments System (CHIPS) in New York, which determines the net balances between the participating banks and allows for payment to take place.

Forward contract transactions

A forward contract is one in which a buyer and seller, almost always at least one party being a bank, agree to exchange a given amount of currency at a given exchange rate, termed the forward rate, on some future agreed date, usually within a year.

Swaps

Before we consider currency swaps we are going to discuss interest rate swaps. This market is huge and this is a good place to consider them.

Interest rate swaps

Before we talk about what a swap is and how it works, it is really helpful to make clear why swaps are possible.

Key concept

A swap enables organizations to exploit market imperfections. If markets were perfect swaps couldn't be profitable.

Example

Suppose Large Plc can borrow at 3% fixed rate or at LIBOR + 1% and that Smaller Plc can borrow at 5% fixed or LIBOR + 2.5%. What is the market imperfection?

Solution

There are two markets operating here. The first is the fixed rate market and the second is the floating rate market.

Both markets consider Smaller Plc to be riskier than Large Plc and so charge Smaller Plc a risk premium.

Borrower	Fixed Rate	Floating Rate
Smaller	5%	LIBOR + 2.5%
Large	3%	LIBOR + 1%
Difference	2%	1.5%

The risk premium in the fixed rate market is 2% (5% – 3%) while the risk premium in the floating rate market is only 1.5% (LIBOR + 1% – (LIBOR + 2.5%). So while both markets consider Smaller to be riskier, their assessment of the appropriate risk premium is different and this is a market imperfection.

The size of the market imperfection is 0.5% (2% – 1.5%). While that might not seem very much, on loans of perhaps as much as a billion pounds that represents a valuable opportunity to reduce costs for large companies and other organizations.

Causes of market imperfections

Market imperfections are created by barriers set up to prevent arbitrage from operating to reduce differences in two or more markets.

Some of those barriers may have been intentionally created, by legislation usually, often with a desire to protect a domestic market from competition.

Other barriers are about the perceptions of market participants, with lenders or investors in one market holding different views about a particular business than those in another market. That can be caused by a tendency to view a business which is better known (for example by being a domestic company as compared to a foreign company) as being more creditworthy.

Suppose, for example, that a UK company seeks to set up an Indian subsidiary financed partially by debt. The company will have a credit history in the UK and UK assets. UK lenders are likely to consider the company more creditworthy than an Indian lender might. To the Indian lender, the company's credit history is based on its UK activities. The Indian lender is likely to charge a risk premium to lend to the UK company, unlike a UK-based lender.

The UK company might prefer to borrow in rupees because it will help to reduce translation risk and economic risk: we will discuss these risks in the next chapter. But a rupee loan will cost more than a sterling loan because of the different perceptions of the riskiness of the company. A currency swap will enable the company to borrow in the currency it wants to use at the lowest possible cost.

Now we have explored the idea of market imperfections in more detail, we can look at how **interest rate swaps** work.

An interest rate swap generally requires a financial intermediary, a bank, to arrange and manage the swap.

Two companies each arrange a loan at the most beneficial interest rate they can. In our example above, Large would borrow at the fixed rate because it gives the biggest discount compared to the rate Smaller can borrow at: 2% in the fixed rate market as compared to 1.5% in the floating rate market. Equally, Smaller would borrow in the floating rate market because that charged the lower of the two premiums over the rate that Large can borrow at. This kind of swap is called a coupon rate swap. If both interest rates are floating, the swap is called a basis swap. A basis swap will be possible if the two companies are offered different interest rates in different markets and again the market imperfection is the different risk premiums in the two markets.

Activity

Suppose Chane Inc can borrow at 4% fixed or LIBOR + 1.5% while Della Inc can borrow at 5% fixed or LIBOR + 3%. Which borrowing should the two companies take in preparation for a swap?

Feedback

Chane is seen as less risky than Della. Della has to pay a premium of 1% (5% − 4%) in the fixed rate market and 1.5% (LIBOR + 3% − (LIBOR + 1.5%) in the floating rate market. So Chane should borrow at a floating rate and Della should borrow at a fixed rate.

Now we are ready to set out exactly what an interest rate swap is.

An **interest rate swap** is an agreement between two organizations to exchange the interest payments on a notional sum of money, sometimes called the **notional principle**. Generally, the agreement is arranged by a financial intermediary which charges a fee for its services.

The companies involved don't swap loans, just the interest payments on the loans. The length of time of the swap is generally between two and 10 years.

Example

Returning to Large and Smaller, suppose they both seek to borrow €100 million for 10 years.

Suppose Large would prefer to borrow at a floating rate, perhaps because some of its income is dependent on LIBOR, while Smaller would prefer to borrow at a fixed rate, again because some of its income is fixed. But we already know that it would be cheaper for Large to borrow at a fixed rate and Smaller to borrow at a floating rate to maximize the benefit of the market imperfection of the risk premium for Smaller in both markets.

The first step of the swap will be for Large to borrow €100 million for 10 years at 3% and for Smaller to borrow €100 million for 10 years at LIBOR +2.5%.

Next, a financial intermediary, let's call them Big Bank, will set up the following interest rate swap:

Large agrees to pay six-month LIBOR + 0.7% on a notional €100 million for 10 years to Big Bank, who agrees to pay 3.2% to Large in exchange.

Smaller agrees to pay 3% on a notional €100 million for 10 years to Big Bank, who agrees to pay LIBOR + 0.7% to Smaller.

Figure 7.1   Interest rate swap

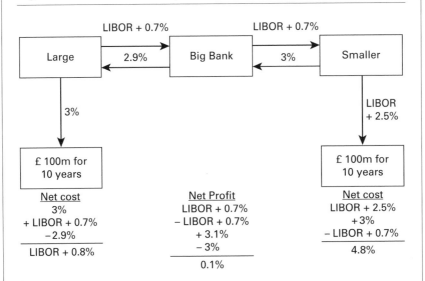

We can see that the total 0.5% we identified to be available due to market imperfections – that is the mispricing of the risk premium levied on Smaller in the two different markets – has been split between the three parties: 0.2% to Large, 0.2% to Smaller and 0.1% to Big Bank. As long as there are market imperfections, banks and borrowers will enter into swap arrangements of various kinds in order to benefit from them.

In the example above, we saw the companies borrowing at either a fixed or floating rate, depending on which gave them the best deal, and by entering into a swap arrangement they were able to take on the liabilities of a loan with a different method of calculating interest rates. This can not only save the company money but also lower its risk. For example, according to the April 2016 Bank for International Settlements (BIS) survey mentioned earlier in this chapter, the daily turnover of swaps was around $1.85 billion, so the market is truly vast.

Currency swaps

The **currency swap market** is another huge market. This time the swap involves different currencies and can be used to manage both interest rate and exchange rate risk. A company might find it cheaper to borrow in its domestic currency but in order to hedge it might prefer to borrow in a local currency. By undertaking a currency swap the company can have the best of both worlds: the lower cost and the currency exposure it seeks.

Just like with an interest rate swap, the principals are not exchanged. The cash flow obligations associated with the principal, that is the interest payments and capital repayments, are swapped.

To avoid default risk, the two counterparties have the 'right to offset', which means that if one party defaults on a payment the other company is able to also withhold a matching payment. One advantage of a currency swap is that because the principals are not swapped they don't have to be reported in the companies' financial statements, which can improve the impression created of the company. At the end of the swap period there is an agreement to swap the maturing principals at a pre-agreed exchange rate, effectively a long-term forward rate.

The reason for this is that the total cost of a loan depends on both the interest rate and also any exchange rate gain or loss on the repayment of the principal. We have already thought about the relationship between interest rate differentials and forward rates in Chapter 6 and will consider this in more detail in Chapter 9, but for the moment it is enough to say that if you borrow money in a currency which depreciates against your domestic currency you will need less of your domestic currency to repay the principal than if it hadn't depreciated, and this gives you an exchange rate gain. Multinational companies are concerned with the total cost of a loan rather than the cost of just the interest element of the loan. Consequentially, it is essential that the principals are exchanged at maturity.

Initially, currency swap arrangements only swapped fixed rate loans but today most swaps involve both a currency swap and an interest rate swap, that is, swapping fixed and floating exchange rates. As with a straight interest rate swap, a financial intermediary would arrange the swap in exchange for a fee but this time the swap payments are guaranteed by the financial intermediary, who must have a very high credit rating themselves, thus eliminating credit default risk.

We have only considered the simplest swaps, vanilla swaps, but in practice swaps can be very complicated, with more than one swap linked with a single loan.

Swaps are not the only possibilities for companies wishing to reduce the costs or the riskiness of borrowing. There are a number of ways of fixing an interest rate on future borrowing.

Forward-forwards

A **forward-forward contract** enables a company to fix the interest rate on a future loan or deposit. In practice, a company can buy a forward-forward contract or they can create one using other contracts. A forward-forward can be a bespoke contract, written specifically for the firm buying it.

Key concept

Bespoke contracts are also called **over the counter (OTC)** because they are not standardized and thus are not traded.

It is easiest to explain forward-forward using an example.

Example

Careful plc wishes to borrow $10 million eurodollars in six months' time and repay it in 12 months' time. The company is concerned that interest rates will increase in the next six months.

First, the company could fix the interest rate at today's rates by borrowing and lending in the money markets. Suppose Careful can borrow and lend at LIBOR + 1%. Then it could borrow $10 million for 12 months at LIBOR + 1% today and at the same time it could deposit $10 million for six months, again at LIBOR + 1%.

Then for the first six months, Careful would have a loan and savings of $10 million with the same interest rate and for the following six months it would have the loan it needed at a cost locked into at the time the need for the loan was identified. Interest rate risk is avoided.

In practice, there is likely to be a small interest rate differential between the rates at which Careful can borrow and lend – that is how banks make some of their money – and there is also likely to be a difference between borrowing and lending over six months and 12 months.

Activity

Look up today's LIBOR rate. You can find it online or in print newspapers like the *Financial Times*.

Feedback

Hopefully by now you are asking me which LIBOR rate you should use; there are many different LIBOR rates quoted. One reason for the different rates is that generally, but not always, investors require a higher return to lend money over a longer period of time than over a short period of time. So generally, LIBOR3, the rate for a three-month deposit, will be lower than

Figure 7.2   History of eurodollar LIBOR rates, 1 January 1999–31 October 2016

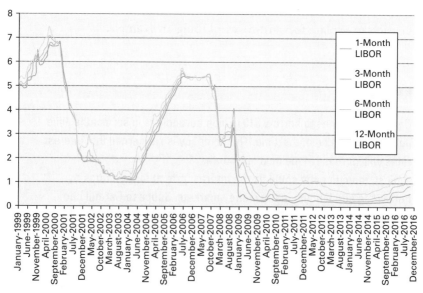

SOURCE Fedprimerate.com

LIBOR12, the rate for a 12-month deposit. There are other reasons for different LIBORs, including the currency in which they are denominated. While LIBOR stands for the London Interbank Offered Rate, it is a global interest rate.

The graph in Figure 7.2 shows LIBOR rates since 1999.

Example

Returning to Careful plc and using the above LIBOR figures, we can calculate exactly how much our loan and saving are going to cost or return to us.

The LIBOR rate on 31 October 2016 is shown in the chart above: 12-month LIBOR is around 1.75% while six-month LIBOR is around 1.3%.

Careful is going to borrow sufficient money now to be able to receive $10 million in six months' time. At a deposit rate of LIBOR + 1%, which is 1.3% + 1% or 2.3%, Careful will have to borrow $9.864365 million ($10 million/(1 + 0.02.3 x 6/12)) now. At the end of the 12-month period, Careful will have to repay a total of $10.135635 million ($9.864365 million x 1.0275).

You might want to go through this again step by step to be sure you understand what we did:

1 We have borrowed money for 12 months and so will use the 12-month LIBOR rate for our loan but we deposited money for only six months so will use the six-month LIBOR rate for deposits.

2 We could now calculate the effective rate of our borrowing $10 million in six months' time for six months using arbitrage. Effectively we are borrowing $10 million in six months' time and repaying $10.135635 in 12 months' time.

3 That is an effective interest rate of 1.36% for six months but we always state it in terms of an annual rate, so 2.72% (1.36% x 6/12).

4 If we deduct the 1% risk premium this suggests that the six-month forward LIBOR rate for six-month borrowing is 1.72% (2.72% - 1%).

5 If the rate is higher or lower than 1.72%, there are arbitrage opportunities which would be used and the rates would swiftly shift to prevent such opportunities being available.

Forward rate agreement (FRA)

Forward-forwards are less widely used today as businesses have moved to using **forward rate agreements**, which are over-the-counter forward contracts. Like a forward-forward, FRAs allow companies to fix an interest rate, called the contracted rate, for a short-term future period of time. In many ways, FRAs are similar to swaps. Businesses seeking to protect themselves against increases in the market interest rate would buy an FRA while businesses concerned about falls in interest rates would sell an FRA. Speculators use FRAs to bet on future interest rates. The specific interest rate used for determining the market rate is called the reference rate.

Once again, interest payments are exchanged by one party paying the difference between the two interest charges while, again, the currencies are not exchanged. If the reference rate is above the contracted rate the buyer of the FRA receives the difference. When the reference rate is below the contracted rate the seller of the FRA receives the difference.

Example

Expanding Inc is planning a substantial investment in four months' time which will be funded by a $700 million loan in four months' time for six months. Growth figures in the United States are causing concern to Expanding that short-term interest rates might rise. To hedge the risk of interest rate rises, Expanding will buy a US $4 x 6 2.5 – 2.75% pa FRA, that is a forward rate agreement for six months, starting in four months' time, paying 2.5% on deposits and charging 2.75% on borrowings.

Expanding can't protect itself from increasing interest rates if the market generally believes that interest rates will rise but it can protect itself from unexpected increases. Once the FRA has been bought, Expanding will be certain of paying 2.75% on its borrowings. Suppose that in four months' time Expanding has to pay 3.1% for its borrowing. Then it is able to recover 0.35% (3.1% – 2.75%) from the seller of the FRA.

But if interest rates were at 2.6% then Expanding would be required to pay 0.15% (2.75% – 2.6%) to the seller of the FRA.

Note then that Expanding is locking in to an exchange rate. It can no longer benefit from lower rates of interest but is of course protected from higher than expected interest rates.

We have now considered a number of relatively simple derivative instruments which can be used to reduce the risk faced by a multinational company.

But financial markets can, and do, create new financial instruments to meet the needs of their customers. Given that, it is easy to understand that there are other widely used derivatives available to those who wish to reduce their risk or speculate on movements in markets.

Eurodollar Futures

One important financial instrument is Eurodollar Futures. These futures are traded on the Chicago Mercantile Exchange (CME), the London International Financial Futures Exchange (LIFFE) and the Singapore International Monetary Exchange (SIMEX) in $1 million amounts and have expiry dates in March, June, September and December. When issued, they will have a maturity of up to three years. Eurodollar Futures enable companies to fix a future interest rate as FRAs do but they are market to market. It is easiest to explain market to market by using an example.

Example

Suppose a company buys a Eurodollar Futures contract when the index is at 97.5. The implied LIBOR3, that is the LIBOR rate for the next three months, is 2.5% (100 – 97.5). In other words, the index is equal to 100 – LIBOR3. By buying a bond the company is exposed to changing interest rates in the same way as someone who was borrowing $1 million. So, if interest rates go down the company will be better off and if interest rates rise the company will be worse off. Selling a bond would have the same effect as depositing $1 million, with falling interest rates reducing the value of the bond and increasing interest rates increasing the value of the bond.

The value of the Eurodollar Futures contract will be $993,750 which is $1 million (1 – 0.025(90/360)) where 0.025 is the annualized interest rate, LIBOR3, 90 is the number of days in the contract (three months) and 360 is the number of days in the year. You can think of this as the present value of $1 million in 90 days with an opportunity cost of 2.5%. We will discuss this in more detail in Chapter 10. Equally, you can think of this as the amount of money you would have to deposit today at an annualized interest rate of 2.5% in order to have $1 million in three months, or 90 days' time.

Then at the end of each working day the gain or loss on the contract over the previous day is calculated.

Suppose the index moves to 97.7 at the end of the next day of trading. The implied forward rate is now 2.3% (100 – 97.7). The actual forward rate might not be 2.3%, partly because the dates now don't match exactly and partly because markets are driven by factors other than LIBOR3.

The new value of the futures contract will be $99,4250, ie $1 million (1 – 0.023(90/360)). This is an increase of $500 ($994,250 – $993,750) and the $500 will be paid into the company's margin account at the end of the day. Equally, had the value of the contract fallen by $500 then that amount would have been withdrawn from the company's margin account at the end of the day.

> We can see then that a borrower looking to fix the price of a loan would sell Eurodollar Futures contracts. When the interest rates fell, the cost of the loan would fall but the Eurodollar Futures would require money to be deposited. If interest rates rose the cost of the loan would increase but the Eurodollar Futures would increase in value.

In the next chapter we will consider the forward contract, which is another financial instrument for dealing with currency risk and a way in which currency and money markets can be used to create a hedge: another way of reducing risk.

Summary

The foreign exchange market is the biggest financial market in the world with over $5 trillion of currency traded every working day of the year. The market is also largely unregulated, making it a very cheap market to buy and sell in. We defined the terms used in the market then focused on swaps, firstly interest rate swaps and then currency swaps.

A swap is used to exploit a market imperfection, generally that the risk premium for a company is mispriced in one of the markets. The swap enables the company to reduce its cost of borrowing by exploiting the mispricing.

We then explored other financial instruments that enable a company to reduce the uncertainty of borrowing such as forward-forwards and forward rate agreements.

Questions

Question 1

If one party of a swap benefits from the swap is it true that the other party will have lost money? Explain your answer.

Question 2

How can Apple use a forward rate agreement (FRA) to fix the rate of a six-month $100 million loan to be taken out in three months' time?

Question 3

Suppose that Tesco would like to borrow yen for five years at a fixed rate while JLR would like to borrow floating rate pounds for five years.

Tesco can borrow at 4.75% fixed rate yen or floating rate pounds at LIBOR + 0.5%.

JLR can borrow at fixed rate yen at 5.15% or floating rate pounds at LIBOR + 1.05%.

Determine the range of possible savings that Tesco could make via an interest/currency rate swap with JLR.

08
Determining and managing exchange risk

At the end of this chapter you will be able to:

- identify and discuss the different types of exchange risk;
- identify strategies for reducing transaction exposure;
- construct a money market hedge to hedge a transaction risk and compare to the equivalent forward rate hedge to select the optimum hedge;
- discuss hedging and economic exposure.

Introduction

In previous chapters we discussed the determinants of exchange risks and suggested that companies may suffer losses due to changes in exchange rates. In this chapter we are going to look in detail at the risks faced by companies trading internationally and the strategies they can take to reduce or eliminate those risks. Finally we will consider the benefits, as well as the costs, of hedging risks.

Risks

Companies face three different kinds of exchange risk:

- translation risk;
- transaction risk;
- economic or operating risk.

We will discuss each of these in turn and then consider how a company can manage these risks.

Translation risk

Translation risk is the risk that exchange rate movements will have an impact on the published financial statements, the income statement and the statement of financial position of companies.

We can see how this works with a simple example.

Example

Growing plc, a UK company, wishes to set up a subsidiary in France. Growing needs to borrow money to buy assets in France.

Suppose Growing borrows £100m in the UK, converts it into euros at a rate of £1:€1.20 and then invests the money in assets in France. At the end of the company's financial year they will have to publish consolidated accounts which must include the results of the subsidiary in France. The relevant extract from Growing's opening balance sheet of the subsidiary will be:

Extract from opening statement of financial position

	£'m
Net assets	100 (€120m /1.2)
Long-term loan	100

Note that the loan is denominated in sterling so no currency conversion is needed.

Suppose that by the end of the financial period the exchange rate has become £1:€1.30. Now the extract will look like this:

Extract from closing statement of financial position

	£'m
Net assets	92.31 (€120/1.30)
Long-term liability	100
Loss on foreign exchange	7.69

Nothing has changed within the company but the exchange rate change has led to a loss having to be reported due to the exchange rate changes. Most businesses dislike having to report losses like this one even though no actual loss has been incurred. The good news is that if the company plans carefully it is likely that this kind of loss can be reduced or even eliminated.

Suppose, instead of borrowing in the UK, the company had borrowed the money to buy the assets in France. Let's look again at the extracts from the statement of financial position.

Extract from opening statement of financial position

	£'m
Net assets	100 (€120m /1.2)
Long-term Loan	100 (€120m/1.2)

Extract from closing statement of financial position

	£'m
Net assets	92.31 (€120/1.30)
Long-term liability	92.31 (€120/1.30)

No matter what the exchange rate is now, the assets and the liabilities have the same value and there can't be an exchange rate gain or loss.

This is an example of a **hedge**.

Here the company has an exposed position in that it holds assets denominated in another currency and the value of the assets in the consolidated accounts will vary if exchange rates fluctuate. This hasn't been changed by taking out a hedge.

The hedge has been created by borrowing in euros rather than in pounds sterling. When the company borrowed in pounds sterling the loan itself did not carry exchange risk but by borrowing in euros an exchange risk arises on the consolidation of the accounts. So before, only the assets were exposed to exchange risk but once the loan was taken out in euros, both the assets and the liability were exposed to exchange risk.

You might be wondering how increasing the risk helps the company.

In this case we have what is called a **perfect hedge**. That means that any loss due to exchange rate changes in one of the items is exactly set off by a matching gain on the other item.

In this case we showed what happened when the pound weakened against the euro and the exchange rate moved from £1:€1.20 to £1:€1.30. After the depreciation of the pound the assets were worth less in the consolidated accounts but the fall in the value of the assets was exactly offset by the fall in value of the liability.

These two risky positions taken together are not exposed to translation risk.

Activity

Draw up the extracts from the financial statements if, instead of weakening, the pound strengthens to £1:€1.1.

Feedback

This time the extracts look like this:

Extract from opening statement of financial position

	£'m
Net assets	100 (€120m /1.2)
Long-term loan	100 (€120m/1.2)

Extract from closing statement of financial position

	£'m
Net assets	109 (€120/1.1)
Long-term liability	109 (€120/1.1)

This time the pound has strengthened and the reported value of the assets has gone up. But the value of the liability has gone up by exactly the same amount. Once again the company has reported neither an exchange rate loss nor gain so the hedge has continued to work.

Please note that the original position, showing a loss on translation, does not involve any change in the cash flows since all of the debt is paid in pounds sterling and the amount repaid is unaffected by the exchange rate between the pound and the euro.

By changing that arrangement to borrow in euros, we may have eliminated the translation risk but we have created a cash flow stream of interest and capital repayments in euros which is subjected to exchange risk. So eliminating translation risk has been achieved but only by creating a new risk and this time the risk does affect cash flows. That may not be an insurmountable problem, as we will discuss when we consider both **transaction risk** (netting off) and **economic risk** (matching streams of cash flows).

While I might not be too concerned about translation exposure, since it doesn't involve cash flows, finance directors tend to worry about anything which makes the accounts show a loss on translation and in practice will often hedge translation risk.

Transaction exposure

Transaction exposure arises when a company has to pay or receive an amount of currency that is not its domestic currency and on exchange into the domestic currency the amount is not as expected due to changes in the exchange rate.

Remember that if a multinational company needs to pay an amount of foreign currency it is said to be short in the currency. In contrast, if it is expecting to receive an amount of foreign currency then it is said to be long in the currency.

In order to manage the transaction exposure, an MNC must first determine how much exposure they actually have. Which gives us an interesting question to ask: should each subsidiary in an MNC arrange its own transaction exposure or should the MNC as a whole deal with the transaction exposure of the group? Before we attempt to answer this question we should say that in general, reducing a company's transaction exposure costs money in the form of fees and other costs.

Activity

Suppose Sprawling PLC is based in the UK and has subsidiaries in the United States and the eurozone, as well as in other parts of the world. Root Inc is a US subsidiary of Sprawling and is currently expecting to receive €20 million from a eurozone customer on 31 January while Branch, a subsidiary in the UK, needs to pay €20 million on 31 January to a eurozone supplier.

What is Sprawling's exposure from the two transactions?

Feedback

This is a very simple situation. One subsidiary has to pay euros while another is expecting to receive the same number of euros on the same date. Clearly it is not necessary to hedge either transaction because there is no risk or exposure.

But neither subsidiary alone could be expected to identify the matching transaction so in order to do this it is necessary for the MNC to act as a single entity rather than as a collection of companies. In practice this can be a serious difficulty to an MNC with subsidiaries attempting to reduce the impact of change on their own results without reference to the impact on the group as a whole. In addition, a number of companies have got into difficulty because of a lack of understanding of how hedging works or what is needed to be hedged. We will discuss some of these cases later in this chapter.

What we have done here is called **netting off.** MNCs often have transactions between subsidiaries as one subsidiary sells goods or services to other subsidiaries in the group. In our activity we had a very simple situation. In practice, with more transactions and more currencies, we use a simple matrix.

Example

Suppose an MNC determines that the following amounts are owed between subsidiaries in the group.

Table 8.1   Proportion of GDP spent by governments 2014

Debt (in £'000) due from company based in	Payment (in £'000) due to company based in				
	Canada	US	Germany	Turkey	Japan
Canada	–	50	100	30	50
US	70	–	40	70	60
Germany	110	40	–	30	40
Turkey	20	60	20	–	60
Japan	20	70	30	30	–

We can see that the Canada subsidiary owes the equivalent of £50,000 to the US subsidiary, which itself owes £70,000 to the Canadian subsidiary.

Instead of the subsidiaries each paying the full amount owed to the other subsidiary, the costs of currency exchange can be reduced and the need to hedge can be reduced by the US subsidiary paying the equivalent of £20,000 (£70,000 – £50,000) to the Canadian subsidiary.

Table 8.2 Largest countries in the world by GDP adjusted for purchasing power parity 2011

Net debt (in £'000) due from company based in	Net payment (in £'000) due to company based in				
	Canada	US	Germany	Turkey	Japan
Canada					
US	20 (70–50)				
Germany					
Turkey					
Japan					

SOURCE IMF

Can you fill in the rest of the table?

Feedback

Table 8.3 Largest countries in the world: GDP per citizen in 2015

Net debt (in £'000) due from company based in	Net payment (in £'000) due to company based in				
	Canada	US	Germany	Turkey	Japan
Canada	–	0	0	10	30
US	20 (70–50)	–	0	10	0
Germany	10	0	–	10	10
Turkey	0	0	0	–	30
Japan	0	10	0	0	–

SOURCE IMF

After the netting-off exercise it is apparent that the exposure of the MNC is very much lower than appeared at first.

An MNC might go even further. It might argue that the US dollar and the Canadian dollar are positively correlated with each other. So while you can't net off the US dollar and Canadian dollar transactions and eliminate exchange risk, you might be able to net them off and reduce the risk to an acceptable level. In this case the Japanese subsidiary owns the equivalent of £10,000 US dollars and is owed £30,000 Canadian dollars. These might be netted off to show a net amount of only £20,000 Canadian dollars owed to the Japanese subsidiary.

Having netted off the amounts due and owed the MNC can now decide whether it wants to hedge these transactions.

The hedge takes the form of taking up an equal but opposite exposed position to the transaction to be hedged. So to hedge a long position a company would take up an equivalent short position and to hedge a short position it would take up an equivalent long position.

We will spend most of the rest of this chapter studying the main means of hedging a transaction but first we need to make a very important point.

What can we hedge?

Suppose in the run up to the US election, when Donald Trump and Hillary Clinton are pretty much neck and neck in the polls, a US company decides to place an order for some equipment costing £10 million from the UK. At the time of writing the consensus is that the foreign exchange market has valued the dollar as if Hillary Clinton is going to win. Hence if Hillary Clinton actually won, you wouldn't expect much change in the value of the dollar from the value at the time of writing, September 2016. If Donald Trump won, the value of the dollar might change to reflect that new information. Let's suppose that if Donald Trump won the dollar would be expected to fall, and indeed did fall.

It is possible today to hedge the dollar so that if Donald Trump won and the dollar fell in value, the transaction wouldn't cost any more than if Hillary Clinton won and the dollar didn't fall.

Here is a graph of the US dollar against the UK pound for the six months from April to September 2016.

We can see that the exchange rate has not moved significantly since July.

But if we look back at June we can see there was a big shift in the exchange rate between the two countries. The dollar appreciated against the pound by around 15% over a day or so. This sudden and significant shift occurred as a result of the June UK referendum vote on whether to leave the EU. The markets believed that the vote would be to remain and priced the pound accordingly. The vote to leave was unexpected and the market reacted after the result was known, leading to a fall in the value of the pound.

These are both examples of unexpected changes in exchange rates and can be hedged against.

Hedging in many ways is similar to insurance. You can use hedging to protect yourself from unexpected changes, just as you can insure yourself against accidents in your car. But you can't hedge against expected changes, just as you can't insure yourself against the loss of value of a car or the cost

Figure 8.1 US dollar against the UK pound April–September 2016

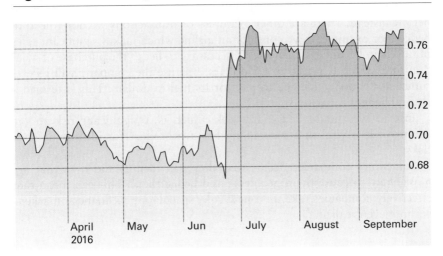

of servicing a car. If a company tried to hedge an expected change then it would find that no one was willing to enter into a contract with it except at a price that was sufficiently high that the other party was fully compensated for the loss they were highly likely to incur.

Timing of a hedge

Suppose a company decides to order goods for €1 million from an Italian company. When should it hedge the transaction?

There are a number of points we could hedge a transaction at:

- when the decision to place the order is made;
- when the order is placed;
- when the goods arrive.

When is the right time to hedge? Remember, by hedging we are going to take up an equal but opposite exposed position in order to eliminate the transaction risk we would otherwise have.

The ideal time to hedge would be once the decision to place the order has been made. Otherwise there is some exchange rate exposure.

If we are considering an order to supply goods then the date on which the order is accepted, or quoted for, should be the date from which a hedge should be entered into.

What should we hedge?

This is a very important question. Hedging is not free and may not have any real benefit to a company.

The first thing we can already say is that we shouldn't hedge things we don't need to. For example, we don't have to hedge transactions that we can net off instead. There are other examples of transactions we don't need to hedge. For example, if we consider an airline which makes significant sales of tickets in US dollars, then it isn't necessary to hedge the purchase of aviation fuel, which is priced in US dollars, because the company will receive sufficient US dollar income to pay for its fuel in dollars. This is termed a **natural hedge**.

Instead we should hedge any risk which is a significant risk to the company. It is vital that a company has a procedure for identifying such risks.

Sometimes companies decide that they will identify the risks that are most likely to cause them problems and hedge those. This can mean that effectively companies take up a new role, speculating in financial markets, without even realizing it.

CASE STUDY   Laker Airways

An old but very straightforward example involved a UK airline, Laker Airways, which was declared bankrupt in 1982. Laker Airways were offering low-cost flights between Gatwick in the UK and New York City at a time when there were very few low-cost airlines.

Laker were selling tickets denominated in pounds so most of their income was in sterling. But they leased their planes from Boeing, borrowed dollars, and aviation fuel was denominated in US dollars, so much of their expenditure was in dollars. Laker faced many problems, including recessions in both the UK and the United States, and high interest rates, but a major cause of the company's bankruptcy was that the board assumed that there would be exchange rate stability between the pound and the dollar and so did not hedge to protect the company from any fall in the value of the pound. The pound did indeed depreciate from about $2.20 to the pound to only around $1.60. The failure to hedge such a decline in value caused Laker's costs to soar to unsustainable levels.

A hedge that backfired spectacularly was entered into by Metallgesellschaft AG in 1993. While this hedge didn't involve currencies, it was a really simple error and easy to understand.

CASE STUDY   Metallgesellschaft AG

Metallgesellschaft AG sold oil-based products and decided to offer its customers 10-year fixed-price deals. This was very popular with the company's customers, who happily signed contracts, which meant that Metallgesellschaft bore all the risk of increases in oil prices for 10 years.

Metallgesellschaft recognized that they had agreed to shoulder the risk of oil price increases and decided to hedge their exposed position. Since they were short in oil and so at risk if oil prices went up, they decided to buy oil futures which would increase in value if oil increased in price. But the futures contracts were only short term, up to around a year at most, while the contracts they were meant to hedge were for periods of up to 10 years.

The company effectively speculated on oil prices increasing. If that had happened, the futures contracts would have provided a handsome return which could then have been used to subsidize the losses that would have been realized in the future. In fact, the price of oil fell significantly, leading to losses on the futures contracts. That fall should have been matched by an increase in profits on the fixed-price contracts entered into but those profits would not be realized for up to 10 years. The company lost 1.3 billion dollars on its futures contracts despite closing their positions to limit the losses, which nearly forced the bankruptcy of the company.

We've now spent some time considering the nature of a hedge against trans- action risk, what can be hedged, what can't be hedged, and what can go wrong. Now let's turn our attention to the mechanics of hedging.

We are going to look in detail at two methods, **money market hedging** and **forward contracts**. We will talk a little about the use of **options**. There are other ways of hedging transaction risk, such as futures contracts, which we won't be able to consider here.

Money market hedge

The first hedge we will look at is the **money market hedge**. Later on we will want to compare hedges and so we will always assess the cost of a money market hedge on the date the hedged payment is made or received.

A money market hedge requires the company to borrow and invest money to create a hedge for a transaction that will take place at some future date.

Let's start by hedging a receipt.

If we are receiving an amount of foreign currency at some date in the future we are long in the currency.

To hedge we need to arrange a second position which is short in the foreign currency. So we will borrow the foreign currency. For a total hedge we will need to borrow sufficient currency so that when we repay it, on the same date as we receive the foreign currency we need to repay exactly the same amount of currency as we receive. We need to take account of interest payments when making this calculation. Once we know how much money we are going to borrow we will want to exchange it at today's rate, the spot rate, for our domestic currency. We will assume that the domestic currency we now have will be deposited in a bank account and remain there until the date the foreign currency is received.

All these transactions should be arranged at the same time so there is certainty about the entire hedge.

Example

A UK company, Derby plc, has received a firm order from a German company which is worth £10 million at today's exchange rate. Payment will be in euros in six months' time. Interest rates in the UK are 4%–5% and in Germany they are 3%–3.5% and the spot rate is £1:€1.16.

Show the money market hedge that Derby could enter into to hedge the receipt.

Solution

First we need to do some arithmetic.

We need to start at the end of the process and then work backwards to the present.

Derby is going to receive the equivalent of £10 million at today's spot rate, which is €11.6 million (10 x 1.16).

Derby is going to borrow exactly the right number of euros to mean that it has to repay €11.6 million in six months' time. The interest rate that Derby is going to borrow at is 3.5%. We always use the interest rates in the country we are going to borrow or deposit in, and borrowing costs more than savers earn on deposits so the rate is 3.5%. But the 3.5% is an annualized rate and Derby is only going to borrow the money for six months so the actual interest rate is going to be 1.75% (3.5% x 6/12).

So Derby is going to borrow an amount of money that, once interest at 1.75% is added, will equal €11.6 million. That is, €11.6 million/1.0175 or €11.4 million.

Derby is going to take the €11.4 million that it has borrowed and convert it into pounds at the spot rate of €1.16:£1, providing it with €11.4 million/1.16 or £9.828 million.

Derby will take the £9.828 million it has and deposit it in a UK account at 4%, which is 2% (4% x 6/12) over six months, giving Derby £10.025 million (£9.828 million x 1.02) on the date that the customer pays the bill.

This example raises a number of interesting questions. The first is about whether the company would profit from the transaction. Derby won't know for sure whether it profited from the hedge until after the six months has passed and it will know what the future spot rate will be. However, don't forget that the company is attempting to hedge a foreign currency receipt, not to make a profit on the hedge.

Forward contract

A **forward contract** is a contract between a bank, or other financial intermediary, and their customer, often an MNC. A forward contract is a contract to exchange a fixed amount of currency at a fixed exchange rate on an agreed future date. The rate used is called the forward rate. We discussed the parity conditions in Chapter 6 and argued that the forward rate is affected by interest rate differential between countries. The forward rate is generally seen to be an unbiased estimator of the future spot rate.

The table shows the pound spot and forward rates. Note that if you look at the euro line you can see that the spot rate was €1.2750, the one-month forward rate was €1.2743, the three-month rate was €1.2731 and the one-year rate was €1.2658. Over time you can see that the pound was forecast to fall slightly in value against the euro. Generally the forward rate is determined by reference to interest rate differentials.

Figure 8.2 Pound spot forward against the pound

Dec 19		Closing mid-point	Change on day	Bid/offer spread	Day's mid		One month		Three month		One year		Bank of Eng. Index
					High	Low	Rate	%PA	Rate	%PA	Rate	%PA	
Europe													
Czech Rep.	(Koruna)	35.2685	0.1168	399 – 971	35.3190	35.0700	35.2118	1.9	35.1790	1.0	34.9050	1.0	–
Denmark	(Danish Krone)	9.4828	0.0098	798 – 858	9.5053	9.4624	9.4777	0.6	9.4684	0.6	9.4106	0.8	–
Hungary	(Forint)	403.730	4.3015	438 – 022	404.110	398.480	403.798	-0.2	404.358	-0.6	406.374	-0.7	
Norway	(Nor. Krone)	11.5062	-0.0712	969 – 155	11.5979	11.4542	11.5142	-0.8	11.5287	-0.8	11.5506	-0.4	91.3
Poland	(Zloty)	5.4344	0.0191	317 – 370	5.4646	5.4057	5.4411	-1.5	5.4518	-1.3	5.4826	-0.9	
Russia	(Rouble)	92.3619	-3.4770	885 – 352	98.6313	91.7539	95.3032	-37.0	98.9579	-26.7	108.105	-14.6	–
Sweden	(Krona)	12.0756	0.0257	686 – 825	12.1177	12.0004	12.0719	0.4	12.0632	0.4	12.0126	0.5	79.8
Switzerland	(Fr)	1.5340	0.0007	333 – 346	1.5377	1.5311	1.5329	0.8	1.5304	0.9	1.5165	1.2	146.9
Turkey	(New Lira)	3.6188	-0.0076	177 – 199	3.6527	3.6088	3.6433	-8.1	3.6889	-7.9	3.9033	-7.3	–
UK	(£)	1.0000	–										
Euro	(Euro)	1.2750	-0.0017	747 – 753	1.2779	1.2719	1.2743	0.6	1.2731	0.6	1.2658	0.7	88.0
SDR		1.0757	0.0008										93.4

Americas

Country	Currency												
Argentina	(Peso)	13.3708	0.0008	671 – 744	13.4081	13.3457	13.6802	–27.1	14.4388	–29.6	18.6375	–28.3	–
Brazil	(Real)	4.1430	–0.0144	419 – 441	4.1753	4.1223	4.1743	–9.0	4.2420	–9.3	4.5831	–9.6	–
Canada	(Canadian $)	1.8136	–0.0010	131 – 140	1.8229	1.8097	1.8144	–0.5	1.8160	–0.5	1.8234	–0.5	100.2
Mexico	(Mexican Peso)	22.8211	0.0770	159 – 263	22.9390	22.6618	22.8479	–1.4	22.9189	–1.7	23.3059	–2.1	–
Peru	(New Sol)	4.6103	0.0124	089 – 116	–		4.6282	–4.7	4.6607	–4.3	4.8129	–4.2	–
USA	(US $)	1.5636	–0.0001	634 – 638	1.5682	1.5609	1.56..	0.3	1.5625	0.3	1.5602	0.2	96.7

Pacific/Middle East/Africa

Country	Currency												
Australia	(A$)	1.9186	0.0021	180 – 192	1.9227	1.9087	1.9226	–2.5	1.9299	–2.3	1.9595	–2.1	98.5
Hong Kong	(HK $)	12.1253	–0.0020	234 – 271	12.1614	12.1034	12.1236	0.2	12.1179	0.2	12.1002	0.2	–
India	(Indian Rupee)	98.9525	0.1845	320 – 729	99.1460	98.5570	99.5881	–7.7	100.672	–6.8	105.336	–6.1	–
Indonesia	(Rupiah)	19529.4	–113.989	905 – 968	19685.3	19472.2	19633.9	–6.4	19839.9	–6.3	20825.3	–6.2	–
Iran	(Rial)	42178.4	–126.937	297–	42353.9	42170.3	–	–	–	–	–	–	–
Israel	(Shekel)	6.1265	–0.0398	207 – 323	6.1734	6.1141	6.1254	0.2	6.1206	0.4	6.0885	0.6	–
Japan	(Yen)	186.741	0.9088	686 – 796	187.240	185.990	186.633	0.7	186.459	0.6	185.267	0.8	122.8
Kuwait	(Kuwaiti Dinar)	0.4575	0.0001	568 – 582	0.4585	0.4563	0.4575	0.0	0.4576	–0.1	0.4583	–0.2	–
Malaysia	(Ringgit)	5.4359	0.0202	328 – 389	5.4519	5.4241	5.4492	–2.9	5.4719	–2.6	5.5537	–2.1	–

(continued)

Figure 8.2 (Continued)

Dec 19		Closing mid-point	Change on day	Bid/offer spread	Day's mid		One month		Three month		One year		Bank of Eng. Index
					High	Low	Rate	%PA	Rate	%PA	Rate	%PA	
New Zealand	(NZ $)	2.0151	-0.0020	142 – 160	2.0189	2.0069	2.0209	-3.4	2.0315	-3.2	2.0810	-3.2	125.1
Philippines	(Peso)	69.9320	-0.0257	152 – 488	70.1322	69.7722	70.0227	-1.6	70.1565	-1.3	70.8193	-1.3	–
Saudi Arabia	(Riyal)	5.8700	0.0004	688 – 711	5.8861	5.8593	5.8678	0.4	5.8649	0.3	5.8675	0.0	–
Singapore	($)	2.0582	0.0028	574 – 589	2.0645	2.0524	2.0598	-0.9	2.0613	-0.6	2.0604	-0.1	–
South Africa	(Rand)	18.1042	0.0833	940 – 143	18.2358	18.0436	18.1966	-6.1	18.3728	-5.8	19.2427	-5.9	–
Korea South	(Won)	1723.09	0.3359	255 – 362	1727.55	1713.70	1725.07	-1.4	1728.52	-1.3	1734.68	-0.7	–
Taiwan	($)	49.4995	0.0790	908 – 081	49.4029	49.0659	49.1820	0.4	49.1174	0.7	48.6763	1.1	–
Thailand	(Baht)	51.3917	-0.0720	538 – 295	51.6380	51.2670	51.4629	-1.7	51.5686	-1.4	51.9638	-1.1	–
UAE	(Dirham)	5.7432	-0.0002	424 – 440	5.7600	5.7332	5.7421	0.2	5.7394	0.3	5.7324	0.2	–

SOURCE Euro Locking Rates: Austrian Schilling 13.7603, Belgium/Luxembourg Franc 40.3399, Cyprus 0.585274, Finnish Markka 5.94572, French Franc 6.55957, German Mark 1.95583, Greek Drachma 340.75, Irish Punt 0.787564, Italian Lira 1936.27, Malta 0.4293, Netherlands Guilder 2.20371, Portuguese Escudo 200.482, Slovakian Koruna 30.1260, Slovenia Tolar 239.64, Spanish Peseta 166.386. Bid/offer spreads in the Pound Spot table show only the last three decimal places Bid, offer. Mid spot rates and forward rates are derived from the WM/REUTERS CLOSING SPOT and FORWARD RATE services. Some values are rounded by the F.T.

Example

Suppose instead of a money market hedge Derby decided to use a forward contract. They have been quoted a forward rate of €1.20:£1.

They are going to receive €11.6 million in six months' time. Their forward contract will be to buy £10.175 million (€11.6 million/1.14).

We can now compare the forward contract and the money market hedge.

The total the company will receive using the money market hedge is £10.025 million, while using a forward contract they will receive £10.175. In this case Derby would prefer to receive the higher amount and so would use a forward contract.

Activity

Now it is your turn. In this activity the company is going to have to pay foreign currency rather than receive it. You need to think about which currency you need to borrow in when setting up the money market hedge. If you are going to receive foreign currency you want to borrow that currency so that you can pay it back with the money you receive. If you are going to pay foreign currency you will want to borrow in the domestic currency and deposit foreign currency so that you will have sufficient foreign currency to be able to pay your debt. Don't forget to allow for the effect of interest too.

Nottingham is going to pay $10 million in four months' time. The spot rate is $1.25:£1; the four-month forward rate is $1.22:£1. Interest rates in the UK are 3%–4% and in the United States are 2.5%–3.4%. Devise a money market hedge and a forward contract that Nottingham could use to hedge the transaction.

Feedback

Money market hedge. At the same time Nottingham will:

1 *borrow £s;*

2 *convert the pounds into dollars;*

3 *deposit the dollars in a US bank account for four months.*

In four months' time Nottingham will use the money on deposit to pay the $10 million dollars they owe.

Now we can add some numbers to the plan.

If the company is going to have $10 million in the account, which will earn 2.5% annually for four months or 0.83% (2.5% x 4/12), it will have to deposit $9.918 million ($10 million/1.0083).

To obtain $9.918 million the company will have to borrow £7.934 million ($9.918 million x 1.25).

The £7.934 million plus interest at 1.33% (4% x 4/12) will have to be repaid in four months' time. The total to be repaid is £8.04 million (£7.934 million x 1.0133).

Forward contract. To set up a forward contract the company will have to arrange to buy $10 million in four months' time at a cost of £8.197 million ($10 million /1.22). The company would prefer to pay £8.04 million than £8.197 million so will use the money market hedge.

Comparison of money market hedge and forward contract

Both money market hedges and forward contracts are used to hedge future foreign currency transactions. They both involve taking up the opposite position of the original position being hedged. A money market hedge requires the company to borrow money, which may affect its financial statements and its ability to borrow more money.

A money market hedge requires knowledge of the spot exchange rate and the interest in both countries.

A forward contract requires knowledge of the forward rate.

Other hedging strategies

Two other hedges for transaction risk are **options** and **futures markets**. While both of these also involve taking an opposite position to the position being hedged they are fundamentally different because a company can end the hedge before the date of the transaction if they choose to.

We will start by considering options.

The holder of an option has the right but not the obligation to do something. A call option gives the holder the right but not the obligation to buy currency, commodities or equities while a put option gives the holder the right but not the obligation to sell currency, commodities or equities. If the holder decides to use the option we say the option is exercised. If the option is not exercised it is said to be allowed to lapse. Options expire if not exercised in a given date and will have a life of up to a year.

Example

Sheffield plc buys a call option for £5,000 to buy €10 million at a price of £1:€1.15. The option expires in three months' time. Sheffield now has the right to buy euros at a fixed price, called the strike price or exercise price, of €1.15 at any time in the next three months. Suppose Sheffield has done this to hedge a payment of €10 million which it needs to make in exactly three months' time.

Why might Sheffield not exercise the option in three months' time?

Solution

Suppose in three months' time the spot rate is £1:€1.10. Then Sheffield can exercise the option and get €1.15 for each pound, meaning that the actual cost in pounds of the payment is £8.7 million (€10 million/1.15). If Sheffield hadn't hedged the transaction they would have had to pay £9.091 million (€10 million/1.1).

But suppose the spot rate in three months' time turned out to be £1:€1.20. Then if Sheffield bought euros at the spot rate it would only cost them £8.333 million (€10 million/1.12) which is less than they would have to pay if they exercised the call option they bought. So the deal costs Sheffield less if they allow the option to lapse rather than exercise it.

This gives two big advantages over the money market hedge and forward contract we've already thought about. First is that if the exchange rate moves to the benefit of the option holder they can allow the option to lapse and take the profit offered by the favourable exchange rate. The second benefit is that the company is not locked into the hedge position, so if for some reason the payment is not made the company is not left holding €10 million with the exchange risk that that creates. It might be, for example, that the order was placed and the hedge taken out but that subsequently the supplier was unable to supply the goods or services ordered so no payment was needed.

The reason options are not the standard hedging technique is because they are more expensive than money market hedges or forward contracts. They can be particularly useful though if there is uncertainty surrounding the transaction, either in terms of whether the payment will be needed or in terms of the exchange rate fluctuations.

Options are examples of derivatives. The hugely successful investor Warren Buffett famously called derivatives 'weapons of mass destruction' in 2002, well before the global financial crisis, which was certainly made worse by the use of derivatives. Worryingly, he repeated his claim in 2015. But while derivatives can be used to create and increase risk they can also be used as hedges where they can reduce risk. It is not derivatives themselves that are dangerous, it is the way they are used.

Futures are another example of derivatives and again can be used to reduce, or increase, risk. We have already seen how they can be misused in the example of Metallgesellschaft above.

Futures contracts are also contracts to buy or sell a given amount of a currency or commodity at an agreed price at an agreed future date but this time the holder is obliged to undertake the transaction. In practice, few futures contracts result in the actual delivery of the currency or commodities because they are 'closed' by the holder taking out a second futures contract that exactly offsets the first. And just like options they can be used to speculate or hedge.

Economic exposure

Economic exposure is the risk that changes in exchange rates lead to future cash flows being different to those that were expected. You have probably realized that this means that all the transactions that we've just been discussing are also examples of economic risk, and you are right. But economic risk includes transactions that haven't been entered into yet. So if we take the example of the fall in the value of the pound as a result of Brexit, and a US company is selling goods to the UK, let's try to identify the economic risk.

First, any transactions entered into and denominated in pounds prior to the referendum will lead to fewer dollars being received than expected.

But unless the company can pass the loss due to the depreciation of the pound on to its customers it is going to be unable to earn the same number of dollars for its sale of goods in the future as it did before the pound depreciated. This is true regardless of whether the goods were invoiced in pounds or dollars. So the depreciation of the pound is going to adversely affect the company indefinitely.

While we can use financial instruments to avoid unexpected losses in the short term, we will have to find other ways to hedge our exposed positions.

There are a number of things that multinational companies can do to protect themselves against economic exposure. As you read about them try to identify the actions taken by some of the multinational companies you are aware of.

If a company can create demand for its assets that are not highly dependent on price, that is they are not very price elastic, they are less vulnerable to exchange rate changes. To achieve this, companies will try to protect their brand name and image and to create very differentiated products that people want to own regardless of the price. Apple is a good example of this kind of strategy. Can you think of some more?

Another effective strategy is to adopt a flexible approach to sources of raw materials and location of production. The more flexible a company can be, the more easily it can limit price increases. Given this, it is apparent that manufacturing abroad actually reduces total risk even though it creates additional risks.

Incurring costs in currencies in which the company generates revenues achieves a natural and long-term hedge. This is along the lines of the netting-off strategy we have already considered in this chapter. If a subsidiary incurs costs in the local currency which can all be covered by the revenue generated in the local currency, then it is only the excess revenue, which ultimately might be expected to be repatriated to the parent company, that is subject to exchange risk.

Consider the case of a domestic company which sources raw materials locally, produces locally and sells locally. Such a company might at first sight appear to have very little exchange risk. In practice this isn't the case, as if the domestic currency appreciates, foreign competitors might seek to export to the market where their products appear cheap.

Tourism is vulnerable to this problem. Currently the pound is weak and many people are choosing to holiday in the UK rather than abroad where their pounds don't buy as much foreign currency as they used to. Equally, foreign tourists find that the UK offers good value for money. So a weak pound provides a boost to the tourism industry. By the same token, a strong pound makes the UK a less attractive holiday destination both for UK residents and everyone else. This is a good example of the exchange risk that a domestic company can face.

Multinationals who believe that a local currency is about to depreciate, or appreciate, can often take action to reduce their exposure.

If a multinational believes that a local currency will depreciate in the near future it would choose to short the currency. That is, it would seek to get rid of as much as possible of the local currency it holds and even to borrow in the foreign currency. No one wants to hold more of a currency they think will reduce in value than they have to and borrowing in a depreciating currency reduces the real amount you have to repay.

So if a multinational believes a local currency will depreciate it will attempt to:

- reduce the length of time debtors take to pay their balances;
- reduce the amount of local currency held;
- buy raw materials or components now rather than wait for prices in the local currency to increase;
- borrow locally;
- delay paying creditors.

If the multinational believes the local currency is going to appreciate it will take the reverse action. in particular:

- hold the local currency;
- pay creditors early;
- defer buying raw materials or components.

Summary

In Chapter 8 we have considered the type of exchange risks faced by MNCs: translation risk, transaction risk and economic risk. In each case we identified the potential risk and the time at which it would arise and then we discussed a variety of hedging strategies that could be used to reduce or eliminate the risk. Strategies we found we could use included matching assets and liabilities to reduce translation exposure. We then used netting to determine the group's real transaction exposure and then applied money market hedges and forward contracts to cover the exposure we identified. We also considered the use of options to hedge transaction exposure. Options are more expensive than money market hedges and forward contracts but provide the opportunity to make a profit. We saw what could go wrong if a company miscalculated the scale of hedging needed or misunderstood the true nature of the risk.

Finally we assessed exposure to economic risk and identified strategies to reduce economic exposure.

Questions

Question 1

In order to eliminate all risk on its exports, a US company decides to hedge all its actual and budgeted sales for the next two years.

What risk is the company exposed to? How could that risk be managed?

Question 2

A US company expects to receive a payment of £4 million in three months' time. The current spot rate is £1:$1.30 and the 90-day forward rate is £1:$1.26.

The interest rate in the UK is 1%–3% and in the US is 1.5%–4%.

Construct a money market hedge and a forward contract to hedge the receipt and recommend one to the company.

Question 3

A Chinese company is part of a consortium of companies involved in building the UK's new nuclear power station at Hinkley Point. The company will be required to invest about £50 million in assets in the UK, which will be financed by subsidized loans provided by the Chinese government. The company will employ a significant number of staff in the UK and will have to incur expenses in the UK as well as making sales in pounds to other members of the consortium in the UK.

What foreign currency exposure will the company be exposed to?
What steps can it take to reduce its economic exposure?

09
Financing international trade

At the end of this chapter you will be able to:

- discuss a range of sources of international finance accessible by MNCs;
- discuss the work of financial intermediaries;
- discuss the origins and current state of the euro currency market;
- calculate the true cost of borrowing in a foreign currency.

Introduction

Throughout this book we have suggested that multinational firms have advantages over purely domestic firms that make them more competitive despite the additional costs and risks they may have to bear.

Sourcing finance, both long term and short term, is one important example of this ability to reduce costs through being a multinational rather than a domestic company.

If costs of finance are lowered, companies are able to invest in projects which would otherwise be unprofitable. In addition, funds may be limited in a purely domestic market, whereas this is much less likely to be the case in the global financial market.

As the world has become more and more globalized and capital has been able to move freely between countries, it has become increasingly important for companies to seek the capital they need to operate and grow from sources all over the world in order to minimize costs and to take advantage of opportunities such as the hedging opportunities we discussed in Chapter 8.

We will start with an introduction to capital and capital markets. As before, if you have not studied corporate finance before, the following section will serve to prepare you for the main body of the material in this and the following chapters. If you have studied corporate finance before, you might find the following section a useful refresher or you may wish to skip over it.

Sources of funds

Few companies can thrive and grow without using external sources to fund their working capital or their investment in new assets and expansion into new markets. One of the reasons for the success of privatized businesses is that they are able to borrow money, whereas state-owned operations often have very limited capability to borrow money.

Most businesses are able to generate funds internally through their retained profits or retained earnings but this is not usually enough to fund all the future projects the company has decided to invest in.

External sources of funds are short-term external funds such as borrowing in the money markets, and longer-term external funds such as equities, corporate bonds and bank lending.

Short-term sources are often used to finance international trade, particularly to fund the delay in receiving payment from exports compared to domestic customers.

In this chapter we will focus on long-term sources of funds.

Fundamentally there are two kinds of long-term funding: debt and equity. In practice, there are hybrid instruments which include elements of each but mostly companies issue either debt or equity.

Equity funding or shares

When a company issues shares in exchange for cash they are inviting people – the public or large institutions mostly – to invest in the company. In exchange for buying shares in the company the investor, now a shareholder, gains:

- The right to receive their share of any dividends paid by the company.
- The right to vote at the company's AGM and at other times. Votes will include the appointment of directors and auditors as well as other matters put to them.
- The right to a share of the assets if the company is wound up, ie ceases to trade and is shut down.

A shareholder would hope to receive capital growth, that is that the share value goes up as well as dividends during the period in which the shares are owned or held. The shares are not usually redeemed – bought back by the company – but shareholders are free to sell their shares at any time.

The cost of equity

Because shareholders are uncertain about the return they will receive, since dividends are discretionary and capital growth is uncertain (higher risk), they require a relatively high level of return to invest in a company. If you are not sure about this, go back and read the section on risk and return in Chapter 1.

In addition, there is generally no tax relief on dividends. These two together make equity expensive for a company; they are expected to pay high levels of dividends and don't get tax relief on the payments.

Debt

People who buy corporate bonds in a company are effectively lending money to the company and so are talked about as being debtholders. Debt can be corporate bonds but might also be a bank loan or a debenture. We can consider all of these as long-term debt.

The definition of long-term debt varies. We can take it as being any debt that doesn't mature – become due for repayment – in the next 12 months

Debt holders are entitled to pre-arranged interest payments, that is a fixed amount on fixed dates in the future. They have certainty. Some debt carries variable rates of interest but the payments are largely certain. They are also generally entitled to receive their capital back again at some predetermined date in the future. Again, some debt has a variable redemption date but there is considerable certainty about the capital repayment.

Bonds held to the redemption date do not offer capital growth, although bonds redeemed early will be sold for a different amount to the sum paid for them, so may have some capital growth.

Because there is tax relief on interest payments and the payments to bond holders are lower, debt is cheaper than equity.

While banks do still provide an important source of borrowing, in some countries there has been a significant shift away from banks and towards issuing bonds, an example of a financial instrument in many developed countries, especially the United States and the UK.

Very large loans are often made by a syndicate of banks, with one bank taking on the role of lead bank, because the banks wish to spread the risk. This enables companies to borrow amounts that exceed the maximum amount that any one bank is willing, or able, to lend to one business.

Domestic financial markets

Financial markets, or capital markets, are the place, not necessarily a physical location, where savers or investors can find satisfactory ways of depositing or lending their savings with borrowers who have suitable risk and return profiles. Equally, a capital market is a place where a borrower can go to obtain the funds they need to invest in their business. The banks and other financial services organizations such as pension funds facilitate the transfer of funds from savers to borrowers and are termed financial intermediaries.

Activity

One of the simplest examples of a financial intermediary is the old-fashioned building society. In a building society, individuals saved money for a variety of reasons, but an important one was to save the deposit to buy a house. Suppose a depositor had decided to make regular savings, intending to use the money to pay for a holiday next year. What does a depositor require from such an investment?

Feedback

Sometimes it can be hard to think of things that are very obvious but bear with me. If I were saving for a holiday next year, these are the things I would want:

- *For my money to be risk free. I want to be sure it is safe and I want certainty.*
- *To be able to save small amounts of money, perhaps regularly, perhaps when I have it.*
- *A return, some interest from the building society, because they have had the use of my money while it has been saved with them.*
- *To be able to withdraw my money when I want to. Some investors agree to a notice period to earn a higher return but they still want to be able to withdraw their funds at the end of the notice period, which might be three months or as long as a year or two.*

In addition to taking deposits from savers, building societies lend people money, mortgages, to enable them to buy a house.

Activity

If you were borrowing money to buy a house, what would be the characteristics of the loan that you would want?

Feedback

Most mortgages are for relatively large amounts of money over a long period of time: 25 or 30 years is not uncommon. Unlike, say, an overdraft, which the bank can demand is repaid at any time, there is no possibility of the

*building society demanding early repayment of the loan unless the borrower
has defaulted on payments.*

*Borrowers expect to pay agreed amounts, sometimes fixed for a number
of years, probably each month. Usually the amount they pay is a combination of the interest due on the loan and some of the capital. As time goes
on, the interest element gets lower, as the capital reduces, and the amount
of capital repaid increases. This describes a simple repayment mortgage, the
most popular mortgage available. There are many variations on this, interest
only and endowment mortgages being two, but we will focus on repayment
mortgages.*

So there is a real mismatch between what savers want from a building society – to make small deposits without risk and to be able to get the money
back fairly quickly – and what lenders want – to borrow large amounts of
money over long periods of time.

Building societies and other financial intermediaries meet the needs of
their savers and borrowers, undertaking what is called transformation. They
transform savers' deposits into borrowers' loans.

The transformations needed are:

- **Maturity transformation.** To take short-term deposits and turn them
  into long-term loans. This is done by taking in deposits for many savers,
  retaining some of those deposits to return to savers who want their money
  back, and lending the rest. Providing there isn't a 'run on the bank', when
  a loss of confidence in the bank leads to many savers wanting their money
  back at the same time, savers should always be able to withdraw their
  deposits when they want to.

- **Size transformation.** To take small deposits from savers and turn them
  into large loans. This is done by aggregating the deposits of many savers
  to provide the large sums that homebuyers require.

- **Risk transformation.** Individuals borrowing money to buy their house
  have some risk of default. Perhaps the loss of a job, illness or a relationship breakdown can mean that a homebuyer can no longer meet
  their mortgage payments. Building societies take steps to minimize the
  risk of this happening by checking the creditworthiness of borrowers
  and trying to ensure that the debt is affordable. They also keep the
  deeds of the house so that if the borrower cannot repay their mortgage
  the property can be repossessed and sold to repay the debt if necessary.
  But they also 'spread the risk' by taking the deposits from many savers
  and transforming them to create loans to many borrowers. Building
  societies and other financial intermediaries have statistical software
  which enables them to predict what proportion of their borrowers
  are likely to run into financial difficulties in any given period of time.
  They then provide for those losses when calculating how much interest to charge borrowers and how much interest they are able to pay to
  depositors.

Financial markets do more than provide opportunities for borrowers to raise finance and savers to invest; they also provide a place where savers can withdraw their savings by selling their shares. This is called a secondary market. The primary capital market is the place where securities are bought for the first time from the company or its agents.

Financial markets also need to have a sound legal system that enables rights, particularly property rights, to be enforced.

A well-functioning capital market will be allocatively efficient, that is the funds available will be allocated to the organization that can make the best possible use of those funds.

One of the most interesting aspects of finance is that it is a service industry and survives and thrives when it meets the needs of its customers. Financial instruments and ways of working are designed to meet a perceived need. If the need turns out to be real, then the financial instrument is retained, otherwise it is withdrawn. Capital markets and banks are in a constant state of evolution and must react and innovate to survive in the rapidly changing world in which we find ourselves.

In the 1980s, the financial markets in the United States and the UK were deregulated along with the markets in many other developed countries including Japan.

One of the outcomes of this was a significant decline in bank lending and a shift in all developed countries towards companies issuing corporate bonds, commercial paper and other financial instruments via capital markets because of the lower costs.

Institutional investors in particular were enthusiastic because they prefer the certainty of the cash flows from bonds to the uncertainty of equities. Issuing securities via capital markets is termed **securitization**. Borrowing from a bank is called using **financial intermediation** and the bank is termed the **financial intermediary**.

Securitization became popular because deregulation reduced the costs of using financial markets and enabled companies to reduce costs by avoiding the use of a bank whose costs were going up as a result of increasing global demands for banks to have a stronger capital base. This shift towards securitization was more pronounced in some countries than others. Countries like Germany, where companies retain their very strong relationship with the banks, still use banks for long-term finance. However, the continued use of bank finance, because the financial markets are not providing access to the cheap debt, is widely thought to contribute to the lack of success of companies relative to those in countries that do have such financial markets and thus greater access to the capital they need to grow.

In addition to deregulation, national financial markets have become increasingly integrated. Financial centres are in competition with each other and we see stock exchanges around the world in merger talks with each other to further reduce costs, though few have actually gone through. At the time of writing, the German Börse in Frankfurt has agreed to take over the London Stock Exchange, despite the Brexit vote.

At the same time, companies are increasingly seeking arbitrage opportunities to reduce costs by exploiting regulatory differences between markets, forcing further deregulation and cost cutting on the markets themselves and their regulators.

At the start of this section we talked about innovation in financial markets in the sense of creating new financial instruments that individuals and businesses wanted to hold. That innovation might be the creation of tax-efficient financial instruments to exploit opportunities in the tax system, but as often as not it is about modifying the risk of financial instruments. If a company can issue a financial instrument that meets the needs of a niche market it can lower the required return on the instrument and thus reduce the costs to the company. This competitive edge is unlikely to provide a long-term advantage as competitors quickly enter the market with similar products and the demands of the niche market are soon satiated.

These same processes are at work internationally to provide businesses with the low-cost securities that meet their needs, wherever they are in the world.

When a bank lends money to a company it incurs costs in deciding if the company is going to be able to repay the interest and capital as they fall due. Similarly, when a company issues securities into the market, each putative investor will need to decide if the company is a good investment. This can only be done if sufficient reliable information is available. As the global market becomes more integrated, for example companies' annual reports become increasingly comparable, the costs of obtaining that information continue to fall, even for foreign firms, and securitization becomes even more attractive.

International financial markets

Most domestic financial markets also operate as international financial markets, attracting international investors and non-resident companies seeking finance in new markets. Successful international financial markets require light regulation to allow innovation and minimize costs. The most important global financial centres are London, New York and Tokyo, all of which benefit from light regulation.

Eurocurrency markets or offshore financial markets

Eurocurrency markets are so called NOT because they have anything to do with the euro – they don't – but because they originated in Europe some 70 years ago. Today they are also termed **offshore financial markets**.

A eurocurrency is a currency on deposit in a bank in a country that is not its country of origin. It generally refers to freely convertible currencies such as the dollar, the pound sterling, the yen and the euro. Banks that accept such foreign currency deposits are called eurobanks and they also lend foreign currency. Eurodollars are the most widely available of the euro-currencies but the market quickly changes in response to economic and political events.

Eurosterling then is the term to describe UK pounds on deposit anywhere in the world except in the UK. Equally, euroeuros are euros on deposit anywhere in the world except in the eurozone.

History of the eurocurrency market

During the 1950s, the Soviet Bloc had US dollars which it wished to deposit to earn a return. But they feared that if they deposited them in a US bank they would be at risk of being seized to pay for war reparations after the Second World War. So instead of approaching a US bank, they sought to deposit the dollars in European banks, primarily in France and the UK. These banks then lent their dollars to other banks and borrowers.

Central banks then began to deposit dollars in order to earn a higher return. Commercial banks followed suit because in addition to earning a higher return they were able to negotiate the period until maturity to suit their needs.

The London insurance industry also received premiums in dollars and deposited their dollars in European banks.

The market continued to grow, mostly through the lack of regulation, which we will discuss in the next section. In 1957, the UK government sought to restrict sterling lending due to the Suez Crisis and banks, in response, lent dollars instead.

The following year there was a relaxation of exchange controls through-out Europe, which meant that dollars earned from international trade could be held rather than sold immediately to the central bank as had been required before 1958.

Over time London became the principal market for trading the dollar outside the United States, partly because of the eurodollar market.

The eurocurrency market today

The eurocurrency market is a money market; loans for periods ranging from overnight to nearly a year are made. The market is very liquid and has grown considerably over time, the main reason being the lack of government regulation or interference in the market.

Eurobanks are subsidiaries of major international banks. Eurodollar bank loans are also called eurodollar credits or just **eurocredits**, a term which applies to all eurocurrencies, not just dollars.

The debt instruments available on the eurocurrency market are termed the **euronote market**. The debt instruments are split into two groups: those with underwritten facilities and those which have non-underwritten facil-ities. More recently, euronotes, which are issued by MNCs and have an interest payment and a fixed redemption date at which the capital will be repaid, have become more popular. Some of the euronotes can be continu-ally rolled over, creating a source of intermediate-term financing for MNCs. The commercial banks underwrite the notes for the MNCs.

The eurocurrency market is able to offer competitive returns to investors and charge low rates of interest to borrowers. This means that the spread – the difference between borrowing and lending interest rates – is very small in the eurocurrency market, often less than 1%.

There are a number of reasons for this:

- The eurocurrency market is a wholesale market. The minimum size of transactions is half a million dollars. It is much cheaper for a bank to deal with a small number of large transactions than to have to deal with many low-value transactions, as retail or high street banks have to.

- The borrowers in the eurocurrency market are multinationals, governments, supranational organizations and banks, all of whom generally have very good credit standing (meaning there is little default risk) and that means that they are able to borrow at very low interest rates.

- Eurobanks have very low overheads. They don't need a high street presence and the low number of transactions and customers means they don't need high numbers of staff. In addition, they have low compliance costs because they have low levels of regulation. For example, they don't have to pay deposit insurance fees and they don't need to maintain a capital reserve of the size required by most regulators.

Usually the interest rate is linked with the London Interbank Offered Rate (LIBOR). Most of the loans are for a fixed period of up to six months.

The eurocurrency market has a multiplier effect on the number of dollars in circulation. That is, $100 deposited in a eurobank turns into $1,000. It works like this:

Example

For every $100 deposit, if a bank holds 10% in reserve (called fractional reserve banking), it can lend out $90 of the initial deposit.

This $90 deposit in turn generates a $9 reserve in the next bank and an $81 loan.

This generates another $81 deposit, an $8.10 reserve in the next bank and a $72.90 loan. The sum of $100 + $90 +81 + $72.90 + ... eventually reaches $1,000, or $100 divided by the percentage reserve.

A 2016 study by the Federal Reserve Bank found that the average daily turnover of eurodollars was around $250 billion (Federal Reserve, 2016). This is a very large amount and makes it very difficult for the United States, and other countries, to control their money supply.

Figure 9.1   Overnight money market volumes

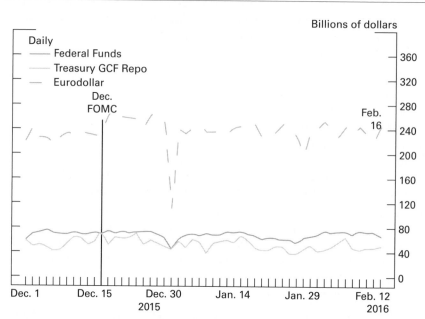

SOURCE For Treasury GCF Repo, Depository Trust & Clearing Corporation (DTCC); for Federal Funds and Eurodollar, Federal Reserve (FR 2420)

The eurobond market

Eurobonds are bonds issued or sold outside the country in whose currencies they are denominated. The bonds are generally dated between five and 30 years. In the early years, eurobonds were physical documents and were delivered to the buyers, but today they are electronic. The first eurobond was issued in 1964 by an Italian company for $15 million eurodollars. The eurobond was designed in London, issued in Amsterdam and paid in Luxembourg in order to take advantage of Luxembourg's low tax rates. The bond enabled European investors to have a low-risk bond and diversify into US dollars. After that, multinational companies, governments and supranational bodies such as the IMF and the World Bank made issues of eurobonds.

Today a bond issue can be for over $1 billion and is usually issued by an international syndicate and categorized according to the currency in which it is denominated. One member of the syndicate will probably underwrite the issue which means that it is certain to be a success, that is all the eurobonds will be sold. A eurodollar bond that is denominated in US dollars and issued in Japan by an Australian company would be an example of a eurobond. The Australian company in this example could issue the eurodollar bond in any country other than the United States.

Eurobonds are attractive sources of finance for companies because they give issuers the flexibility to choose the country in which to offer their bond according to the country's regulatory constraints, interest rates and the extent to which the market is liquid. They may also denominate their eurobond in their preferred currency. Eurobonds are attractive to investors because they generally have small par, or face, values and are very liquid.

In the UK, eurobonds are issued by the Certificateless Registry for Electronic Share Transfer (CREST) and are generally 'bearer bonds', which means that the holder of a bond is deemed to be its owner, just as a five-pound note is a bearer bond. This means there is no register of owners and enables investors to evade taxes by failing to declare their income. The eurobond market has been an important source of finance for companies as bank funding has reduced, especially in countries with only a limited capital market. Today the market is worth around $100 trillion of debt, although the bearer bonds and the lack of regulation make it difficult to be certain of the exact size.

In the last few years the market has allowed some smaller issues to take place. The disadvantage of this is reduced liquidity because it becomes harder to find a buyer and seller for smaller issues but it has enabled medium-sized companies to access the eurobond market.

Another growth area is companies and governments from emerging markets who otherwise might have limited access to long-term borrowing.

We have evaluated the financial markets where multinational companies seek the long-term financing they need; in the next section we will evaluate the range of methods that can be used by multinationals to raise finance in those markets.

Foreign bonds

A **foreign bond** is a bond issued in a country by a company which is not resident in that country. Foreign bonds are part of the domestic bond market and are subject to the same laws. They are denominated in the local currency. However, they may have to comply with additional rules and regulations. Foreign bonds are often used by companies who undertake a significant amount of business in the domestic economy. Companies will often seek to issue foreign bonds if the local interest rate is lower than the company's home interest rate in order to reduce costs. The bonds may be fixed or floating rate or be equity related.

The bonds appeal to investors who are generally domestic and can use the bonds to add foreign securities to their portfolio, but because they are denominated in the domestic currency they don't carry exchange risk.

Foreign bonds are inherently riskier than domestic bonds so provide a higher return.

A foreign bond issued in the United States is called a Yankee Bond. One issued in Japan is a Samurai Bond, Bulldog Bonds are issued in the UK, Matilda or Kangaroo Bonds are issued in Australia, Maple Bonds are issued in Canada and Dim Sum Bonds are issued in Hong Kong.

Global bonds

Global bonds were first issued by the World Bank. They are issued in several countries at the same time using a single currency, which is generally the domestic currency. Such an issue allows a company or even country to access different markets. The issuing organization generally has a high credit rating so low default risk. A global bond generally leads to lower borrowing costs and also tends to raise a company's profile and broaden its investor base.

Global bonds tend to be issued by the largest of companies, such as Apple, Dell and so on, and each issue can be for $15 billion or more; the total for 2016 is likely to be over $600 billion for US industrial companies alone.

Foreign bank lending

Many banks set aside some of their funds to lend internationally. This is the foreign bank market and is another important source of finance for companies.

Foreign equities

Investors understand that being diversified by holding securities in a wide variety of companies can reduce risk without reducing return. In the UK we have a saying, 'Don't put all your eggs in one basket', by which we mean that it is better not to rely on a single investment, or asset, but rather to have a range of investments or assets or opportunities generally. I often pose a problem about a farmer to my students.

Example: diversification

A farmer can grow only two crops, rice and sunflowers, and his growing seasons have an equal chance of being very very wet or very very sunny. When the farmer plants his seed, he doesn't know what kind of summer weather he is going to experience that year. I ask my students what they would do if they were the farmer. My students find this a very simple problem to solve and correctly suggest that our farmer should plant half rice and half sunflowers.

We can think about the farmer a little more. What would happen to a farmer who planted just sunflowers every year, or indeed just rice every year? We would expect him to be able to harvest a full crop in half the years and no crop at all in the other half of the years. So on average he will get half a crop a year. The problem comes if his crop fails for several years on end. Our farmer might have to give up farming while waiting for good years to return. So the expected return each year is half a crop and the risk, as measured by volatility, is very high.

If instead our farmer planted half a crop of sunflowers and half a crop of rice then he can be certain of harvesting half a crop each year. He won't get a great crop but he also won't have a year with no crop at all. His volatility is now zero; there is no risk. We have complete certainty that we will get half a crop each year.

Now let's consider the expected return. If he planted only one kind of crop his expected return was half a crop. Now he is planting both crops his expected return is still half a crop. So we have managed to reduce our farmer's risk while not reducing his expected return.

Diversification is about investing in a range of assets or financial securities in order to reduce your level of risk; if you are careful you can reduce your risk without suffering a loss of expected return. Diversifying internationally is better than just diversifying domestically for two reasons.

The first reason is that you will have investments that don't suffer from the same systematic risks as each other. We discussed this in Chapter 1. So if, say, we invest in securities in the United States and in India, then if US interest rates rise, an example of a systematic risk, the US investment may suffer but the Indian investment won't be affected.

The second reason is that the economies of the United States and India are not strongly positively correlated with each other. In 2013, the correlation between the US and Indian stock exchanges was 0.375. Our rice and sunflowers above have strong or perfect negative correlation, which is −1. Perfect positive correlation is equal to +1. So correlation of 0.375 is positive but it is only a weak correlation. If one economy is doing badly the other economy probably won't be doing so badly. For these reasons, holding shares in a foreign company, without taking on exchange risk, is very attractive to investors seeking international diversification.

An important part of diversification for investors is international diversification, so holding shares in a foreign company is a very attractive prospect for them.

Companies may choose to issue equity in more than one country for a number of reasons:

- To obtain a wide, well-diversified shareholder base which helps to protect against the specific risks of a national stock market, such as a referendum. This may also help to protect the company from a hostile takeover bid or reduce the risk of state interference or even nationalization.

- To make an issue that is too big for a single market to cope with, particularly if the domestic market is relatively small.
- To attract new shareholders overseas, which might increase demand for shares and thus increase their value.
- To improve corporate governance for companies whose domestic market doesn't have strong corporate governance standards. This should improve corporate performance.
- To raise the company's profile in the new market, and potentially the region.

The United States is a particularly attractive place to seek an international listing and some international companies go straight for a US listing without listing on their domestic exchange first. Most exchanges allow foreign companies to list on them but naturally they require them to comply with the same regulations as domestic companies. These can be onerous and are an expense that has to be considered before seeking such a listing. Perhaps for this reason there has been a decline in recent years of foreign companies listing in the United States.

The true cost of borrowing internationally

In this chapter we have discussed the wide range of financing options that are available to an international company. We have thus far focused on the interest rate cost of borrowing but there is another potential cost. If a company borrows in a currency which is not the domestic currency, then it will have to make interest payments but it will also have to repay the capital. If the debt is denominated in an appreciating currency, paying interest and repaying the capital will cost the company more than if it wasn't appreciating.

First we need to be able to calculate the interest rate using compound interest.

Example

A company borrows €1,000 on 1/1/16 and has to repay €1,300 on 1/1/21, five years later. What is the effective annual interest rate?

Solution

The interest paid is €300 and we need to work out what annual rate would give a total interest payment of €300. We can use this formula:

$$(R/L)^{1/N} - 1$$

where

R is the amount repaid;

L is the amount borrowed; and

N is the number of years of the loan.

$$(1,300/1,000)^{1/5} - 1 = 1.05 - 1 = 0.05 \text{ or } 5\%.$$

Now try the following activity.

Activity

Suppose a UK company borrows $1 million using a eurodollar 10-year loan when the exchange rate is $1.32:£1. Just to make our calculations easier let's assume that the interest is rolled up so that the company needs to repay $1.2 million in 10 years' time when it turns out the exchange rate is $1.2:£1. The company converts the dollars into pounds as soon as it receives the loan and repays the loan but converting pounds into dollars after 10 years.

How many pounds does the UK company receive from the loan in the first place?

How many pounds does it have to repay in 10 years' time?

What is the interest cost of the loan as a percentage ignoring exchange rate changes? Hint: use compound interest technique here.

What is the total cost of the loan as an annualized percentage?

Feedback

The company would receive £ 757,575 ($1 million/1.32) immediately.

In 10 years' time the company will have to repay £1 million ($1.2 million/1.2).

The annualized interest cost of the loan is 1.84% ((1,200,000/1,000,000)^{1/10} – 1).

The total cost of the loan is 2.8% ((1,000,000/757,575)^{1/10} – 1).

Because the dollar has appreciated it has cost the company more to repay the loan than it otherwise would have. Once the depreciation of the pound has been taken into account, the loan has cost much more than it at first appeared: 2.8% per annum rather than 1.84 % per annum when interest only was considered.

But borrowing in a foreign currency might provide a useful hedge for a company. We discussed the details of hedging in the last chapter, and how borrowing in a foreign currency might help a company hedge. Consider the following example.

Example

A US multinational company sells 30% of its production in the United States and the remaining 70% is sold in over 50 countries all over the world.

The company cannot produce its goods anywhere except in the United States. Describe its economic exposure. How can a foreign currency loan reduce its economic risk?

Solution

The company is well diversified so it has only limited exposure if another currency moves significantly against the US dollar.

The economic risk is about changes in the value of the US dollar. If the US dollar weakens then the company will be able to reduce the foreign currency prices of its goods without suffering any loss in dollars received and thus may be able to increase the volume of sales.

But if the dollar appreciates in value the company will have to increase the foreign currency prices of its goods in order to generate the dollars it needs to cover its costs and earn a profit. Increasing prices abroad is likely to reduce sales and enable competitors to increase their market share.

If the company has foreign borrowings then it will have to pay interest and repay the capital in the foreign currency. So if the dollar weakens, the cost of borrowing increases, as we saw above, and if the dollar strengthens, the cost of borrowing falls.

Since this is the opposite of the sales position, international borrowing can help to reduce the company's level of risk. Large US companies like General Electric and Boeing do exactly this to hedge their sales.

This chapter in particular is just an introduction to a very interesting topic. In practice, companies have a wide range of options and choices when seeking to raise money. For example:

- How long a period should borrowings be made for? The longer the term of the loan, generally the more expensive the borrowing is.
- Should the company use currency swaps, interest rate swaps or parallel loans? In practice, large companies do use these complex arrangements to reduce the cost of financing.
- Should the company use fixed rate or floating rate borrowing?

Summary

In this chapter we have considered the opportunities for raising equity and borrowing for domestic companies and MNCs, and appreciated the additional opportunities available to MNCs. We considered the importance of financial intermediation.

We have briefly discussed the important markets for companies to borrow in, including some discussion of their creation. Many of these markets are lightly regulated, which enables them to offer lower-cost financing while paying high rates on deposits. Light regulation also reduces the ability of governments to restrict lending and enables MNCs to access the funds they need without restriction.

Finally we began to think about the true cost of borrowing when borrowing in a foreign currency. The cost is dependent not only on the interest rate and level of tax relief, but also on any appreciation or depreciation of the currency.

Questions

Question 1

Why might a UK firm seek a listing on the New York Stock Exchange? What are the costs of doing this?

Question 2

How has the way companies raise money changed over the last 20 years? What has driven the changes? What has enabled the changes to take place?

Question 3

When an MNC decides to borrow money using a currency other than its own, what factors should it consider?

10
International investment appraisal

At the end of this chapter you will be able to:

- discuss the uses and limitations of the net present value (NPV) investment appraisal technique;
- calculate the NPV of a foreign project;
- discuss the other factors a company will take into account when making an investment decision.

Introduction

If you have studied corporate finance before you will have come across the idea of investment appraisal. But for those of you who haven't and for those readers who need a reminder we will start by reviewing the net present value technique of investment appraisal. Once we have done that we will extend it to the special difficulties faced by companies undertaking investment appraisal in other countries.

Investment appraisal

One of the important decisions companies have to make is about **capital expenditure**, perhaps acquiring a new facility or buying new equipment or machinery.

Capital expenditure has some special characteristics and problems, in particular:

- Large amounts of money are often involved and the decision affects the business for several years so it is potentially a critical decision for the future success of the firm.
- The data is likely to include estimates several years into the future. It is notoriously difficult to forecast accurately far into the future so inevitably the decision has to be made using data which is not accurate.

While considerable effort has been made by academics to find effective ways of evaluating such projects, no single method has been found that doesn't have serious limitations. Business people solve the problem by using one or more of a range of techniques to try to obtain the information they need to make good decisions.

We are going to focus on the **net present value** method but there are others, particularly Accounting Rate of Return, Internal Rate of Return, and Payback. Each has their advantages and limitations.

Net present value

The net present value method is a discounting cash flow technique applied to cash flows.

Discounting cash flow uses the idea that cash in the future is worth less than cash today.

Activity

If you were offered £1,000 now or £1,000 in five years' time, which would you rather have, and why? Assume that you don't need £1,000 now.

Feedback

Most people are clear that they would rather receive £1,000 now than wait five years. There are three reasons for this preference:

1 *Inflation makes money worth more today than it will be worth in the future. Even if inflation is very low, say the UK government's target of 2% over a few years, it makes a difference to the purchasing power of the money.*

2 *If you had £1,000 today you could do something with it; at the very least you could deposit it in a bank and earn some interest. Unless there is a better use of the money, we call the interest you could have earned on the money the opportunity cost of money.*

3 *There is a risk that you won't ever receive the money in five years' time.*

Now we know that money received on different dates is worth different amounts we can't simply compare two amounts of money arising at different times any more than we can add $7 and €5 and get 12. Just as we would have to convert these two sums of money into a single currency before we can add them together, we have to convert money received at different times into the equivalent amount of money received, or paid, on the same date. By convention we usually convert all amounts of money received in the future into the equivalent value of money received today, called the present value. That is, if someone offered to lend you £1,000 now or give you £1,100 in two years' time we would find the equivalent value in today's terms of £1,100 received in two years' time. Then we could compare the two amounts to decide which we prefer.

We use the idea of **compound interest** to help us solve this problem.

Activity

Supposing you put £1,000 in the bank and earned interest at a rate of 9% a year. How much would you have in the bank at the end of each of the following five years?

Feedback

Table 10.1 The value of the money at the end of each year

	Amount in the bank	Interest for the year	Amount in the bank at the end of the year
Today's date 1/1/X2	£1,000	£90 (£1,000 × 0.09)	£1,090
1/1/X3	£1,090	£98.1 (£1,090 × 0.09)	£1,188.1
1/1/X4	£1,188.10	£106.93 (£1,188.10 × 0.09)	£1,295.03
1/1/X5	£1,295.03	£116.55 (£1,295.03 × 0.09)	£1,411.58
1/1/X6	£1,411.58	£127.04 (£1,411.58 × 0.09)	£1,538.62

The same example is set out as a graph in Figure 10.1.

So we can say that £1,188.10 received in two years' time is worth the equivalent of receiving £1,000 now.

The generally accepted way of using this technique is to restate all future cash flows in today's equivalent cash flow.

So we would say that receiving £1,411.58 in four years' time is the equivalent of receiving £1,000 today. Put another way, an individual would be indifferent to receiving £1,000 now or £1,411.58 in four years' time.

Figure 10.1

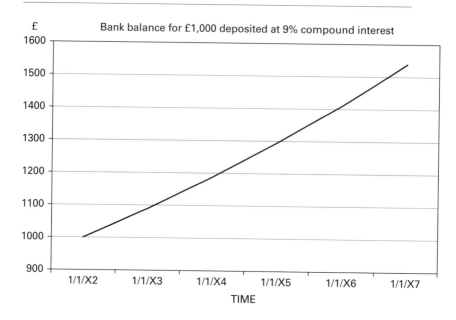

£   Bank balance for £1,000 deposited at 9% compound interest

TIME

Activity

Supposing you were offered £120 in two years' time or £100 today and interest rates are at 10%. Which would you rather have? You should calculate the value of the future cash flows in today's terms.

Hint: look at the activity above. We worked out how much money there would be in the bank at the end of a year by multiplying by 1 + interest rate. Effectively we worked out how much we would have at the end of the second year by repeating that process. We can say that we multiplied by $(1 + interest\ rate)^2$. But you need to reverse this process. Effectively you are asking yourself, how much do I have to put in the bank today to have £120 in the bank in two years' time? You can do this by dividing by $(1 + interest\ rate)^2$.

Feedback

£120 received in two years' time has a value today of £99.17($£120\ /(1.1)^2$). *So we would prefer to receive £100 now rather than £120 in two years' time.*

Present value

We call the £99.17 you just calculated the present value of the future cash flow.

Activity

Now try this activity. It is similar to the last one. If you were offered £1,420 in four years' time or £1,000 today, which would you choose?

Feedback

The correct answer is £1,420 in four years' time because once restated into today's terms, £1,006 (£1,420/(1.09)^4), we can see that the present value of £1,420, £1,006, is more than £1,000. Many students answer £1,000 now because they think the £6 difference is not enough to compensate them for the four-year delay. This is a mistake. The £1,411.58 is full compensation for the delay in receiving the money. The additional £8.58 (£1,420 - £1,411.58) received is additional to the full compensation needed.

Choosing between investments

Supposing we were considering two banks' accounts, one of which offered a return of 9% and the other offered 10%. Which one would we prefer to invest our money in?

We already know that we would prefer more return to less return so we can easily decide we would prefer the account offering 10%, all other things being equal. Which one will have the higher NPV? Well a moment's thought should persuade you that the present value of the investment at 10% will be higher than the investment earning only 9%. If you are not sure, try it and see.

So when we have two real-world projects to decide between and we don't know the return on the two projects we can pick the one offering the higher return simply by picking the one with the highest NPV.

Choosing the appropriate discount rate

So far we have just assumed that we will use current interest rate. In practice, companies have to decide what rate to use. This is a very interesting problem. Let's start by thinking about why we chose the rates we used in the activities above. We used the interest rate that is the subject of the question to borrow or deposit money at. We said before that that was the opportunity cost of money, the best use of the money. So, if we use the same logic for a company we should use the rate at which the company can 'borrow' money. In terms of a company it is probably easier to think of it as the rate which the company has to pay to raise money, which might be debt or equity.

We call the amount that a company has to pay for its capital the weighted average cost of capital or WACC.

But there is another issue here and that is about the riskiness of the project. In Chapter 1 we agreed that the higher the risk the higher the required return. But if we discount every project at the company's WACC and accept any project with a higher present value than its cost we are not using that rule.

Activity

Suppose a company was faced with two potential projects that did follow the risk and return relationship we identified, that is that the riskier project offered higher returns. Suppose both offered a positive NPV, which project would the company choose?

Feedback

The company would choose the project with the higher NPV because it gave the higher return, which also means it was the riskier.

So, a company will always tend to choose riskier projects over less risky projects if it uses the NPV method.

One solution to this problem is to use a higher discount rate for riskier projects. But that leads to still more difficulties that are beyond the scope of this book. We will come back to this point at the end of the chapter.

Relevant cash flows

Now that you know how to 'discount', that is to find the present value of a future cash flow, we need to spend a little time deciding which cash flows we should include in our net present value calculations for a project.

The key point is that we should only include cash flows that are relevant to the decision to be made, which we will assume is about whether to undertake a project or not. It is easiest to identify cash flows that are not relevant. Costs, such as depreciation, which are not cash flows should be ignored since there is no alternative use for the cost.

First, we can ignore any cost that has already been incurred, even if it hasn't yet been paid for. Such a cost will be incurred regardless of whether the project goes ahead or not.

Second, we should only include cash flows as they arise. For example, if the project requires the purchase of new equipment, we include the cost when the equipment is paid for rather than when it is ordered or arrives.

Third, we can ignore any cash flow that would be incurred regardless of whether the project is going to be undertaken or not. Let's consider an example here.

Activity

Pottery Inc is evaluating a project to manufacture a new range of tableware. The company currently employs a designer at a cost of $50,000 a year. If the new project is undertaken, the designer will work full time on the new project and a junior designer will be taken on to work on other projects at a cost of $30,000 a year. If the project is not undertaken, the existing designer will work on other projects and a new junior designer will not be employed.

What is the relevant cost?

Feedback

The designer earning $50,000 will be working on the project and the prospective designer, who won't be working on the project, will be paid $30,000 if they are taken on. At first sight it might be tempting to include the cost of the senior designer, as they are working on the project. But this would be a mistake.

The designer earning $50,000 will be paid by the company regardless of whether the project is accepted or rejected. Their costs can't be a relevant cost because they don't change if the project is accepted.

But the junior designer won't be appointed if the project doesn't go ahead so their salary and other expenses are actually relevant costs.

One last thing: how to deal with inflation

We did identify inflation as one of the reasons for cash flows at different points in time being worth different amounts. Now we are going to discuss how to deal with inflation.

It turns out that it doesn't matter if you use cash flows that have been adjusted for inflation or those that have not, provided you are consistent. That is, you will come to the same decision if you adjust all the numbers to allow for inflation as you would if you didn't adjust any of the numbers for inflation. In practice, it is generally much easier to use cash flows which have not been adjusted for inflation but if you do that you need to make sure that none of the figures include any adjustment for inflation. That means you need to use real interest rates for your cost of capital rather than nominal or inflation-adjusted interest rates. Interest rates quoted by banks and others do include an allowance for inflation so you will need to reduce them to adjust for inflation. We did this in Chapter 6.

International cash flows

There are two new issues we need to consider once we attempt to calculate the net present value of an international problem. The first is to decide which cash flows we wish to discount. The second is to decide which exchange rate we should use if we are going to exchange one currency for another at some future date.

We will start with the first issue: which cash flows we wish to discount. The answer to this lies in the fundamental assumption about companies. We assume that all companies seek to maximize shareholder wealth. Now we need to decide which shareholders' wealth we are attempting to maximize. A subsidiary might not be wholly owned, for example; do we need to maximize the wealth of the minority interest of a subsidiary? The answer is that the group as a whole is responsible for maximizing the group's shareholders' wealth.

Now we know we are interested in maximizing the parent company's shareholders' wealth we can think about which cash flows are the relevant cash flows.

Activity

Suppose Minion Ltd is a subsidiary of Big Fish plc and the directors are evaluating a proposal to build a centre to develop virtual reality applications in India. The centre will cost £10 million to build and it is thought it will generate a positive cash inflow of £1 million a year for 15 years. However, the maximum amount the subsidiary is allowed to remit back to the UK each year is £500,000 due to a local covenant imposed on it by the local state. Identify the relevant cash flows which will be used to assess the viability of the project.

Feedback

We have agreed that the shareholders of Big Fish are the key group. Now we need to decide which cash flows are relevant to Big Fish's shareholders. While Minion is generating cash at the rate of £1 million a year, only £500,000 is remitted back to the UK and is then available to Big Fish to either pay out in dividends or invest in future profits.

We are interested in the cash flows available to the parent company, so in this case we will include £500,000 a year in the calculation. Of course, Minion may be able to reinvest the surplus cash and generate yet more profits in the future and those should be included in the calculation at the time that they are remitted to the parent company.

Exchange rates

We will use forecasts of inflation and the purchasing power parity relationship, as we considered in Chapter 6, to determine the exchange rate that we should use to convert local cash flows into the domestic cash flows we are going to discount.

Taxation

The company is likely to have to deal with both local taxes and domestic taxes. Taxes are like any other expense; we just need to identify the cash flows and then discount them according to the date on which they are due to be paid or received. Taxes generally don't take account of inflation and are one important reason why it is easier to calculate the net present value without adjusting for inflation.

Overall strategy

1   We need to start by identifying which ultimate cash flows we are concerned with. This is generally, but not always, the cash flows arising in the parent company rather than the subsidiary. In practice, this usually means that you need to calculate the relevant cash flows arising in the subsidiary and then determine the cash that will be remitted back to the parent. You are likely to need to determine a suitable exchange rate between the local currency and the domestic currency using purchasing power parity to achieve this.

2   Then take account of any additional relevant cash flows. For example, if the subsidiary will pay a management fee to the parent as part of the project then you will have an expense in the subsidiary's accounts, which will be eligible for tax relief, and a receipt in the parent company's accounts, which will be relevant and is probably subject to tax in the home country.

3   Now discount the cash flows at the parent company's WACC, adjusted for risk if required.

Example

Sunday plc is considering an investment on Mars, which has the currency bars and has spent £1 million on a feasibility study.

Investment costs are £500m immediately and £200m next year, both on capital items.

Spending on working capital will be £50m immediately. Sunday will invest sufficient money from the UK to Mars to cover the capital costs and the initial working capital at the time the expenditure will be incurred.

Sunday expects profits of 50 million Mars bars a year in real terms.

Tax on Mars is at 10% a year and tax relief is given on capital investments at 10% a year flat rate.

The current exchange rate is £10 to 1 bar.

Inflation in UK is expected to be 3% and on Mars is expected to be 7% throughout.

Tax in the UK is 25%.

Sunday's cost of capital is 8% and Sunday will charge an additional 5% for the extra risk of the project.

The project will end after 10 years.

Required

Find the NPV of the project.

Solution

We will make the following assumptions:

The cash flows are stated at today's value, ie the real value rather than their nominal value. We are going to work with inflation-adjusted figures, because it is much easier, so we will have to adjust the numbers for inflation.

We assume the discount rate given is adjusted for inflation.

Let's start by using the purchasing power parity theory to estimate the future exchange rates.

The current exchange rate is £10:1bar or £1:0.1bar. Inflation is 3% in the UK and 7% on Mars.

The exchange rate in Year 1 is going to be: 0.1 x 1.07/1.03 = 0.104 or £1:0.104 Mars bars. You can either remember the formula, which is current exchange rate x (1 + home inflation)/(1+ local inflation), or you can remember that the currency with the higher inflation is expected to devalue and deduce the formula. Now, can you work out the forecast exchange rate for Year 2? Use the forecast rate for Year 1 and then apply the purchasing power parity formula again. Working 1 shows the forecast exchange rates for all years.

Table 10.2 Working 1: Exchange rates

Year	£1:bar
0	0.1
1	0.104
2	0.108
3	0.112
4	0.116
5	0.121
6	0.126
7	0.131
8	0.136
9	0.141
10	0.146
11	0.152

Now we need to determine all the cash flows arising in the subsidiary. The £1 million feasibility study is a sunk cost so we can ignore it.

Let's move on to the investment in capital items and the initial working capital. We will include the immediate costs at their given value but the capital costs for next year will have to be adjusted for inflation so the cash flow we will include will be £200 million adjusted for inflation. There is some uncertainty about whether the inflation rate to use should be the home rate or the local rate. Since the expenditure is on Mars, we will use 7%. Provided you stated clearly which you were using you wouldn't be wrong to use the home rate. This is one way in which academic questions can be harder than situations that arise in the 'real' world.

Table 10.3   Working 2

Year	Capital expenditure Mars bars' million	Working capital Mars bars' million
0	50	5.00
1	20.231	

The capital expenditure in Year 2 has been adjusted to reflect inflation on Mars and the expected spot rate at the time the expenditure is incurred. That is £200 million x 0.1038 x 1.07 = 22.23107 million Mars bars.

Working capital

We've accounted for the initial investment in working capital but inflation means that the nominal amount invested in working capital increases each year. If that isn't clear then consider a business that sells cars in a chain of car showrooms which are subject to inflation at 7% a year. Suppose the cars in the showroom are worth £50 million at the start of the year. If the company has exactly the same range of cars in the showroom a year later, how much would they cost now? The answer is £53.5 million (£50 million x 1.07). So, the company will have had to increase its investment in working capital by £3.5 million (£53.5 million − £50 million). The same calculation needs to be made each year and the new investment needed due to constant inflation will be a little higher in each successive year. What would happen to the working capital if the owner decided to retire and close the business down? In the final year of business he would sell all his cars but wouldn't replace them with new stock, giving him the present value equivalent of £50 million of extra cash.

In Sunday's case, at the end of the project's life, the company will convert the working capital, inventory, debtors and cash less creditors into cash and remit it back to the parent company.

Working 3 shows the increased investment in working capital needed each year and the reversal of those increases at the end of the project's life. The initial £50 million will also be released as an additional cash flow in Year 10.

Table 10.4 Working 3

Year	Working capital Mars bars 'm
0	−5.00
1	−0.35
2	−0.37
3	−0.40
4	−0.43
5	−0.46
6	−0.49
7	−0.53
8	−0.56
9	−0.60
10	9.19

For the next calculation we will need to deal with profits rather than cash to calculate the tax payable. We won't include profits in our final calculations, just cash flows. In practice, in this and many other situations, the big difference between profits and cash flows is the depreciation.

Working 4

We will start by increasing the real profits to calculate nominal profits. But the profits are stated before depreciation so we need to deduct the depreciation, at 10% flat rate a year, to get the taxable profits.

Once we have the taxable profits we can calculate the Martian tax, which is 10% of the taxable profits. Note that while the profits go up each year due to inflation, the depreciation is locked in to the original cost and doesn't change with inflation. Finally, we can find the cash flow by deducting Martian tax from the profit/cash flow.

The profit in Year 1 is 50m bars in real terms and 53.5 bars (50m x 1.07) in nominal terms.

Depreciation in Year 1 is 5m bars (50m/10) and in Year 2 is 7.22m bars ((50m + 20m x 1.07)/10).

The Martian tax in Year 1 is 4.85m bars ((53.5 – 5) x 10%).

The cash flow after tax is the nominal profit – tax.

Remember that depreciation isn't a cash flow so we need to ignore it in our cash flow calculations. We needed it to calculate the Martian tax.

Table 10.5   Working 4

Years	Nominal profit 'm bars	Depreciation 'm bars	Martian tax 'm bars	Cash flow after tax 'm bars
1	53.5	5.00	4.85	48.65
2	57.245	7.22	5.00	52.24
3	61.25215	7.22	5.40	55.85
4	65.5398005	7.22	5.83	59.71
5	70.12758654	7.22	6.29	63.84
6	75.03651759	7.22	6.78	68.26
7	80.28907382	7.22	7.31	72.98
8	85.90930899	7.22	7.87	78.04
9	91.92296062	7.22	8.47	83.45
10	98.35756786	7.22	9.11	89.24
11		2.22	−0.22	0.22

Now we can calculate the cash flows remitted back to the UK by converting Mars into pounds at the rate we calculated in Working 1.

Discount rate

We are told that the company wishes to use a discount rate equal to the cost of capital of 8% plus a risk premium of 5%, giving a discount rate of 13%. This will already include an allowance for inflation so we don't need to adjust it any further.

We can now deal with the cash flows arising in the UK by discounting them at 13% to determine the net present value.

The UK cash flows are the amounts sent to, and remitted from, Mars together with the UK tax payable at the rate of 25%.

Table 10.6 Working 5

Years	Cash flow after tax	Capital cash flows	Working capital	Net cash flow	Exchange rate	£'m remitted back to the UK
0		-50	-5.00	-55.00	0.1	-5.50
1	48.65	-22.2310	-0.35	26.07	0.103883495	2.71
2	52.24		-0.37	51.87	0.107917806	5.60
3	55.85		-0.40	55.45	0.112108788	6.22
4	59.71		-0.43	59.28	0.116462528	6.90
5	63.84		-0.46	63.38	0.120985344	7.67
6	68.26		-0.49	67.76	0.125683804	8.52
7	72.98		-0.53	72.46	0.130564729	9.46
8	78.04		-0.56	77.48	0.135635204	10.51
9	83.45		-0.60	82.85	0.14090259	11.67
10	89.24		9.19	98.44	0.146374535	14.41
11	0.22			0.22	0.152058983	0.03

Since the net present value is positive we can say that the method suggests the project should be accepted.

Limitations of the net present value methodology

There are many reasons for having concerns about the use of this method to evaluate projects. In particular:

- it doesn't have a robust way of dealing with risk;
- it appears to be very accurate but most of the numbers are actually estimates and the method relies on good estimates.

Brealey and Myers famously stated that 'A Project Is Not a Black Box' (Brealey and Myers, 2003). That is, in practice, managers do not just accept a project and then let it run without any further input. Projects that are not performing well will be reviewed by management and steps will be taken in the light of the performance. That might range from ending the project early to investing in assets, people or increased expenses like marketing. The net present value method does not take account of this activity.

While there is value in appraising projects, and rejecting those which seem unlikely to be financially successful, we also need to acknowledge that companies will also take account of strategic issues. For example, a car maker might decide to enter the Formula One racing championship for the first time. If they calculated the net present value of such a decision it is unlikely that the car would do well in its first year so the NPV is likely to be negative. But at the end of the first year the company would have a choice, called a real option, to take part for a second year or to withdraw from the championship. Having that real option has value to the company and the more uncertain the choice the greater the value of the option. When the value of the option is included as a positive cash flow, in this case arising in Year 1, the NPV might change to be positive.

Brealey and Myers (2003) give a great example of real options involving airplanes in their book on corporate finance. Should a carrier buy one large plane or two smaller planes? If they buy two smaller planes their running costs will be higher as both planes need a pilot and so on. But if they buy two smaller planes they have more options; for example at the end of the year they could sell one of the planes if fewer seats were sold than predicted. Including the value of this option can make buying two planes a more attractive option.

A successful MNC will be able to identify and value the real options that are created from the decisions they are taking today and so make better decisions.

Summary

Investment appraisal is a key activity of a finance department. In this chapter we focused on the most widely used method of investment appraisal, the net present value method. First we set out the method of calculating the net present value of a project in a local country. The first step is to identify the local cash flows and then determine the cash flows into the home country. Then the net cash flows in the home country can be deduced and it is those cash flows that are discounted.

Finally we discussed the significant limitations of the method.

Questions

Question 1

Inflation in Kenya is 10% and in Tanzania it is 5%. The spot rate is 1 KES shilling:21.6 TZS shilling. Using purchasing power parity, forecast the exchange rate between the two currencies for each of the next six years.

Question 2

After the vote to leave the EU the pound fell in value and the government talked of cuts in corporation tax. Do these changes make the UK more or less attractive to invest in?

Question 3

Local Inc has been set up to undertake a single project with a 10-year life in a foreign currency. Local has undertaken a net present value computation and the project has returned a positive net present value.

Distant plc, a company from another country, is considering buying Local and undertaking the project itself. If none of the cash flows change is it necessary for Distant to also undertake a net present value calculation?

11
Investing directly in foreign enterprises

At the end of this chapter you will be able to:

- discuss the theories that explain foreign direct investment;
- explain how companies come to be multinationals;
- briefly describe MNCs in the 21st century.

Introduction

In this chapter, we will discuss the theory behind the creation of multinationals. Then we will explore the reasons for companies becoming multinational companies, and finally we will investigate the processes that are undertaken to allow them to become multinationals. A multinational company is generally defined as a company with facilities and assets in more than one country controlled by a parent operating from the home country. In practice, multinationals tend to be large and to have a parent company controlling their global operations. At the time of writing there are considerable political and economic changes taking place and multinational companies, as well as domestic companies, will quickly adapt to those changes. A truly multinational company will take account of global factors when planning its adaptations rather than focusing on changes in one country or region of the world. In practice, today almost all large companies in the United States and Europe are multinationals.

You might have noticed that after the Brexit vote in June 2016 the FTSE 100 rose while the pound fell. The large number of MNCs listed in the FTSE 100 explains what happened.

The MNCs generate significant income in dollars which they then convert into pounds sterling to calculate their profits. As the pound fell, the dollars and other foreign currency they earn bought more pounds than previously. Thus the falling value of the pound increased their UK profits, leading to a rise in the value of the companies.

Multinational companies are also called transnational, international or stateless companies. It is perhaps this final term that suggests that these companies can be truly independent of any individual country and its government.

In the 2016 *Forbes* list of the world's largest companies, four Chinese banks and three US investment companies made up the biggest seven companies in the world. The remaining top 10 companies were Apple, ExxonMobil and Toyota. The largest European company is the UK bank HSBC in 14th place, followed by the German companies Allianz and Volkswagen in 21st and 22nd place respectively. From this we can see how very large many banks now are, and that is perhaps concerning after the global financial crisis when some banks were criticized for being 'too big to fail'.

The theories about foreign direct investment (FDI)

FDI refers to the practice of investing in real assets, such as property and equipment, in a country other than your home country.

We need to consider the following issues:

- Why do companies directly invest in other countries?
- How do international companies compete with the local competition in the host country?
- Why do companies choose to undertake direct investment rather than exporting or licensing their products?

Activity

Using your own country, compare and contrast the advantages and disadvantages of a domestic company competing with an MNC seeking to enter the market. You should think about internal and external factors and consider the political, economic, legal and cultural aspects of your country.

Feedback

At first sight the MNCs are at a considerable disadvantage to the local companies they are going to need to compete with. Local companies will have a much better understanding of the market in which they are operating. An incoming MNC will need to gain an expertise in the legal environment, the banking sector and the business culture of the country as well as understanding the peculiarities of the local market.

In addition, the local company will be well known and trusted by its investors, suppliers, customers and employees and potential employees.

The MNC will also have to address the problem of long chains of command, which will require additional time, attention and control, leading to increased costs, and determine how much autonomy to give the new subsidiary. The MNC will also incur additional costs for communication, administration and transportation.

But an MNC does have significant advantages over a purely domestic firm. They may have valuable brands that help them penetrate the new market, and are likely to benefit from economies of scale, particularly in terms of research and development.

There are other, not-so-obvious advantages. For example, an MNC can take advantage of differences in tax rates to arrange for its profits to be taxed at lower rates by arranging for the profits to arise in a low-tax country.

Additionally, if a domestic company is based in a country which is in recession, the company just has to take whatever steps it can to protect itself and wait for better times, but an MNC has many options including relocating the operation to a different country.

Economic theories of FDI

Market imperfection theory

Market imperfections refer to differences between markets which create opportunities for exploitation. Take the example of a UK MNC which has a subsidiary in Ireland. The corporation tax rate in the UK is currently 20%, while in Ireland it is only 12.5%. If the UK parent sells goods to the Irish subsidiary at cost to be sold on to the public, all the profits on the activity will arise in Ireland and thus will be taxed at the lower rate of 12.5%. If the UK parent sold the goods at cost plus an element of profit to the Irish subsidiary, some of the profits would arise in the UK and be taxed at 20%, leading to more tax being paid. This is a clear and simple example of market imperfection. The difficulty is that governments and citizens often disapprove of such activities and companies such as McDonald's and Starbucks attract significant bad publicity for their legal tax avoidance policies.

There are other examples of market imperfections including:

- Information is not freely and quickly available, leading to consumers buying from market leaders rather than smaller businesses with equivalent products.
- Product differentiations. These differences are often exploited by companies who use branding to create and maintain product differentiations to increase their sales. Apple, among others, exploits this market imperfection.

- Some companies have better marketing skills which they can use to generate increased market penetration. One example of this is Disney, which is able to create merchandise linked with films such as *Frozen* that is able to command a significant price premium over similar products without a film link.

- Companies with trademarks and patents can benefit financially by using them to sell more goods and services. We have seen the legal struggles between Apple and Samsung where each seeks to protect its own advantage.

- Some markets provide easier access to capital than others. One criticism of Germany and other European countries is that it is much harder to raise capital than in the United States. Certainly, more venture capital is issued in the United States than in Europe, so a US company is likely to find it easier and cheaper than a European competitor to raise funds for future investment.

The market imperfection theory claims that these advantages MNCs have over domestic companies help to compensate them for the additional costs of operating internationally and explain the existence of MNCs.

Product life cycle theory

The product life cycle theory argues that there are five stages in a product's life cycle:

- introduction;
- growth;
- maturity;
- saturation;
- decline.

The product life cycle theory suggests that early in a product's life cycle all the parts and labour associated with that product come from the area in which it was invented. After the product becomes adopted and used in the world markets, production gradually moves away from the point of origin. In some situations, the product becomes an item that is imported by its original country of invention.

A commonly used example of this is the invention, growth and production of the personal computer with respect to the United States. In the new product stage, the product is produced and consumed in the United States: no export trade occurs. In the maturing product stage, mass-production techniques are developed and foreign demand (in developed countries) expands; the US now exports the product to other developed countries. In the standardized product stage, production moves to developing countries, which then export the product to developed countries.

The model demonstrates dynamic comparative advantage. This is a very important point. The early thinkers about globalization such as Adam Smith believed that every country had its own strengths, fishing or agriculture for example, and that each should stick to what they did well and trade with other countries to obtain the goods that they were not so good at producing. Modern thinking accepts that comparative advantage is dynamic and that, for example, as a workforce becomes better qualified or a country improves its infrastructure, it can change its comparative advantage as compared with other countries. Changes in macroeconomics such as oil prices or demand for oil may also lead to changes in comparative advantage.

The eclectic theory

John Dunning's eclectic theory (Dunning, 1980), which I introduced in Chapter 1, links together three elements of comparative advantage: location advantage, ownership advantage, and internalization advantage. Dunning proposes that FDI will take place when three conditions are satisfied.

First, the firm must own some unique competitive advantage that overcomes the disadvantages of competing with foreign firms in their own market. This is called the ownership advantage and might be a brand such as Disney or Apple.

Second, it must be more profitable to undertake a business activity in a foreign location than a domestic location. This is called the location advantage. One example is the relocation of business to produce in low-wage economies such as China.

Third, the firm must benefit from controlling the foreign business activity, rather than hiring an independent local company to provide the service. This is called the internalization advantage. An example of this might be a superior inventory management system that helps reduce costs. We will discuss this issue of control later in this chapter.

International portfolio diversification theory

In Chapter 1 we explored the relationship between risk and return and reviewed the capital asset pricing model, which suggested that risk could be split into two elements: systematic risk and specific risk. Specific risk is the risk that only affects a single company. Examples are the problems that Samsung have had with phones exploding and VW's problems with emissions. I'm sure you can think of many more.

Systematic risks are risks that affect every business, though not to the same extent. So, every business will be affected by changes in oil prices, for example. But some businesses, for example an app-writing business, will not be greatly affected by this, while others, for example a transport company, will be significantly affected because fuel costs make up a high proportion of their costs.

Systematic risks that affect a domestic company include:

- recession in the home country;
- changes in tax rates, exchange rates or interest rates in the home country;
- civil unrest including strikes in the home country.

The impacts of those same risks are different for MNCs than domestic companies.

Example

Suppose the government of a country, Eurostan, increases interest rates and that leads to an appreciation of the currency.

Now let's explore the impact of such an appreciation on three companies.

Company A is a large domestic company in Eurostan.

Company B is an MNC with the parent company based in Eurostan. About 50% of the company's production and sales are in other countries.

Company C is an MNC based in another country. Company C has a large subsidiary in Eurostan which manufactures and sells in the country.

Company A will find that any imports it needs for production are cheaper but, more importantly, competing goods imported into the country, for example from Company C, are cheaper for customers to buy and so Company A is likely to find its sales falling due to the increased competition. There is little that Company A can do to protect itself from its increased competition.

Company B will have the same problem with cheaper imported goods competing with its domestic products and it will also find it more expensive to export goods produced in Eurostan. But only half of its production and sales will be adversely affected. Company B may move some more production to its overseas subsidiaries, enabling them to export goods back to Eurostan at more competitive prices.

Company C may also shift production from Eurostan to other facilities to take advantage of the opportunity to send cheaper goods into Eurostan.

So we can see that MNCs are much less affected by these kinds of risks in either their home country or any local country they are working in.

As time goes by the world economy is generally becoming less diversified but the benefits are still considerable.

In practice, the benefits of the reduction in total risk, systematic and specific risk, and of diversification more than compensate for the increased risks – exchange rate risk, country risk – and the additional costs of operating in other countries, that an MNC takes on.

The creation of a multinational

We have had multinational businesses for centuries, among the earliest being the East India Company, formed in 1600, and the Dutch East India Company, formed in 1602.

The first multinational companies in more recent times were seeking raw materials such as oil, gas, coal and metals. As we can see from the *Forbes* list mentioned above, such companies are still among the largest global companies even now.

After the end of the Second World War, the next wave of multinational companies was seeking new markets for their products. Early market-seeking companies included Coca-Cola, Nestlé, IBM, McDonald's, Volvo and Sony. Accessing new markets can bring economies of scale but can also ensure the survival of the company if the home market declines. One example of this is tobacco companies who are facing falling numbers of smokers in their original markets.

More recently, multinationals have been looking for low-cost production facilities, generally achieved by moving into a low-wage country such as Mexico or China. Examples include Apple and Dyson. Many of these companies are moving to gain a competitive edge, lower prices, over their competitors in a move to ensure their survival. In more recent times, as low-cost countries have a more highly educated workforce, companies seeking to cut costs have even moved their research and development departments to low-wage economies. For example, Intel has moved its research and development department to India.

In addition, companies have sought to become multinationals for the following reasons:

- To seek the benefits of operating in multiple markets in order to minimize costs, benefit from country risk diversification and seek new opportunities.
- To obtain new knowledge, for example acquiring companies in other countries to gain their specialist knowledge and patents.
- To retain their existing domestic clients who increasingly need MNCs to service their needs as they themselves become MNCs. Banks and accounting firms have particularly taken this approach as their clients have become multinationals.

The process of becoming a multinational company

Companies generally become multinational companies in a number of stages or steps. These tend to be small steps forward in response to opportunities or threats that present themselves rather than through following a strategic plan.

Exporters

Initially companies become exporters, perhaps using an agent, responding to demand for their goods and services. Exporting does not require investment in new infrastructure and so is low in risk. Profits are quickly received but exporting is relatively expensive and volumes are limited, so market penetration and profits tend to be lower than in subsequence steps.

As demand grows and the company gains knowledge about the new market, they may shift away from using intermediaries such as export agents to dealing directly with agents and others within the local country and as their knowledge of the market increases, to setting up a sales subsidiary in the local country, including some service facilities such as warehousing and aftersales service. Finally, they manage their own distribution network.

Local manufacturing

Exporters may then move to manufacturing locally.

Activity

What are the advantages of manufacturing locally over simply exporting?

Feedback

You may have some of the points below:

- *orders can be satisfied more quickly;*
- *goods can be modified or designed to meet the needs of the market more easily;*
- *production schedules can be tailored to the needs of the local market;*
- *there is more certainty of supply for customers;*
- *the cost of sales will be lower, increasing profits;*
- *aftersales services can be offered or expanded as needed;*
- *as the company shows a commitment to the local market, sales are likely to increase. It is sometimes seen that exports from the home country increase after the local sales facility is established as demand for goods not manufactured locally increases.*

Manufacturing locally can be achieved in a number of ways. A firm could undertake the manufacturing themselves either by growing organically or by acquiring a local firm to manufacture locally. Alternatively, a company could work with a local company to produce their goods locally. Such an agreement might be via a licence or it could take the form of a joint venture with a local firm.

In practice, the best choice for a company may vary from time to time so it is essential for managers to constantly monitor and manage their strategy in response to constantly changing circumstances such as:

- new information;
- changing market perceptions;
- change in the risk and return characteristics of each option;
- experience.

In the second section of this chapter we will evaluate the various strategies used by companies to invest directly in other countries.

Licensing

One of the steps that companies seeking international expansion can take is to grant a licence to a local company to manufacture their goods. The company then receives royalties on the local company's sales.

There are some advantages to licensing:

- it requires little investment;
- financial risks are limited;
- the goods are in the marketplace more quickly when manufactured by an established business than if a new production facility is needed.

However, the disadvantages are significant:

- the profits earned are lower than from manufacturing;
- maintaining the quality of goods is more difficult when they are being manufactured and sold by a third party;
- it is difficult to prevent the licensee from exporting production which may then compete directly with the company's own businesses;
- the local firm is effectively gaining all the MNC's expertise so licensing can create competition.

Organic growth vs growth by acquisition

At its simplest, organic growth tends to be slower and cheaper while acquisitions tend to be faster but more expensive. In practice, some expansions will be into markets which do not have a suitable company to acquire, perhaps because the market is very underdeveloped and so organic growth becomes the only option.

Acquisition allows the parent to quickly transfer its skills and knowhow, for example patents and trademarks, to its newly acquired subsidiary, which itself has a good understanding of the local market.

In practice, larger, highly experienced and well-established companies are more likely to use organic growth than smaller, younger companies.

Factors to consider when choosing the method of FDI

Companies usually have some form of intangible capital that gives them a competitive advantage over other companies; it might be their brand or a patent or even their inventory management system. The nature of that intangible capital can make one form of international expansion more advantageous than another.

Where the competitive advantage is directly about the product, for example a new drug for high blood pressure, then the best way of distributing the drug is probably exporting it.

In contrast, if the competitive edge is in the form of a process or method that can be formally and objectively recorded and replicated, then licensing becomes a good choice. McDonald's is an example of this kind of competitive edge and the company expands by franchising new outlets as well as managing some themselves.

However, if the company's competitive edge lies in its organizational skills and those skills cannot be replicated, then setting up a local subsidiary is likely to be the only way to fully exploit the company's advantages. The term organizational skills is wide ranging and includes a good understanding of markets or excellent quality control or customer service.

Fundamentally, if a company can make more money by maintaining control of its assets, tangible and intangible, than it can by selling or licensing them, then it should undertake FDI. Otherwise, exporting or licensing is more attractive.

Multinational companies in the 21st century

We have already agreed a definition of an MNC but now we are going to discuss the characteristics of most MNCs.

MNCs are generally very large in terms of both their assets and sales and operate in more than one country. MNCs tend to use professionally qualified and experienced staff in management as well as in technical areas, and they often invest in staff development. Policy is set by the parent company, which also controls the operations of the subsidiaries. This is essential. If subsidiaries are given too much control, they may make decisions which are not in the best interests of the group as a whole.

MNCs tend to be **oligopolies**, that is control of their business sector is held by a small number of large MNCs. Oligopolies are able to manipulate the market because each company in an oligopoly tends to understand the other companies and the likely impact of their actions on the other companies. A good example of an oligopoly is the UK supermarket sector, which is dominated by a small number of large companies. They learned many years ago that cutting prices soon led to price wars, which might benefit their customers but at the expense of their profits, so they all tend to limit themselves to price matching and compete in terms of quality rather than price. The move of low-cost German competition into the market has somewhat disrupted things.

Twenty-first-century MNCs diversify into other countries largely to reduce their total risks via international diversification. As the global economy becomes more and more integrated, the benefits of international diversification are somewhat eroded but given the Brexit vote and other recent political and economic shocks to countries, it becomes a more attractive strategy. In addition, modern MNCs continue to exploit market imperfections to lower their tax bills, lower their cost of capital and improve cash flows. These benefits help MNCs compete with the purely domestic firms who we know are at a significant advantage to MNCs in many ways.

In Chapter 10 we used the net present value method to assess potential projects; however, in practice companies need to take a more strategic view of potential projects. The net present value might be an important element of their decision making but there are other factors that need to be taken account of too.

Much of an MNC's strategy will be about creating, sustaining and defending the competitive advantage, or barriers to entry, that we talked about earlier in this chapter.

MNCs who are innovative, such as technology companies and pharmaceuticals, use their cutting-edge products to compete. Their competitors are constantly striving to erode any competitive disadvantage they are at by innovating themselves. Thus, such companies must continually introduce new products or find ways to differentiate their current products. These companies invest heavily in research and development.

Other MNCs can be considered to be mature. These companies are selling standardized products which are not innovative. Mature MNCs still seek to create and maintain barriers to entry by using economies of scale, including manufacturing in low-cost countries, to reduce costs. They will also use advertising and marketing to differentiate their products and deter others from entering the market because of their strong brands. Mature MNCs will also seek new markets for their products, such as tobacco and soft drinks, which are suffering declining demand in their domestic markets.

Finally, an MNC becomes **senescent,** meaning that products are standardized, any organizational competitive edge has been eroded, and technological skills are no longer superior to those of competitors. All the barriers to entry have been removed and the MNC resorts to seeking new markets with little competition and moving to low-cost countries to minimize costs. While there may be little competition initially, local firms are quickly able to compete with MNCs that cannot find new competitive advantages.

Reasons for FDI revisited

Given the above, it is apparent that many companies are driven to become MNCs more by the need to survive than by the desire to grow.

MNCs seek to manufacture abroad either to seek a competitive advantage or to seek to erode another company's competitive advantage. Such MNCs need to be constantly aware of changes which may make moving production from one low-cost country to another even lower-cost country worthwhile. They will need to take account of taxation, exchange rates, inflation, particularly wage inflation, and government stability and attitude to FDI to make decisions and changes in any of those variables that may mean that a new decision should be made.

Companies in industries requiring innovation will seek to grow to enable them to absorb the high research and development costs they need to incur. Without such expansion, their costs would be high compared to their sales. We see this in the mergers and takeovers in the pharmaceutical industry in recent years. In technology companies, we see the same products, the iPhone for example, sold around the world as it takes global sales to be able to absorb the high research and development costs.

It is very important to these large companies to have assured sources of the raw materials and components they need to satisfy their markets. One strategy to achieve this is to acquire supplier companies. Another is to adopt multiple sourcing, where two or more suppliers are used to guarantee supply. For the same reason, many companies choose to manufacture in more than one country, even though it may cost more than manufacturing at a single facility. The reduction in risk of interruption of supply by using multiple facilities makes the additional costs worthwhile. Multiple facilities provide an MNC with the flexibility to move production quickly from one site to another to take advantage of small cost benefits, for example a shift in exchange rates, or to avoid conflicts with governments or groups such as unions seeking to bring pressure to bear on the company.

While countries are less heterogeneous and more dynamic than suggested by Adam Smith, countries or regions of countries often do have a competitive edge over other countries, for example banking and insurance in London and computing innovation in Silicon Valley in the United States. Sometimes MNCs expand into regions in order to learn from the companies already there. Such a move can make it easier to recruit staff with the desired knowledge and experience. It is also likely that the company will become more competitive by the simple act of competing for business with market leaders in their own market. This is one reason protectionism fails. When a government protects a domestic industry from global competition the industry is not exposed to, and forced to compete with, the best in the world and so does not gain the experience which would make it a better company.

CASE STUDY Wal-Mart

We are going to consider the attempts by Wal-Mart, the world's largest retailer, to expand from its domestic market, the United States, into a number of countries in recent years, including the UK, where it took over Asda in 1999. Previously it had invested in China in 1996, Germany in 1997 and South Korea in 1998. In total, Wal-Mart currently operates in 27 countries and about 40% of its turnover is generated outside its domestic market.

Wal-Mart opened its first shop in China in 1996, but 20 years on has only 400 stores in the world's most populous country. While Wal-Mart in China sources almost all its products locally, it is generally seen as not understanding that local consumers are somewhat suspicious of the US company and its warehouse style of shop; they are more interested in the quality and authenticity of the products in stores than they are tempted by lower prices. Wal-Mart also finds itself competing with the Sun-Art Retail Group, which is a local company that modelled itself on Wal-Mart but had the benefit of understanding the market and having the trust of consumers. Sun-Art creates the sense of a street market or marketplace in its stores, which is something customers are familiar with. Wal-Mart is shifting its offering away from its large stores, employing more Chinese staff, and slowly building its market share in China.

Wal-Mart expanded into Germany in 1997 by acquiring two existing supermarket chains. However, these two chains made up only a very small share of the German grocery market and from the beginning, Wal-Mart faced fierce competition from Aldi and Lidl. In 2006, Wal-Mart withdrew from the German market.

It is likely that the failure of Wal-Mart to thrive or even survive in Germany is down to a number of factors.

Wal-Mart failed to understand the tastes of its new customers and was not big enough to gain customer acceptance. German customers were not used to the US culture of large, brash stores which showed insufficient regard to environmental issues. Germans tend not to smile at strangers, so the requirement that customers should be greeted with a smile by store staff might have been seen as off-putting rather than welcoming.

Wal-Mart was unprepared for the strong unionized labour force in Germany which was reluctant to adopt some of the Wal-Mart culture introduced by the strongly Americanized management; for example, Wal-Mart employees are required to begin each day with motivational chanting of the company's name.

Wal-Mart found it difficult to obtain the planning permissions it needed to expand quickly and broke the law with prices that were sometimes too low. It also required staff to report misconduct by other staff and banned sexual relationships between staff members. In a court case in 2006 between Wal-Mart and the unions, this ethical code was found to be unethical and Wal-Mart withdrew from Germany.

In 1998, Wal-Mart expanded into South Korea by setting up 16 supermarkets, repeating its mistakes of the year before in Germany, where they were not able to benefit from the economies of scale they needed. Wal-Mart focused more on the financial advantages – a weak local currency and strong economy making entry into a growing market cheap – than on the culture of the country. Wal-Mart did not understand the shopping culture in South Korea, where a high-quality experience is valued much more than saving money. Their stores just didn't offer the luxury goods or environment offered by the domestic supermarkets and demanded by the market.

In 1999 in the UK, Wal-Mart bought Asda, one of the big four supermarkets chains, for £6.7bn. By 2003, the new subsidiary of Wal-Mart had overtaken Sainsbury's to become the UK's second-largest retailer behind Tesco. Asda's low-cost approach was a good match with Wal-Mart's strategy, which might be behind Wal-Mart's decision to transfer the ownership of Asda to a wholly owned UK subsidiary leave a British board in charge of Asda: not their normal strategy. Prior to the takeover, Asda had enjoyed considerable success with its George brand of clothing and Wal-Mart has adopted the George name and range in its stores in several countries including the United States, Canada, Argentina, China, India and Japan. The Asda name has been retained but there has been some rebranding of some stores to Asda Wal-Mart.

Perhaps, in the end, the success of Wal-Mart in the UK, as compared to China, Germany and South Korea, has more to do with the similar culture of the two countries than with the financial fundamentals.

A final word

In many ways, MNCs are the inevitable consequences of the neoliberal global environment which has dominated the world economy since the 1980s. But just as neoliberalization and globalization have their critics, so do MNCs.

MNCs are criticized for dominating markets and using the economies of scale which provide them with a significant competitive edge, making it difficult for small local companies to succeed or even survive.

Some MNCs are also criticized for using their monopoly, or market strength, to make excess profits by overcharging consumers. Some are also accused of other unethical practices such as using child labour or paying workers very low wages, as well as showing little regard for environmental factors, creating pollution and consuming non-renewable resources.

Summary

All MNCs invest in assets in other countries and at some point most invest directly into foreign enterprises. We began this chapter by studying the economic theories which seek to explain why companies invest in assets in other countries. We then looked in more detail at the process of becoming an MNC and compared organic growth with growth by acquisition. We ended the chapter by taking a detailed look at modern-day MNCs, including a case study on Wal-Mart.

Questions

Question 1

Like Wal-Mart, Tesco has actively sought to expand internationally using a range of strategies including takeovers, joint ventures and organic growth. And like Wal-Mart, Tesco has enjoyed mixed fortunes; it was forced to withdraw from the United States, for example. Pick one or more countries where Tesco has successfully established a presence and compare them with one or more countries where it has been forced to withdraw after failing to create a profitable local business. Can you identify the reasons for the success and failure of these projects? Is Tesco's experience similar to that of Wal-Mart or different?

Question 2

By reference to the Wal-Mart case study and your work in Question 1, critically assess the theories of FDI in the chapter.

12
Country risk analysis

At the end of this chapter you will be able to:

- explain the risks that make up country risk;
- source evidence of the scale of those risks for a single country;
- discuss the practical difficulties facing companies operating outside their domestic country and outline some of the strategies that can be used to reduce those risks.

Introduction

Country risk analysis is undertaken in order to assess the risk that the company's cash flows remitted from an overseas operation back to the home country will be less than expected due to the risks inherent in investing in that country.

In contrast, **sovereign risk analysis** is an analysis of the ability of a government to pay its debts as they fall due. The credit rating agencies, Moody's, Standard and Poor, and Fitch, publish credit ratings of countries as a measure of each country's sovereign risk.

There are many ways in which a company may be adversely affected by a local country's economics or politics, ranging from war to rules on capital flows of cash out of the country.

Country risk analysis is dynamic, requiring constant review by MNCs seeking to protect their existing subsidiaries as well as determining the location of new subsidiaries or other business activities such as sourcing raw materials or components or exporting.

As we will see, forecasting is unreliable and so MNCs prize flexibility and stand ready to move production quickly to respond to changing political, economic and financial environments. For example, in 2016 the UK company Smiffys decided, given the uncertainty of Brexit and the potential consequences of a 'hard' Brexit, to relocate its headquarters to an EU country.

In this chapter we will consider many different kinds of risk but essentially our concern is always that the actual cash remitted will be less than expected.

Political risk – a first look

Political risk is primarily about the impact that a government, local or domestic, can have on the cash flow of an MNC or any of its subsidiaries. At its most extreme, a company could be threatened with being taken into state ownership by a host government. For example, at the end of 2015, the UK government considered nationalizing Rolls-Royce Engines to force a merger between the company and BAE Systems in order to protect national security. In the end, the government didn't nationalize Rolls-Royce but the risk was certainly real at the time.

Not all political risks are as dramatic as the Rolls-Royce example but the impact on cash flows can be significant.

For example, changes in international trade agreements like Brexit may lead companies to change their plans for FDI or even to move production from one country to another.

Changes in tax rates, especially corporate tax rates, can also impact on cash flows, although MNCs are able to take action to shelter profits from higher tax rates, as we will see in Chapter 14.

Micro risks

Political risks may be specific to a firm, termed **micro risks**, or firm-specific risks. This often takes the form of governance risk, which is a goal conflict between the company and the local or host government. We saw this in the Rolls-Royce incident described above in 2015. Many governments want to acquire their military supplies from a domestic firm or from a country to whom they are closely aligned and are unwilling to use a company with a parent based in another country.

Macro risks

Political risks might be country specific, or **macro risks**; they are nationwide but can affect MNCs too. An obvious example is the vote for Brexit, where all businesses operating from the UK have already seen a fall in the value of the pound and are currently dealing with the uncertainty of the negotiations between the UK and the remaining EU countries.

A government which prevents funds leaving the country, corruption and protectionism are other examples of country-specific political risk. Any MNC seeking to assess the present and future macro risks will need to assess both political and financial factors.

Political factors would include the attitude of the local government to MNCs. Many welcome MNCs as investing money in their country and providing jobs and training for the population. The relationship between the local government and the domestic government is also key. Sanctions between the two, for example, could be very disruptive to an MNC. The stability of the local government, its relationships with its neighbours, and its vulnerability to terrorist attacks are other key factors. Financial factors to consider include economic growth, interest rates, exchange rates, inflation, public sector deficits, unemployment and the balance of trade.

Finally, political risks may be global risks such as cybercrime, the rise of civil war and a refugee crisis, or climate change.

An MNC will maintain constant vigilance, scanning global data to identify increasing political risks to enable pre-emptive action to be taken where possible.

Economic factors

MNCs will also wish to monitor the economic environment of a country they seek to invest in. The key factors for economic growth are interest rates, exchange rates and inflation.

An economy is more likely to grow if interest rates are lower because low interest rates tend to lead to increased spending and reduced saving rates.

Lower exchange rates tend to favour exporters who find that they can sell their output more cheaply into international markets. A weaker currency can also reduce demand for imports, which may benefit local producers. In contrast, a strong currency favours importers while at the same time increasing the cost of international sales. There is a widely held view that economies benefit from stable exchange rates.

Inflation of around 2–2.5% is generally seen to be ideal for a modern economy but high inflation can lead to an increase in interest rates, a fall in the exchange rate and a weakening of demand as consumers lose purchasing power. Together these pressures can reduce growth in an economy.

There is clearly a link between political risk and economic factors. For example, a government seeking to stimulate the economy might cut interest rates significantly, leading to increased demand and thus creating increased inflation. In addition, forecasting the future direction of these economic factors is notoriously difficult.

Cultural risks

There are some simple reasons for an MNC to suffer loss of cash flows because of the culture in the local market. We have already considered some of these in Chapter 11, when we looked at Wal-Mart's activities in the UK, Germany, South Korea and China. In this chapter we will formally identify the cultural risks facing many MNCs.

The first hurdle facing them is the cultural preference to buy local goods. There is a current push in the United States to buy goods 'Made in America' and many other countries have similar views about their own goods.

The first risk is that MNCs fail to successfully modify their business to local preferences or even regional preferences within a country. Individuals' behaviour is affected by the culture in which they live, and that includes their attitude to prices and desire for quality products among other things. No MNC is going to be able to substantially change the culture of a country and so MNCs must adapt to local tastes.

Globalization is about bringing standardized world-class products to local markets. For example, an iPhone is identical in every market in which it is sold. But MNCs also need to invest time and money in localization, in tailoring their products and services to meet the needs of local markets. Apple achieves this via the App Store, which offers tailor-made apps.

Other global companies, McDonald's for example, have a global presence with outlets across the world offering a similar range of products and services but within countries the company adapts its offer to meet the needs of local markets. For example, the Indian menu offers burgers, wraps, chips and drinks just as every other McDonald's does but it focuses on chicken and vegetarian food to meet the tastes of the local consumers.

But it is not enough to adapt to a single culture within a country; in practice, consumers within a country are a diverse population and a successful MNC will provide a diverse offering, appropriately marketed to appeal to a number of sectors of the total market.

Culture Plus Consultants (who represent Visa and Disney, among others) describe this as the integration of local features and global ideas.

Just as an MNC needs to adjust its offering to local consumers to be successful it must also adapt its business practices in line with local business practices; this might be as simple as adopting local office hours but will also need to extend to account for economic, political and regulatory influences. An MNC must understand clearly the legal environment in which it operates, for example what protection is offered to brands or patents and the legal requirements it has to accept. Equally, an MNC will need to assess the impact of the local culture on its management practices and make the necessary adaptation. We thought about this when we discussed Wal-Mart's treatment of employees in Germany and the resulting court case against it.

MNCs also need to understand the ethical environment of a local country.

CASE STUDY Doing business in China – cultural differences

In China, business is undertaken within a framework of relationships or *guanxi*. The relationship is built over time by the creation of a series of reciprocal obligations via social exchanges and favours including, sometimes, gifts. This means that many Chinese would prefer to do business with people they already have a relationship with. As a result, an MNC might find it helpful to use a third party who already has a relationship with a company it wishes to do business with to gain an introduction, rather than to approach the company directly. Of course, the third party will have to expend *guanxi* in making the introduction and will expect the MNC to repay the favour.

This sense of trust between business partners in China extends to a company's customers, who value trust as well as price. For example, food retailers need to have the public's trust in the quality of their products as well as offering keen prices.

It is inevitable that such a system can lead to individuals in the MNC being obligated to local businesses in ways which would be unacceptable in the culture of 'arm's-length transactions' in the United States or the UK but which are the normal business practice in China.

In addition, individuals and businesses operating in such an ethical environment need to be sensitive to the state of their relationships with others to avoid creating offence or an obligation which they do not wish to be under. Perhaps when a gift is received the recipient might wish to make a gift themselves to avoid being further obligated.

MNCs also need to be culturally sensitive in their human resource department activities. Not just recruitment but also motivation, feedback and rewards require a good understanding of the local culture to ensure that the MNC gets the best from its staff. Where home-country staff are seconded to a local subsidiary there is a significant risk that the deployment will break down. Reasons range from family difficulties and cultural adaptation to isolation. An astute MNC will ensure that staff to be seconded are carefully selected and prepared for the role and that a strong support network is in place for both its staff and their families.

CASE STUDY Changing consumer behaviour in China

We have already discussed Wal-Mart's activities in China. In 2014, both Revlon and L'Oréal Garnier decided to withdraw from China because of low sales, despite growth of over 10% in the cosmetics market in the country. Chinese consumers are becoming more discerning and will not pay a premium for foreign brands unless they have some clear advantage over locally manufactured goods. As Chinese brands become more competitive, foreign brands will find it increasingly difficult to maintain their market share. Chinese consumers are increasing seeking high-quality goods and interesting brands rather than foreign logos. The demographic most likely to buy Western goods is the urban upper middle class, which is also the fastest-growing group and is expected to include around half the total population of China by 2022. The Chinese media are quick to disclose problems with foreign brands. Surveys have revealed that Chinese consumers are less impressed by foreign brands than in the past, perhaps because the Chinese government has criticized companies including Apple, Nike and Procter and Gamble for failing to provide a satisfactory service to Chinese consumers.

Not all brands suffer the same pressure. Seemingly luxury brands are more sensitive to consumers' changing perceptions and demands, while value brands remain popular with price-conscious consumers wherever they are.

Japanese companies have enjoyed mixed fortunes in China. The territorial dispute between the two countries over the Diaoyu Islands, or the Senkakus, has led to a significant loss of market share for Japanese car manufacturers. However, other Japanese companies, for example the clothing retailer Uniqlo, have been successful in revising their products and marketing to target younger Chinese people who are less subject to government propaganda than their parents.

Major shifts in consumer behaviour and tastes are not confined to emerging markets. Let's look at Japanese consumers for a moment.

CASE STUDY Japanese consumer behaviour

From the middle of the last century, Japanese consumers were interested in the goods produced in, and consumed by, the affluent West, particularly the United States. Japan enjoyed high economic growth until the early 1990s and sought to buy Western technology; initially televisions, washing machines and fridges but over time including cars. While the Japanese increasingly wanted to consume Western goods they also wanted what they saw as the Western lifestyle and women began to stay at home to raise their children, increasing further the demand for desirable Western goods.

During the 1970s, the focus was shifted to the quality of the goods bought and by the 1980s, conspicuous consumption was key, with European goods joining the American goods imported into Japan.

The 1990s brought the end of economic growth and consumers became price conscious, assisted by the arrival of the shopping mall and 'pound' or 'dollar' stores. The 2000s ushered in the 'new rich' who had more money as women re-entered the workplace, wanted luxury brands and were willing to pay for quality products and convenience. But the global financial crisis led to decreased consumption in Japan and a return to being price and value conscious.

Today the Japanese consumer looks much like a Western consumer, using discount retailers and online shopping, buying in bulk to reduce their costs, and taking an increasing interest in the environment (although perhaps unwilling to pay more to be environmentally friendly). The Japanese consumer is spending more time at home and is cooking rather than eating out, even taking packed lunches to work. The focus is on spending time to save money rather than before when they were willing to spend money to save time. There is increased interest in 'own brands' or 'private label brands' which are cheaper than the branded goods they compete with. Department stores are losing sales to shopping malls or speciality shops. Online shopping is enabling consumers to make their own decisions about purchases instead of being led by the consensus of all consumers as in the past.

These are big shifts in consumer behaviour and successful MNCs must constantly monitor consumer culture and quickly react to changing behaviours. Companies like McDonald's, Wal-Mart, Amazon and Ikea have thrived while others have struggled to adapt.

Increasingly, to be successful, foreign companies need to understand the cultures of the countries to which they are exporting.

Political risk: some examples and useful resources

One of the main sources of political risk is **governance risk**: the risk that the parent will not be able to exercise effective control over its subsidiary because of the local country's legal and political environment.

The main difficulty is goal conflict between the objectives of the local government and the subsidiary. In some cases, the government finds the likely consequences of the subsidiary's activities conflict with their own objectives. Examples include: foreign control of key industries such as defence; impact on the local government's economic development; balance of payments; use of foreign or local workers at all levels; and exploitation of natural resources.

Governments can introduce legislation that can seriously affect the ability of a subsidiary to generate cash. This might be environmental: for example, in the UK diesel cars have enjoyed tax breaks but as the evidence mounts against their environmental credentials the government has increased the tax on diesel fuel and in the year to February 2017 diesel car sales fell by 9%. Car manufacturers and other affected businesses will need to react effectively to such changes in legislation and sentiment in order to protect their businesses and exploit new opportunities.

Ideally, potential difficulties will be anticipated and resolved prior to conflict.

Often local governments and companies enter into a formal agreement determining key issues. These might include:

- the nature, amount and timing of remittances to the parent;
- the basis of the calculation of transfer prices;
- the tax treatment of the subsidiary including income taxes, sales taxes, wealth taxes and expenditure taxes;
- the access for subsidiary and parent to local capital markets;
- any requirements for the subsidiary to contribute to the local economy, for example by constructing local infrastructure like roads or schools or making contributions to retirement funds;
- the basis on which local raw materials can be sourced;
- the extent to which home staff can be brought in to work in the local country and the costs to the company of bringing staff into the country;
- the exit strategy of the parent from the project.

We will discuss the difficulties of paying dividends in detail in Chapter 14. It is enough to say here that some local governments find payments such as fees, royalties and payments for goods made to the parent less controversial than dividend payments.

In a 2017 *Financial Times* article, Roger Blitz considers the impact of political risk on the world's leading reserve currencies: the dollar, the pound and the euro.

Blitz concludes that the euro has depreciated against other currencies because of the presidential election in France and the risk that France will vote to leave the EU, along with the pound sterling that is trading at a lower value because of the Brexit vote. The euro has also been affected adversely by the German elections that will be held in 2017. After the shock results in the 2016 UK referendum and the US presidential elections, markets are reacting to future elections even if it is thought very unlikely that there will be another political upset.

Methodology for undertaking country risk analysis

There are several different methods of undertaking country risk analysis. Some data is cheap to acquire and easy to analyse, and financial and economic data tends to fall into this category. Other data is expensive to gather and tends to be subjective and difficult to analyse. The timeliness and accuracy of the data must also be considered.

Given this range of data and analytical techniques you won't be surprised to find that there are a number of methodologies used to undertake country risk analysis. The main methods are given below in order of cost.

Quantitative methods

A variety of statistical techniques including regression analysis can be used to identify most relationships between variables and from that an analysis of the impact of the country's risk on a company in a particular industry can be undertaken. Such techniques merely tell us the possible consequences of a particular change; they don't tell us anything about how likely it is that the change will occur. Quantitative techniques tend not to include subjective data either.

A checklist

The company can create a checklist of all the political and financial factors considered relevant and then allocate each factor a ranking based on either objective data or subjective judgement depending on the factor. The rankings are then converted to a numerical rating which can be used to assess the level of country risk. The exact calculation of the numerical rating will be subjective.

Delphi technique

This is a popular technique used to forecast future scenarios. A group of experts, called panellists, are asked about their views on, say, a country, by completing a questionnaire. Using the results of the first questionnaire, a second questionnaire is completed by the same panellists. The exact methodology used varies and can extend to panellists assessing the questionnaire itself as part of the process. In some ways, the questions that evolve from the process are as useful as the answers, though both are subjective.

Inspection visit

An MNC may arrange to send a delegation to the country to meet with politicians, business leaders and consumers. This is likely to produce an assessment of the country that could not be undertaken in any other way but it is inevitably anecdotal and subjective.

An MNC might use several of these strategies before deriving a country risk rating, which can be a single number generated from combining political and financial findings. In many ways, the final rating is less important than the process undertaken, which will have undoubtedly improved the MNC's understanding and knowledge of the country.

Third-party providers of data and analysis

Companies undertaking country risk analysis can access several services, some free and some paid. We are going to take a look at some of the free ones because it is enlightening to see how each of them assesses risks. You can use them to find out more about any country you are interested in. Many of my students find them fascinating.

Before we look at some of the analysis it will be helpful to explain some terminology.

The **structure** of the economy is a measure of the changing balance of output, trade incomes and employment from primary economic sectors – farming, fishing and mining – secondary economic sectors – manufacturing and construction – and tertiary economic sectors such as tourism, banking and the software industry. While changes in economic structure are normal, the shift from one sector to another can create structural unemployment. One example is the unemployment rate of 15% among construction workers in Colorado in 2010 while national unemployment in the United States was less than 10%.

The trade deficit or surplus refers to a country's exports less its imports. If the result is positive, the country has a trade surplus. The United States is currently running a historically large trading deficit, owing a total of around $7 trillion in 2017. Other countries with large trade deficits are Spain, the UK, Australia and Mexico. A country with a large trading deficit may find that it loses jobs, including high-quality jobs, as manufacturing falls and it is forced to buy imports as locally produced items become unavailable.

The Economist Intelligence Unit

The Economist Intelligence Unit is a paid-for service run by the group that produces the highly respected *Economist* weekly magazine-format newspaper. We are interested in the factors they consider when undertaking their country risk analysis.

The *Economist*'s operational risk model considers the following 10 risk characteristics:

- security;
- political stability;
- government effectiveness;
- the legal and regulatory environment;
- macroeconomic risks;
- foreign trade and payments issues;
- labour markets;

- financial risks;
- tax policy;
- the standard of local infrastructure.

These risk characteristics are subdivided into the impact on different business sectors.

The model also uses qualitative variables such as the likely reaction of the government to various crisis scenarios because it believes this improves the forecasting ability of the model. Each of the quantitative risk factors is given a rating between 0 and 100, with lower numbers meaning the risk is also less. Once the data has been gathered and input into the model, the EIU uses a board of specialists to analyse the model and derive an assessment of each country's risk. If you would like to find out more about the risk factors they use you can get an explanation on the IEU website (IEU, 2010).

Euler Hermes

Euler Hermes is a global consultancy company which produces a number of reports on country risk analysis. On its website, you will find a colour-coded global map, a short report on the politics and economy of each country, and the option to download a long report on each country. In addition, Euler Hermes provides an assessment of the risks of a number of business sectors by country. It is interesting to note from the map that countries often have similar risk rates to their near neighbours.

Euler Hermes's main focus is on default risk, that is the risk that a company will not receive payments from its debtors. Euler Hermes uses data about the structure of the economy, budgetary and monetary policy indebtedness, the trade deficit or surplus, the stability of the banking system, perceptions of the regulatory and legal framework, control of corruption, political stability, social cohesion and international relations.

OECD

The OECD is a supranational organization which works with governments to 'promote policies that will improve the economic and social well-being of people around the world'. In common with other supranational organizations such as the IMF and the World Bank, the OECD collects and analyses data from many countries, including country risk assessment.

The country and institutional risk classification focuses on two risks, the first being the risk that a government may take actions which prevent local cash flows from being repatriated to the domestic country or which reduce the amount of domestic currency received from the local cash flow repatriated. The second element of country risk is the risk of unforeseen events such as earthquakes or extreme weather, and the risk of extreme events such as war or civil disturbances. The OECD primarily uses subjective strategies for determining the risk classification.

Transparency International

TI describes itself as a global coalition against corruption with a mission of raising the global profile of corruption in the public sector. As part of its work it publishes an annual assessment of the level of corruption of countries around the world. Their rankings for 2016 are perhaps predictable, with the least corrupt public sector being found in New Zealand, with Western Europe and North America taking most of the other top spots. Perhaps more importantly, however, TI found that levels of corruption are increasing globally and most interestingly of all they have found a strong correlation between the level of inequality in a country and its level of corruption. You can find all their data and analysis on their website: **www.transparency.org**.

In practice, while it might be possible to forecast some trends such as interest rates and inflation over the short term, many events happen that no one could forecast. To name but a few:

- the terrorist attacks on the World Trade Centre;
- Brexit;
- President Trump's election in the United States.

But it isn't just dramatic events that can change a country's fortunes. In 2000, Venezuela was the richest country in South America with the world's largest oil reserves in its jurisdiction, even though half its population lived below the poverty line. Today Venezuela is likely to default on its debt payments and could collapse economically. Here isn't the place to study the causes of this but it shows us just how quickly a country's fortunes can change.

In practice then, while MNCs should monitor countries they might invest in or seek to export to or import from, it is even more important that they remain flexible, able to react quickly to an ever-changing world, ready to take advantage of opportunities such as a favourable exchange rate, and able to protect themselves from threats.

How can an MNC reduce its exposure to country risk?

There are a number of ways in which an MNC can limit the risk of operating in a local country:

- Borrow funds locally rather than the parent providing the capital needed by the subsidiary. Using one or more local banks to provide capital for the subsidiary means that the MNC has not had to risk all the capital needed for the business and that a local bank is effectively sharing any country risk with the subsidiary.

- Use a joint venture rather than set up a separate subsidiary, thus ensuring that other businesses are committed to the survival of the business.
- Employing local people again ensures that the local community is invested in the MNC's activities in the country.

Investment appraisal

Once the decision has been made to evaluate investment in a project in a country then the country risk rating can be used to decide whether to invest in the country or not, but there are other ways in which it can be used.

First, we could use the country risk to help determine the discount rate to be used when calculating the net present value in an investment appraisal computation. So far we have discounted the company's cost of capital but if we reflect on the fundamental relationship between risk and return we might argue against that if an investment is being considered in a country which is thought to be very risky. On the other hand, we have been arguing that being diversified is very advantageous to an MNC because it enables it to diversify away its systematic risk. So, an MNC might conclude that investing in a country with a high risk rating would be worthwhile provided that the risk factors were different to the factors faced in other economies it is operating in.

Summary

Country risk analysis can be broken down into a number of areas: political risk, economic risk and cultural risk. In recent years, country risk analysis has become more analytical and sophisticated; at the same time there have been a number of shocks in various countries, perhaps the UK and United States being the most surprising, which emphasizes the need for thorough and ongoing analysis of countries of interest to an MNC. We are also living at a time when there is a huge amount of data about any one country and a number of agents interpreting the data, so the opportunities to undertake country risk analysis are plentiful.

Questions

Question 1

Pick a country you know reasonably well and use the online data and analysis sources to undertake a country risk analysis. Reflect on your findings in the context of your personal knowledge of the country: do you agree with the online analysis; are there any surprises?

Question 2

Pick a country that you are interested in but don't know much about. Undertake a country risk assessment using the same online data and analysis sources you used in Question 1. Draw a conclusion about how attractive the country would be to inward FDI given the analysis you have undertaken. By reflecting on your findings in Question 1, identify the additional information you would need to have in order to draw a reliable conclusion about the suitability of the country for FDI.

13
Emerging markets

At the end of this chapter you will be able to:

- discuss the key features of emerging markets;
- identify some of the difficulties facing emerging markets;
- discuss the benefits for MNCs of investing in emerging markets;
- discuss the current impact of emerging markets on the global economy.

Introduction

Since the global financial crisis, the developed markets of the West have offered relatively low rates of growth and all eyes turned to the new exciting emerging markets of the BRIC countries, Brazil, Russia, India and China, to provide the new markets and growth that the world needed. But the emerging markets have now faltered.

In this chapter we will consider what an emerging market is and follow the fortunes of two of them. Finally, we will assess the state of emerging markets today.

What is an emerging market?

The concept of emerging markets appeared towards the end of the 20th century and the term was coined in the 1980s; until then such economies had been referred to as LDCs (less developed countries). There is some sense that the term is not so useful today but nothing has yet replaced it so we will use it for the time being.

There is no formal agreement on what constitutes an emerging market and there are several competing definitions. For example, investment research firm MSCI bases its definition on the number of large companies and the proportion of shares available to the public as well as the market's openness to foreign ownership and capital. In contrast, the FTSE uses a numerical score sheet to determine which countries are eligible for inclusion. As a result of these different measures, MSCI includes South Korea while the FTSE's equivalent index doesn't. We will take a pragmatic view of the general consensus of what is an emerging market.

Broadly speaking, an emerging market is a country which is exhibiting some of the characteristics of a developed economy but which lacks the regulatory infrastructure such as a strong legal system and sound capital markets of a developed country.

While most emerging markets are moving towards becoming developed countries it is possible for a smaller developed country to deteriorate until it is, in fact, an emerging market. Greece is such a country, having been seriously weakened by the global financial crisis and the subsequent euro crisis until it now satisfies the criteria of an emerging market.

The term BRIC was first used in 2001 by Jim O'Neill at the World Bank to describe the world's largest emerging markets: Brazil, Russia, India and China. The next-largest emerging markets by size are South Korea, Mexico, Indonesia, Turkey and Saudi Arabia. Saudi Arabia is not generally considered to be a developed country because of its lack of stable infrastructure and its relatively high levels of corruption and inequality despite its high oil reserves and oil revenues.

Definitions of emerging markets are needed because many investment banks run an emerging market index which investors can use to indirectly invest in emerging markets.

Countries which are insufficiently advanced to qualify as emerging markets are often termed frontier countries.

Characteristics of emerging markets

Emerging markets tend to have low to medium income per capita. They tend to be economies in transition, usually from being a closed economy towards being an open market economy. Governments tend to regulate business rather than leaving the markets to determine what is produced and at what price it is sold. There may also be government restrictions on foreign ownership of shares and companies and the transfer of capital in the form of dividends, loan repayments or even interest payments back to the parent. At the same time, emerging markets find themselves having to create the accountability that is needed in a modern economy.

Typically, emerging markets are fast-growing economies with youthful populations, offering the temptations of high returns to companies and investors. But as we already know, the reason for those high returns is that they are also highly risky investments and in practice often don't deliver the high returns anticipated.

Economic systems

One way of analysing economic systems is to think of them as a continuum, with command economies or centrally planned systems at one extreme and free market economies at the other. In a centrally planned system, the government owns the country's economic resources and the state plans the production. In a free market economy, individuals and businesses own the economic resources and market forces drive production. In practice, there are no countries at either of these two extremes. An economy between these two extremes is described as a mixed economy, where ownership of the resources of production is split between the government and individuals.

The World Bank publishes the proportion of countries' GDP that is spent by the government. This is sometimes talked about in terms of the size of the government. As you might expect, this data is difficult to obtain and the figures given here are from 2014, the most recent available.

Table 13.1 Proportion of GDP spent by governments 2014

Country	General government final consumption expenditure (% of GDP)
Developed countries	
France	23.9%
Canada	21.2%
UK	19.4%
Germany	19.2%
USA	14.4%
Emerging markets	
Brazil	20.2%
Russia	19.1%
China	13.8%
India	10.6%

We can see from the above table that among the developed economies, France and most other developed economies have a relatively high level of government spending. This covers welfare expenditure, education, health, defence and other services such as the police and rubbish collection. The percentage expenditure of the United States is much lower and is probably what we would expect from a country which has a much smaller welfare state than Canada and Western European countries.

There is a real split among the BRIC countries, with Brazil and Russia having percentages in line with the developed world while China and India have significantly lower percentages. At the end of 2016, Brazil passed a law to cap increases in government spending to inflation only until 2037. Providing the economy grows over the next 20 years, that will result in a fall in the percentage of GDP spent by the government.

Russia is also reducing government expenditure, although its military spending is high.

So all the countries we are looking at have mixed economies, although the amount of government spending does vary widely from country to country.

In a centrally planned economy the focus is on the welfare of the group and the aim is to create equality in the group. While these are laudable goals, in practice such systems didn't create economic growth or provide incentives for individuals to create wealth, neither did they meet the needs of their consumers. Ultimately this is one reason for the collapse of the communist system in countries like Russia at the end of the 20th century.

In a mixed economy the focus is on economic stability, with steady growth and low rates of unemployment along with an equitable distribution of wealth. Governments who do not achieve this find themselves under pressure from opposition parties, the media and their own citizens. But in practice, state-owned industries are less efficient than privately owned industries and prices and taxes tend to be higher. During the 1980s, many economies, led by the UK and the United States, privatized many state-owned industries with a resulting increase in growth and profitability. Privatized industries were able to borrow money to invest without government restrictions and could abandon unprofitable business in order to invest in more profitable activities, giving more choices to consumers. While the law of supply and demand is key to a free market economy, governments retain a crucial role:

- To provide a strong legal system that is able to ensure that businesses act in a fair way and that consumer interests are protected. Laws to prevent monopolies are an example of this.

- To protect property rights of businesses, for example by enforcing laws protecting trademarks.

- To provide a stable environment for businesses and consumers. That means economic stability, fiscal stability and monetary stability as well as political stability.

Certainly, studies of economies around the world show that free market economies lead to increased wealth for those countries.

The 2017 Index of Economic Freedom lists Hong Kong, Singapore, New Zealand, Switzerland and Australia as the five countries with the most economic freedom in the world (Miller and Kim, 2017).

The index is based on four main measures: the rule of law, the size of government, the extent to which regulation enables businesses, labour and capital to be free, and how open the country's markets are.

You might be interested to know that the UK is in 12th place, the United States 17th and Germany 23rd. In contrast, China is in 111th place, Russia 114th, Brazil 140th and India 143rd.

From this we can see very clearly a difference between the developed countries, with high degrees of economic freedom, and the emerging markets with much lower levels.

We've clearly identified some of the differences between developed markets and emerging markets. Now we can consider the strategies that the governments of emerging markets need to use to shift from a traditional or centrally planned economy towards a free market economy that will increase the wealth of their citizens.

Governments need to manage their tax collection and spending to reduce their budget deficit. This is very challenging, particularly if a country has an ageing population and a falling percentage of people of working age. Governments need to move towards using the law of supply and demand to determine the level of economic activity and set prices. State-owned businesses need to be privatized and private businesses must be allowed to operate. Finally, the barriers to trade and investment must be removed and currency controls need to be abandoned. Effectively, we are describing the neoliberalism supported by the IMF and the World Bank which we criticized in Chapter 4. Perhaps the key is the way in which the reforms are introduced. It is likely that the order in which reforms are introduced is critical.

There are a number of factors that restrict an emerging economy from taking the steps described above to create a free market:

- The citizens of an emerging market lack the managerial experience needed to develop a world-class company. One major benefit of foreign direct investment (FDI) is that the multinational company (MNC) is likely to deploy senior staff into the country and to provide appropriate training to local residents to ensure the success of the business.

- A local business is likely to find that it is unable to raise the capital it needs from the local capital market because it is underdeveloped and there is a lack of funds for investment in the country. Again, FDI can help by providing the essential initial capital for individual businesses and also by contributing to the development of viable capital markets.

- The cultural change necessary to accommodate the needs of a world-class company can be difficult for a country's citizens and organizations. A European example of the need for cultural change is unfolding today in Spain, where it has been customary for employees to take a two-hour siesta in the afternoon, ending the working day at around 7pm. This is proving difficult to manage for families with school-age children and both parents working. Various proposals have been made to enable Spain to move towards the same working hours as its neighbours and partners, including moving the clocks back. Such change takes time and is inevitably unwelcome to some even if others are enthusiastic.

- An adverse impact on the environment may be caused by an incoming MNC or a domestic firm. It can be difficult for the emerging market to successfully protect its environment because of an inadequate legal infrastructure. In 2014, Coca-Cola was finally forced to shut down a plant in Varanasi, India, after over a decade of protests from local people, including a hunger strike in 2006 because the plant's high levels of water consumption lowered the water table and affected local farmers. There were also complaints about polluting effluents discharged by the company. China suffers badly from pollution despite legislation designed to reduce the problem. Air pollution is at an all-time high, with 32 cities on red alert in January 2017 despite legislation to curb air pollution in 2011. CO_2 emissions continue to increase, although the rate of increase is beginning to slow.

Now that we have considered the emerging market environment in some detail we are able to determine the benefits and risks for MNCs investing in emerging markets.

The biggest benefit for an MNC investing in an emerging market is the benefit of diversification. While globally countries are becoming increasingly positively correlated with each other, emerging markets, while positively correlated with developed countries, are less positively correlated than other developed countries with each other. We began to consider the benefits of diversification in Chapter 1 and it has been a key theme in this book. Diversification means that risk is reduced and so even though emerging markets are inherently riskier than developed countries the benefits of diversification outweigh the risks.

The other main benefits of investing in emerging markets are: MNCs being able to access new markets, many of which are growing rapidly; accessing cheap finance provided by governments seeking the benefits of FDI; accessing cheap labour; and enabling their shareholders to increase their global diversification.

Let's consider the example of Jaguar Land Rover, a UK company now owned by an Indian company, and its activity in China.

CASE STUDY Jaguar Land Rover

Jaguar Land Rover (JLR) is a UK MNC which was bought by Tata Motors, an Indian MNC, in 2008. JLR manufactures sports utility vehicles (SUVs) and luxury cars. In 2012, JLR and Chery, a Chinese carmaker, agreed to a joint venture, JLR China, to manufacture JLR's vehicles and engines in China. The deal included a new research and development facility in China. JLR have targeted the luxury segment of the Chinese car market, which is both highly competitive and also a growth market. China was the largest market for JLR's cars in 2016.

At the end of 2016, JLR China appointed its first Chinese director, who reports directly to the UK's chief executive, at the same time as announcing that production in China will increase by 70,000 vehicles a year to a total of 200,000 vehicles.

The following is an extract from JLR's Annual Report 2015/16.

Figure 13.1 Extract from Jaguar Landrover's annual report 2015/16

	UK £m	US £m	China £m	Rest of Europe £m	Rest of World £m	Total £m
31 March 2016						
Revenue	4,529	4,344	4,930	4,109	4,296	22,208
Non-current assets	10,475	18	16	26	137	10,672
31 March 2015						
Revenue	3,564	3,112	7,595	3,200	4,395	21,866
Non-current assets	9,357	16	11	10	32	9,426
31 March 2014						
Revenue	2,989	2,683	6,687	2,978	4,049	19,386
Non-current assets	7,376	13	8	10	17	7,424

In the table above non-current assets comprise property, plant and equipment and intangible assets.

If we start by looking at the figures to 31 March 2016 we can see that the company's sales are pretty much evenly spread across five geographical areas – the UK, the United States, China, the rest of Europe and the rest of the world – although China did generate the most sales. But if we then consider the figures from 2014 and 2015 we see a more interesting picture. JLR's sales in China fell sharply in 2015/16 while sales in developed countries, the UK, the United States and the rest of Europe, rose very substantially. Despite the substantial loss of sales in China in 2015/16, that meant that total revenue increased slightly. This table shows clearly the extent to which diversification can help to protect an MNC against an economic downturn in one of its markets as well as giving an example of the level of risk in an emerging market such as China. It also reveals the lack of correlation between China and the developed world.

The global shift in economic activity

We have spent time considering what an emerging market is and looking at some of them in some detail. Now we are going to look at the global rankings of countries in order to assess the extent to which emerging markets, particularly the BRIC countries, are growing as compared to the developed countries.

Table 13.2   Largest countries in the world by GDP adjusted for purchasing power parity 2011

Rank	Country	GDP $trillion 2016	GDP $trillion 1990	Average annual growth between 1990 and 2016
1	USA	18.6	9.2	2.7%
2	China	18	2	8.8%
3	Japan	4.5	3.8	0.7%
4	Germany	3.5	2.6	1.1%
5	UK	2.4	1.4	2.1%
6	France	2.4	1.7	1.3%
7	India	7.7	1.7	6%
8	Italy	1.9	1.7	0.4%
9	Brazil	2.9	1.6	2.3%
10	Canada	1.5	0.8	2.4%
11	Russia	3.4	2.4	1.3%

SOURCE IMF

It is very difficult to compare countries by GDP, particularly over time. Changes in exchange rates can make it very difficult to compare performance in different countries. The table reports the purchasing power parity-adjusted figures to enable us to calculate the average annual growth but the countries are shown in order of absolute GDP stated in US dollars. That is why some countries' rankings are at odds with their GDP in 2016.

Even given these limitations, this table tells a story of great success for the BRIC countries, which are all now among the biggest economies in the world.

As we can see that while the United States is the largest economy in the world, *Forbes* predicts that China's economy will be larger in 2018. We are living through a period of transition when global economic power is shifting from the developed world to the emerging economies. PwC predicts that the size of the emerging economies will exceed the developed economies by 2050.

However, if we look at the same countries again but instead consider the GDP per citizen, we get a very different view of these countries.

We can see that while China is the second-largest economy its citizens are creating only a quarter of the GDP generated by US citizens. This second table more clearly distinguishes between the developed economies and the emerging markets than the first one does because it takes into account the population of the country.

Table 13.3 Largest countries in the world: GDP per citizen in 2015

Rank	Country	GDP $'000
1	USA	56
2	China	14
3	Japan	38
4	Germany	47
5	UK	41
6	France	41
7	India	6
8	Italy	36
9	Brazil	16
10	Canada	46
11	Russian	26

SOURCE IMF

Activity

In addition to our studies on emerging markets there are some very interesting results in our above analysis. Look again and see what you can find.

Hint: try asking yourself some questions. The first is really to confirm that growth in GDP in emerging markets has been far higher than growth in GDP in the developed world. Now look again at the growth in the North American countries, the United States and Canada, and compare that to growth in countries in the European Union: Germany, France, Italy and the UK.

Feedback

The average unweighted mean growth in the BRIC countries over the last 26 years is 4.6%, while China and India have average annual growth of 8.8% and 6% respectively. The average unweighted mean growth of the largest developed countries over the same period is only 1.5%, less than a third of the growth in the largest emerging markets.

Average growth in North America was 2.55%, twice as high as the 1.2% of the largest EU countries. You might want to investigate this further.

Notice that Japan's average growth over the same period was only 0.7%. Analysts talk about Japan's 'lost decade', referring to the 1990s when growth was much lower than it had been in the previous 45 years after the end of the Second World War.

The Human Development Index

While GDP may be an important measure of the success of an economy there are other factors that are important.

The Human Development Index is a combination of life expectancy, education and income per person and is published each year by the UN. Using this measure, the country rankings are very different, with Norway, Australia, Switzerland and Germany earning the highest scores and the United States and the UK in 10th and 16th place respectively. In contrast, Russia is in 49th place, Brazil is 79th, China is 90th and India is languishing in 131st place. There is a long way to go before all the citizens of the BRIC countries are able to enjoy the standard of living the developed countries are accustomed to.

The future for emerging markets

2016 was generally seen to be a difficult year for emerging markets, due in part to falling rates of growth in China and falling oil prices, although things improved as the year wore on.

For 2017, the fact that the dollar is increasing in value and commodity prices are stable is probably good news for emerging markets but President Trump's protectionist policies may make the US market harder to export to and reduce the number of dollars being invested in real assets in emerging markets. The relationship between the new administration and China is not yet clear but the falling value of the renminbi during 2016 may exacerbate their conflict. Falling emerging market bond prices resulting in increasing costs of borrowing after Trump's election increase the pressure on the emerging markets. Despite their problems, growth across emerging markets is predicted to be over 4% in 2017, much higher than the growth forecast for countries in the developed world. Merrill Lynch raised further concerns about Brazil, despite its improving current account deficit, and Venezuela, which has suffered badly from falling oil prices.

Summary

Emerging markets were the global economic powerhouses of the world until recently, generating growth that the developed world couldn't emulate.

In this chapter we discussed the key characteristics of emerging markets and explored how MNCs can operate in emerging markets. Finally, we looked a little deeper into some emerging markets to find that there is a long way to go before their residents are able to enjoy the same benefits – health, education, housing and so on – that are taken for granted by citizens of developed countries.

Questions

Question 1

Select two contrasting emerging markets, Brazil and China perhaps, and investigate their economic performance at the present time.

Question 2

For a large emerging market, investigate and assess the success, and failure, of MNCs undertaking FDI into the country. Can you see any factors which make success, or failure, more likely?

14
International cash management

At the end of this chapter you will be able to:

- describe the cash flows and real flows between members of an international group;
- critically evaluate centralized and decentralized cash management systems.

Introduction

Cash is often described as the life blood of a company. Certainly, cash flows through all the activities of a company, paid to the company from its sales, either directly from cash sales or later when trade debtors settle their accounts, and then used by the company to pay its liabilities and expenses or invest in assets for the future.

Academics think that about 80% of companies that fail had cash flow difficulties immediately prior to their failure. In practice, companies are most likely to find that they have cash flow difficulties at times when they are growing, termed overtrading, rather than during economic downturns. This rather reflects the evidence that banking crises occur when the economy is booming rather than in economic downturns.

This is all as true for a sole trader as it is for the largest multinational companies, although MNCs have more complex systems and often more opportunities to manage their cash.

In practice, there is often a tension between the liquidity that cash provides and profitability, since capital tied up in cash is not generally generating profits. Too much cash and a firm's return on assets falls; too little cash and a company can suffer increased costs or at worst bankruptcy.

Companies aim to take control of their cash and to make the best use of it. In addition to having to decide how much cash to hold, an MNC will need to decide how to manage the cash it holds; should cash be left with the subsidiaries that are generating it or should the group's cash be managed by the parent? This is a surprisingly complex decision which we will explore, and as we will see there is no right or wrong answer.

The subsidiary's position

Successful cash management is a crucial part of the management of the working capital of a subsidiary. But a local subsidiary of an MNC faces some additional problems compared to a domestic company.

It is likely that more of their costs for raw materials, management charges and patents will be incurred in foreign currencies. Because of exchange rate volatility this makes it more difficult to forecast future payments. In response, the subsidiary is likely to hold larger stocks of raw materials so that it can buy less at times when the exchange rate is worse. A higher level of inventory might also be needed if there is any risk to the supply chain, which is more likely for imported goods. As a result, a local subsidiary is likely to hold higher cash reserves than a domestic company.

Equally, if the subsidiary is an exporter it may find that its volume of exports fluctuates in response to fluctuating exchange rates. This would again lead to the subsidiary holding higher levels of cash and may lead to an increase in trade debtors as the company loosens it credit terms in a bid to boost sales.

Finally, the subsidiary will need to manage its cash surpluses, by putting cash on deposit, and cash deficits, by arranging short-term borrowings.

Centralized or decentralized cash management

When each subsidiary is considering its working capital and cash position it is focusing on its own circumstances. But that means it might make decisions that aren't in the best interest of the group. For example, one subsidiary might have a cash surplus while another has a cash deficit. The group is likely to be better off if one subsidiary lends money to the other rather than using third parties to deal with the two positions. Often one subsidiary will supply raw materials, components or finished goods to other subsidiaries in the group. If the exchange rate between two subsidiaries is volatile they might both choose to hold increased inventory for the reasons given above. This makes sense to each subsidiary but is not in the best interests of the group as a whole, since holding inventory generally has a negative impact on profitability.

In a centralized cash management system, the cash of the entire group is managed by a small number of managers in the parent company.

Activity

Top Dog is the parent of a group of companies. Two of the companies in the group are Tiny, which is based in Kenya, and Titch, which is based in India.
    The companies can borrow and lend at the following interest rates:

Company	Borrow	Lend
Top Dog	6%	3.5%
Tiny	8%	5.5%
Titch	7%	5%

a) Tiny has been offered the opportunity to buy additional components at a 15% discount, which would meet their production needs for six months. Tiny does not have surplus cash and would borrow the 1 million Kenyon shillings needed for the deal.

b) Titch needs to pay a management fee to Top Dog in three months' time but has sufficient cash to pay it now if required.

Top Dog does not currently have any surplus cash.
    For each of the two situations above, identify the optimal decision for the subsidiary and for the group.

Feedback

Tiny can get a 15% discount on the components which will last them for six months. We can assume that Tiny will need to borrow the money at 8% for six months, or a total of 4%. Tiny is likely to consider it worth borrowing and paying 4% of the amount borrowed in interest in order to get a 15% discount. Top Dog may have placed restrictions on the amount of borrowing that Tiny can undertake, so Tiny might have to obtain Top Dog's permission to take out the loan.

From Top Dog's point of view the deal also looks good but they might be able to make an even bigger saving by borrowing at 6%, or 3% for six months, rather than Tiny's 4%.

So in the case of a), Tiny and Top Dog would make the same decision, but in a centralized cash management system the cost of borrowing might be cheaper than in a decentralized one.

In the second example, Titch would prefer to retain the cash and earn an annualized return of 5% rather than pay the money to Top Dog now.

On the other hand, Top Dog would prefer to have the cash now and reduce their borrowing, at 6%, which is less than the interest that Titch can earn on its funds.

So in the case of b), Titch and Top Dog would make different decisions and if Top Dog made the decision, the group's interest expense less interest income would be lower, so once again a centralized system would be better.

One way of running a centralized cash management system is to operate a bank account into which the surplus cash for the entire group is deposited. Minimal operating requirements will have to be established for each subsidiary and any surplus over the minimal can be transferred to the centre. Precautionary balances are held centrally. The managers at the centre then make the key decisions about cash for the group and communicate those decisions to the local managers who then comply with them.

This effectively creates a finance centre for the group which is able to put surplus cash on deposit and can also lend cash to subsidiaries who need additional cash.

The group will need to decide the interest rates to charge and pay to subsidiaries and set the repayment terms to be met by any member with a cash deficit.

The group will also need to determine which currency or currencies to use.

In order for a centralized cash management system to work, the parent must be able to accurately forecast future cash flows for each subsidiary of the group. This requires a fast and reliable system for reporting and dealing with cash inflows and outflows. Subsidiaries will have to report their cash flows and forecasted needs much more frequently than in the past. We'll consider some of these systems later in this chapter.

It is also essential for the MNC to have access to excellent bank services. Without a good relationship with their banks, an MNC risks lost interest income, high fees and poor or inappropriate services. Some MNCs are dealing with too many banks, meaning that balances are not being netted off to best effect, balances may be too low to get the best deals, and the costs of managing banking relations are too high. An MNC must monitor the costs they are being charged by their banks to ensure they are paying the lowest possible amount and at the same time getting the best possible service. It is essential that banks provide fast and accurate reports on transactions so that surplus funds can be quickly reinvested. An MNC should ensure that funds are cleared as quickly as possible to enable them to be put to good use as soon as possible.

There are some significant advantages of such centralization:

- The head office managers probably have more experience and competence than the local managers, leading to reduced costs and better decisions.

- The group will need less cash because the need to hold a precautionary or speculative balance of cash will be less for the entire group than for individual subsidiaries. We saw a great example of this when schools in the UK had their budgets devolved to them rather than being held by the Local Education Authority.

Example

The LEAs had been responsible for many schools and hundreds of teachers so, for example, they were able to estimate how many teachers would leave in a year and knowing how long it took on average to fill a vacancy enabled them to reduce the budget for teaching staff salaries. Once the individual schools managed their own budgets they couldn't make the same kinds of assumptions because they had fewer staff and so schools soon built up cash reserves that were far higher in aggregate than the balance previously held by the LEA.

- Holding lower cash balances should lead to increased profitability and lower financing costs.
- Head office staff are better placed to see the 'bigger picture' and can make better decisions for the group than local managers who have limited access to information about the group.
- Netting off of transactions between subsidiaries is possible; we considered this in Chapter 8. This reduces the need for hedging transactions and so reduces costs.
- The parent company can undertake all the hedging activities for the group, which is likely to be cheaper and more effective.
- The group is likely to be able to negotiate better terms for foreign exchange, loans and deposits because of the large amounts they will be negotiating with.
- Political risk will be reduced because excess cash will not be on deposit in the local country.
- It should lead to increased consistency between different members of the group which will strengthen the corporate identity and avoid customers encountering different experiences with different subsidiaries in the group.

The higher currency and interest rate volatility faced by MNCs today and the increasing drive for profits make most MNCs opt for predominantly centralized cash management. In practice, however, it is not possible to have an entirely centralized cash management system, as there are some limitations:

- Subsidiaries will still have to hold some precautionary balances because the global financial system is not always able to facilitate the rapid transfer of funds in every country.
- Subsidiaries are likely to need to have money on deposit with local banks to maintain local banking relationships and to satisfy the requirements of local customers and suppliers.

- Many local managers find the lack of control of the cash demotivating. One way to address this problem is to amend the criteria on which local managers are assessed. Another is to set interest rates for borrowing from, or lending to, a subsidiary. Local managers are then able to make decisions about what to do with their surplus funds. Because the interest rates are set with regard to the MNC in its entirety they reflect the true opportunity cost of funds to the MNC rather than just to the local company.

- The subsidiary will not be able to take advantage of local opportunities if they have only sufficient cash to meet their ongoing operating needs.

- If the centralized cash management system uses a single currency then the subsidiaries will face transaction risk. A liquid forward market between the chosen currency and the subsidiaries' local currencies will make hedging easier.

- There may be local restrictions on the flow of cash out of the country or tax considerations which limit the amount of cash that can be transferred.

- Where a subsidiary is not wholly owned, there may be some conflict with the other owners that prevent a completely centralized cash management system. A satisfactory cash holding for the MNC may not be satisfactory for the local shareholders.

Reinvoicing centre

Another strategy to improve the cash management of the MNC is the use of a **reinvoicing centre**.

A reinvoicing centre is often located in a low-tax country with a very active money market and currency market. All the subsidiaries in the group sell their output, denominated in their local currency, to the reinvoicing centre, which then takes legal title of the goods. The reinvoicing centre then sells the goods to the group's customers and also invoices any intragroup sales which are invoiced in the buying subsidiary's currency.

This means that all exchange rate risk is contained in the reinvoicing centre, which can then hedge the risk in the most efficient way possible.

A reinvoicing centre can lead or accelerate (make payments prior to the contract date) cash payments or lag or delay (make payments after the contract date) cash payments to move cash from cash-rich subsidiaries to subsidiaries with cash deficits. Often a centralized cash management system includes a reinvoicing centre.

Collection and disbursement of funds

An important aspect of international cash management is taking steps to speed up or accelerate receipts from debtors. There are two main reasons for the delay in receiving payments. The first is the delay between the date the payment was made and the date the receipt was received, perhaps due to delays in the postal system. The second is delays in banks clearing funds. These two delays can combine to delaying a payment by as much as 10 business days.

There are a number of ways of accelerating cash receipts.

Lockboxes

Lockbox banking is a banking service. Lockboxes are post office boxes set up around the world by the bank for its client company. Payments and remittance documents from customers are then deposited in the post office box, or lockbox, rather than mailed directly to the company. The bank recovers the payment and documents from the box each day and couriers the contents to its processing centre, which pays the funds directly into the company's bank account and scans the remittance documents to be sent electronically to the company. The lockbox data is backed up daily. Because the lockboxes are local to subsidiaries and customers of the MNC they reduce the amount of time cash and cheques spend in the mail (the mail float). Lockboxes can also reduce the company's processing costs because the bank manages the bank deposits and creates the accounting records via the lockbox system. Lockboxes are particularly useful if an MNC receives high volumes of payment or high-value cheques. This makes lockboxes a very efficient way of depositing customers' payments.

But there is a risk of fraud; bank employees have been known to take the information in the lockbox and use it to create counterfeit cheques. MNCs should ensure that the bank it uses has sufficient controls in place to minimize this risk.

Electronic payment methods

Trade debtors are asked to make payment via one of a variety of payment platforms. There is generally a fee to be paid for using the service but it is usually sufficiently low that the benefit of speeding up the receipt outweighs the cost.

Blocked funds

Sometimes governments block cash flows out of the country. The parent can respond to this threat in a number of ways. First, they could organize their research and development so that more is undertaken by the blocked subsidiary. This will enable the surplus cash to be used in the local country and may ultimately lead to increased revenues for subsidiaries based in other countries. Second, the parent could adjust the cost of goods sold by other subsidiaries to the blocked subsidiary so that there is less surplus cash in the local country. The cost at which goods are transferred from one subsidiary to another is called the transfer price. Many governments require the transfer price to be the 'arm's-length' cost, that is the price that would be agreed between two unrelated entities. But in practice there are many situations when it is not possible for the arm's-length value to be agreed and the parent company has some leeway to set the transfer price. In the case of blocked funds, adjusting the transfer price of goods sold to and by the subsidiary to minimize the surplus cash arising in the blocked subsidiary can reduce the problem. Note that this same strategy can be used to reduce the amount of tax paid in a high-tax local country.

Finally, the parent could require the blocked subsidiary to borrow money locally to limit the need to send funds out of the country. This has the added advantage of having the local bank to defend the rights of the blocked subsidiary since it then has a stake in the company.

The multinational company's financial system

In the second part of this chapter we will determine and evaluate the MNC's financial system to see how it can add value to the MNC.

The parent company's financial managers will wish to take account of the financial environment in which each of its subsidiaries is operating. For example, they will look at the effective tax rates in each country, the currency used and the ease with which funds can be repatriated from the subsidiary to the parent. Once this has been done the parent can create a financial management plan for the group to determine the optimal profits, cash flows and capital for each subsidiary with the aim of minimizing the group's tax burden, minimizing exchange risk and ensuring cash flows can readily be repatriated to the parent when required. However, the planners are unlikely to be free to arrange their affairs exactly as they would wish to. They will face political, fiscal, foreign exchange and liquidity constraints or potential constraints. With careful planning, the impact of these constraints can be minimized.

The parent company has a number of connections with its subsidiaries. They can be split into financial or cash flows, real flows of goods and services, and decisions that can be made about those financial and real flows. Equally, subsidiaries will have many of those same connections and decisions between each other. This creates a rich network of flows and decisions which provides an MNC with opportunities to create wealth and reduce risk. Such opportunities are not available to domestic companies.

The financial flows between two members of a group are:

• Dividends paid from the subsidiary to its shareholders. When deciding on the dividend policy the group needs to consider a number of factors. The value of dividends that can be paid may be restricted by the profitability of the subsidiary and the amount of cash available to the subsidiary. An important consideration is external shareholders; if some shares are held by third parties then paying high levels of dividends leads to cash leaving the group, perhaps unnecessarily. The company will also need to consider any tax consequences of dividend payments. Dividends tend to be the less tax-efficient way of remitting cash back to the parent because they are paid out of after-tax profits. Most countries apply a withholding tax on dividends, meaning that paying a dividend also means paying tax which might not be recoverable in the future. The timing of any payment is within the control of the group, enabling it to take advantage of any favourable exchange rate. However, governments may have regulations about leading and lagging payments to prevent such planning. Finally, some local country governments resist high dividends paid to the parent, seeing it as cash being syphoned out of the local economy. Such governments may block dividend payments or levy very high rates of tax on them. However, few governments are as concerned with interest on capital repayments made to the parent, and interest payments often attract favourable tax treatment. Parents are aware of all these issues when setting up the capital structure of a subsidiary and often favour lending the subsidiary money over providing equity capital. Host governments are equally aware of the benefits of debt financing over equity for the parent and many have rules about 'thin capitalization', that is they require a certain percentage of the capital to fund the subsidiary to be equity.

- Interest payments and capital repayments. Interest payments are usually eligible for tax relief in the local country but subject to tax in the home country. There is likely to be a formal loan agreement in place so the timing and amount of interest payments are not flexible but capital repayments may offer some flexibility and while they are not eligible for tax relief in the local country they are not taxable in the domestic country and offer a nearly unique method for recovering the investment in the subsidiary without suffering a tax penalty. Generally, local governments are less concerned about interest payments and capital repayments than they are about dividends, making such payments less politically sensitive.

- Payments to the parent for intangibles such as royalties, service charges and fees are another important way in which money can be sent back to the parent from its subsidiaries. These payments are not usually as subject to local government intervention as dividends can be and it is often not possible to determine a suitable 'arm's-length' value for them so the parent has more freedom to fix the amount, if not the timing, of any payments.

- The parent could invest more money in the subsidiary in exchange for shares or equity investment, or the subsidiary could undertake a share buyback and return equity to the parent. A share buyback may create a capital gain and subsequent tax charge for the parent but otherwise these transactions are generally free of tax. A share buyback may be subject to the same difficulties that dividends can suffer from. Investing in new shares is unlikely to be controversial but will increase the need for dividend payments in the future, which may be problematic as we have seen.

- The parent could lend money to the subsidiary. This is unlikely to be difficult and as we have seen, payment of interest and repayment of capital are not usually politically sensitive.

In practice, it often benefits an MNC to break cash flows down into separate flows, such as administrative expenses, licence fee royalties, which tend to be more acceptable to local governments than high dividend payments. The split should be made in such a way that the costs identified can be matched directly against income streams for the subsidiary, thus linking the costs with the benefits they help to generate. Such a split can also allow the group to claim the highest level of tax relief by maximizing before-tax costs.

The real flows between a parent and subsidiaries or between subsidiaries are:

- Tangible assets such as capital goods, raw materials, components or finished goods. In practice, it is likely that such transfers would be both to and from a parent and its subsidiaries, or between subsidiaries. The main considerations are around the transfer prices and the timing of payments. Regulation on transfer prices can be to use the arm's-length value but when that isn't possible, local and domestic governments can require other suitable methods to be used instead such as a fixed percentage mark-up.

- Intangible assets such as technological developments, patents, management skills and marketing expertise. An MNC has more freedom to set the level of charges for these services and licences and to determine the timing of payments. For example, royalties might be sold for a single large payment or alternatively a series of payments, monthly or annual, might be required. These two possibilities have significantly different risk and return characteristics and managers will have to decide which is the optimum strategy.

- Finally, the MNC does have the freedom to determine which currency invoices and other agreements are denominated in. This decision can make a big difference in the value transferred from subsidiaries to their parent. The guiding principle when deciding all these issues should be the maximization of the parent company's shareholders' wealth.

The MNC's financial system can provide opportunities to exploit market differences in a number of ways:

- By arranging for costs and profits to arise in particular ways it is possible to create tax arbitrage opportunities. The simplest example is to use transfer pricing or allocated overheads to shift profits from a subsidiary in a high-tax country to one in a lower-tax country. But there are many other examples. Consider a company which incurs high research and development (R&D) costs. It might choose to use one subsidiary in a high-tax country to undertake all the R&D and once a revenue-generating product has been developed, transfer it to a subsidiary based in a lower-tax country. This gives higher tax relief for costs and lower taxes on the profits. As you can imagine, governments are not enthusiastic about such strategies but in a global economy with highly mobile MNCs it is hard to eliminate such tactics.

- Financial market imperfections, often created by regulations, can be exploited by using the MNC financial system. For example, a group can transfer funds between subsidiaries in order to borrow more cheaply or earn a higher, risk-adjusted, return. We saw how interest rate swaps worked in Chapter 7, but companies can go further. Consider the following example.

Example

A UK parent company has a German subsidiary and a German parent company has a UK subsidiary. Both the subsidiaries wish to borrow money but their size and youth mean that it costs more for them to borrow money than their respective parents. If the two parents take out a loan and then swap with the other group's subsidiary, both subsidiaries are able to borrow more cheaply without the need to exchange currency.

- In the UK, the prices that drug companies can charge the NHS are negotiated with the government department as well as the NHS. By reallocating profits, perhaps by manipulating the transfer prices to increase costs or reduce revenues, it is possible to make the company appear less profitable, enabling a higher price to be negotiated with the NHS and the UK government. This is an example of regulatory system arbitrage.
- Governments sometimes resort to credit controls, perhaps in an attempt to cool an overheating economy down. An MNC can use the financial system to move cash to a subsidiary that is subject to such credit controls.

Governments and regulators are well aware of the strategies being used by MNCs and an MNC would be well advised to exploit arbitrage opportunities with restraint. In recent years, MNCs thought to have paid too little tax locally have been subjected to protests from members of the public.

Summary

In this chapter we returned to the internal operations of the MNC itself and focused on the cash flows and real flows between a parent and its subsidiaries and between common subsidiaries. These flows provide a key opportunity for an MNC to exploit market imperfections to create wealth.

We viewed the MNC from the perspective of both the parent and its subsidiaries and considered the benefits and limitations of both central-ized and decentralized cash management systems. Both have benefits and problems but on balance it is likely that a centralized cash management system will be better able to maximize the shareholder wealth of the parent company.

Questions

Question 1

The current corporation tax rate in Japan is just over 30%, while the US corporation tax rate is 38.9%. How might an MNC with business in both the United States and Japan respond to such a difference?

Currently President Trump is suggesting cutting the rate of corporation tax to 15%. How might our MNC react to such a reduction?

If Trump's proposal was enacted, what would you expect to happen to the amount of profits from MNCs that are subject to US tax?

Question 2

In addition to corporation taxes, the United States charges import tariffs on certain goods. In line with neoliberal policies, these tariffs have tended to be very low and even lower if part of a trade agreement like the North American Free Trade Agreement (NAFTA). President Trump is seeking to increase import tariffs in an effort to reduce imports and increase the number of manufacturing jobs in the United States. How have MNCs responded to President Trump's proposals? How might MNCs use their internal cash flow systems to minimize the impact on any increases in tariffs? What will increases in tariffs mean for US consumers?

A final word

In this book we have studied the financial position of multinational companies and the financial environment in which they operate.

There are two fundamental ideas about finance which we have used to evaluate MNCs: the relationship between risk and return and the impact of diversification on risk and return.

We found ways of reducing the exchange rate risk by hedging both individual transactions and future cash flows. However, probably the most important benefit of being an MNC is the way in which diversification can reduce risk without significantly reducing returns.

MNCs face some additional risks that purely domestic companies don't face, such as exchange risk, political risk and supply chain problems, and the domestic companies they compete with can have significant advantages over MNCs. But while an MNC faces some additional risks, the benefits of diversification are so substantial that the total risk faced by an MNC is generally lower than the total risk faced by a domestic firm.

In our discussion of the financial environment in which MNCs operate, we have discussed many of the financial and economic issues of our times, particularly the global financial crisis and the subsequent euro crisis, as well as some of the other difficulties facing the euro. Other aspects of the current economic environment have not been considered in this book, such as historically low interest rates and the high levels of sovereign debt that many countries are struggling to reduce. I hope that you will be sufficiently interested to read more on these topics yourself.

We are also in something of a state of flux politically, with a wave of populist votes taking place and a view in some quarters that globalization and neoliberalism have had their time, and that a more nationalist stance will be taken by some governments in the future. I hope that you are able to take a more informed interest in such debates having read this book.

Dora Hancock

REFERENCES

Bank for International Settlements (2017) Triennial Central Bank Survey of foreign exchange and OTC derivatives markets in 2016 [online] https://www.bis.org/publ/rpfx16.htm

Barth, J R, Caprio Jr, G and Levine, R (2013) Bank regulation and supervision in 180 countries from 1999 to 2011, *National Bureau of Economic Research* [online] http://www.nber.org/papers/w18733

Blitz, Roger (2017) Political risk returns as driver of forex trading, *Financial Times*, 7 February [online] https://www.ft.com/content/a581d44a-ed43-11e6-930f-061b01e23655

Brealey and Myers (2003) Principles of Corporate Finance, 6th edition, McGraw-Hill

Dunning, John (1980) Towards an eclectic theory of international production: some empirical tests, *Journal of International Business Studies*, **11** (1) pp. 9–31 [online] https://papers.ssrn.com/sol3/papers.cfm?abstract_id=1773302

Federal Reserve (2016) FR2420: Report of selected money market rates [online] https://www.federalreserve.gov/apps/reportforms/reportdetail.aspx?sOoYJ+5BzDZiceJ/KVuLKQ==

IEU (2010) World risk: alert – guide to risk briefing methodology [online] http://viewswire.eiu.com/index.asp?layout=RKArticleVW3&article_id=183328603&country_id=1510000351&refm=rkCtry&page_title=Latest%2520alerts

Malkiel, B G (2003) The efficient market hypothesis and its critics, CEPS working paper no. 91 [online] https://www.princeton.edu/ceps/workingpapers/91malkiel.pdf

Miller, T and Kim, A B (2017) 2017 Index of Economic Freedom, *IEA* [online] https://iea.org.uk/publications/2017-index-of-economic-freedom

Rogoff, Kenneth *et al* (2003) Evolution and performance of exchange rate regimes, IMF working paper [online] https://www.imf.org/external/pubs/ft/wp/2003/wp03243.pdf

Stiglitz, Joseph (2016) *The Euro: And its threat to the future of Europe*, Allen Lane

World Bank (2013) Global Financial Development Report: Bank regulation and supervision survey [online] http://econ.worldbank.org/WBSITE/EXTERNAL/EXTDEC/EXTGLOBALFINREPORT/0,,contentMDK:23267421~pagePK:64168182~piPK:64168060~theSitePK:8816097,00.html

Worstall, P (2016) Bank of England's stress tests worse than useless – they're dangerous, Forbes [online] https://www.forbes.com/sites/timworstall/2016/08/03/bank-of-englands-bank-stress-tests-worse-than-useless-theyre-dangerous/#3fc2bc632c1a

INDEX

Page numbers in *italic* indicate figures or tables.